Policy Discourses in Malaysian Education

Since independence in 1957, Malaysia has become a globally-recognised industrial trading partner. With a 60% Muslim population, it also enjoys the reputation of being a moderate and peaceful nation. However, with just a short time left to realising its Vision 2020 of developed nationhood, the pathway of nation building still seems ambiguous. There is a brewing tension in its race and ethnic relations which has permeated the various fronts, namely politics, society, economics and education. This book analyses the education policies that have been formulated and implemented in Malaysia since independence. It demonstrates how these policy enactments have influenced the nation's growth and transformation, and the challenges faced in creating a model of equity and multicultural co-existence among its racially and ethnically diversified people. Shedding light on these issues, it points towards the major mending that is needed for Malaysia to become a truly developed nation.

Chapters include:

- Education of ethnic minorities in Malaysia: Contesting issues in a multiethnic society
- Access and equity issues in Malaysian higher education
- Graduate employability in government discourse: A critical perspective

This book is a case study on Malaysia that will supplement researchers and advance students in their understanding of a multi-racial society's perspective and attitude towards education.

Suseela Malakolunthu (PhD, Michigan State) is a former Professor and Chair of Educational Research and Consultation at the Universiti Utara Malaysia and founding director of the Leadership for Learning and Research Network at the University of Malaya. She is an awardee of the Fulbright Fellowship for research on 'Multicultural education and leadership' at Stanford University, and she was a visiting professor at the University of Cambridge and a Fellow at the Centre for Commonwealth Education, Cambridge University, UK. Currently, she is a research associate in the Cambridge Schools Leadership for Learning Community Project – an initiative of the Cambridge International Examinations (CIE). Suseela teaches via Coursera and provides consulting services on Teacher development, Educational leadership and School improvement, and participates in International Education Development.

Nagappan C. Rengasamy (PhD) is a Senior Consultant in Technical Vocational Education and Training (TVET) at the Asian Institute of Logistics and PEMM Consultants, Petaling Jaya, Malaysia. He has about 35 years of industrial work experience both in operational and educational capacities. He specialises in strategic management, leadership, creativity, and adult and vocational education, and offers consulting services in professional development programs. He has also taught management subjects in universities.

Routledge Critical Studies in Asian Education

Series Editors:
S. Gopinathan and Wing On Lee

For a full list of titles in this series, please visit www.routledge.com

Asia as Method in Education Studies
Edited by Hongzhi Zhang, Philip Wing Keung Chan and Jane Kenway

Secondary School English Education in Asia
From Policy to Practice
Edited by Bernard Spolsky and Kiwan Sung

A Critical Study of Thailand's Higher Education Reforms
The culture of borrowing
Rattana Lao

Mapping the Terrain of Education Reform
Global Trends and Local Responses in the Philippines
Vicente Chua Reyes, Jr.

Nonformal Education and Civil Society in Japan
Edited by Kaori H. Okano

Knowledge, Control and Critical Thinking in Singapore
State ideology and the politics of pedagogic recontextualization
Leonel Lim

Languages in the Malaysian Education System
Monolingual strands in multilingual settings
Edited by Asmah Haji Omar

Policy Discourses in Malaysian Education
A nation in the making
Edited by Suseela Malakolunthu and Nagappan C. Rengasamy

Making Sense of Education in Post-Handover Hong Kong
Achievements and challenges
Edited by Thomas Kwan-Choi Tse and Michael H. Lee

Policy Discourses in Malaysian Education
A nation in the making

Edited by Suseela Malakolunthu
and Nagappan C. Rengasamy

First published 2017
by Routledge
2 Park Square, Milton Park, Abingdon, Oxon OX14 4RN

and by Routledge
711 Third Avenue, New York, NY 10017

First issued in paperback 2018

Routledge is an imprint of the Taylor & Francis Group, an informa business

© 2017 selection and editorial matter, S. Malakolunthu & N. C. Rengasamy; individual chapters, the contributors

The right of S. Malakolunthu & N. C. Rengasamy to be identified as the authors of the editorial material, and of the authors for their individual chapters, has been asserted in accordance with sections 77 and 78 of the Copyright, Designs and Patents Act 1988.

All rights reserved. No part of this book may be reprinted or reproduced or utilised in any form or by any electronic, mechanical, or other means, now known or hereafter invented, including photocopying and recording, or in any information storage or retrieval system, without permission in writing from the publishers.

Trademark notice: Product or corporate names may be trademarks or registered trademarks, and are used only for identification and explanation without intent to infringe.

British Library Cataloguing in Publication Data
A catalogue record for this book is available from the British Library

Library of Congress Cataloging in Publication Data
Names: Malakolunthu, Suseela, editor. | Rengasamy, Nagappan C., editor.
Title: Policy discourses in Malaysian education : a nation in the making / edited by Suseela Malakolunthu and Nagappan C. Rengasamy.
Description: New York, NY : Routledge, 2016. | Series: Routledge critical studies in Asian education | Includes bibliographical references and index.
Identifiers: LCCN 2016022790 | ISBN 9781138188105 (hardback) | ISBN 9781315642703 (ebook)
Subjects: LCSH: Education and state—Malaysia. | Language and education—Malaysia. | Education, Higher—Malaysia. | Educational planning—Malaysia.
Classification: LCC LA1236 .P65 2016 | DDC 379.9595—dc23
LC record available at https://lccn.loc.gov/2016022790

ISBN 13: 978-1-138-60461-2 (pbk)
ISBN 13: 978-1-138-18810-5 (hbk)

Typeset in Galliard
by Apex CoVantage, LLC

Contents

Acknowledgements		vii
Chapter contributors		viii
1	Introduction SUSEELA MALAKOLUNTHU AND NAGAPPAN RENGASAMY	1
2	Globalisation and the politics of education in Malaysia: Some past and contemporary policy issues K. S. BALAKRISHNAN	15
3	Education of ethnic minorities in Malaysia: Contesting issues in a multiethnic society R. SANTHIRAM AND TAN YAO SUA	29
4	Access and equity issues in Malaysian higher education HENA MUKHERJEE, JASBIR S. SINGH, ROZILINI M. FERNANDEZ-CHUNG AND T. MARIMUTHU	45
5	English as a Malaysian and ASEAN language: Implications for language policy and planning AZIRAH HASHIM AND GERHARD LEITNER	71
6	Technical and vocational education and training in Malaysia: From policy to implementation KEE-CHEOK CHEONG, HWOK-AUN LEE, KUPPUSAMY SINGARAVELLOO AND ABDILLAH NOH	86
7	Education policy and human capital transformation strategy in Malaysia HUSSEIN HAJI AHMAD	105

8 Graduate employability in government discourse:
A critical perspective 125
ZURAIDAH MOHD DON

9 Going forward: The need to rethink education
policies 142
SUSEELA MALAKOLUNTHU AND NAGAPPAN RENGASAMY

Index 152

Acknowledgements

Our motivation to undertake this project of editing a book on the scholarly discourse of education policies and how they have affected the process of nation building in Malaysia was based on two objectives: to make available well-researched scholarly perspectives of the Malaysian experience of nation building via selective deployment of the education factor; and, to provide a reserve of theoretical bases on the events and eventualities of the intermingling of education and nation building within the realm of the historical, demographic and political realities in a globalised world. The aspiration, of course, was grandeur but the challenges appeared to be even greater. It was not an easy task to identify and acquire the necessary crop to project a comprehensive portrayal of the state of affairs. No doubt the literature in Malaysian education does hold numerous publications that may well feed into elucidating the stated objectives but the same could not be obtained in adequate number and scope of coverage on the basis of new research for first time publication. Nevertheless, we consider the venture a reasonable success and deem that the effort would be an added contribution to academia and others who may have particular interest with regard to the intended objectives.

We exercised our discretion as editors in selecting the chapters, although the final decision remained with the publishers. We wanted the chapters to highlight the most recent research for presentation in a scholarly fashion. We strictly wanted to avoid any political or activist undertones. The chapters were to be arranged such that the reader would be able to appreciate them individually against a broader framework of developments in the nation.

Our true appreciation goes to Professor Gopinathan Saravanan of the Lee Kuan Yew School of Public Policy, National University of Singapore, and series editor of the Routledge Critical Studies in Asian Education who actually offered us this opportunity and provided necessary guidance along the way. We thank all the chapter contributors for their willingness and commitment to stay working on the chapters until they were ready for publication, and Routledge for agreeing to put them in print. Finally, we want to thank Alina Ranee for her help with copy editing and her useful suggestions.

Chapter contributors

Hussein Haji Ahmad (Ph.D Stanford) specializes in education policy studies, sociology of educational development, planning, management and leadership. He is currently a Senior Research Fellow in the Department of Educational Management, Planning and Policy, Faculty of Education, University of Malaya.

K. S. Balakrishnan (PhD) is currently a Senior Lecturer and Former Head of the Department of International & Strategic Studies, FASS, University of Malaya. He is a policy consultant for ministries, think tanks, institutes, media and other non-governmental organisations both in Malaysia and abroad.

Kee-Cheok Cheong is Senior Research Fellow, Department of Economics, Faculty of Administration, University of Malaya. His research interests are in development economics with a focus on transition economies, as well as the role of education in development and Chinese overseas. He has published in journals and books in these areas.

Rozilini M. Chung-Fernandez (PhD Leicester) is currently Vice President (Quality Assurance) at HELP University in Malaysia. As a trainer-administrator Rozilini was formerly with the Malaysian Qualifications Agency involved in establishing the Malaysian Qualifications Framework and standards.

Azirah Hashim (PhD) is a Professor in the English Language Department, University of Malaya and currently the Dean of the Humanities and Ethics Research Cluster at the same university. Her research interests include English in Malaysia and in the Region, Language and Law and Academic and Professional Discourse.

Gerhard Leitner (PhD) is a Professor of English Linguistics at the Institute for English Philology at the Free University of Berlin. He is a specialist in varieties of English worldwide, among other interests, and has published widely on these varieties. He has been a visiting professor and external examiner in Malaysia, India, Singapore and Australia.

Hwok-Aun Lee is Senior Lecturer in and Head of the Department of Development Studies, Faculty of Economics and Administration, University of Malaya. His research interests include affirmative action, inequality, labour, social policy, and education.

T. Marimuthu (PhD Manchester) currently serves as an Adjunct Professor at Asia e-University. Formerly he was a Professor of Social Psychology of Education at the University of Malaya and Chairman of AIMST University, Kedah. He was a member of Parliament and a Deputy Minister of Agriculture, Malaysia.

Zuraidah Mohd Don is Dean of the Faculty of Languages and Linguistics, University of Malaya, Chair of the Council of Language Deans, and Chair of the English Language Standards and Quality Council. She is on the editorial board of five international journals, including ISI and Scopus-Indexed journals.

Hena Mukherjee (EdD Harvard), formerly Lead Education Specialist for South Asia at the World Bank, and founding head of the Department of Social Foundations, Faculty of Education, University of Malaya, is an independent international education consultant focusing on higher education.

Abdillah Noh is Assistant Professor and Deputy Dean at the Tun Abdul Razak School of Government, Universiti Tun Abdul Razak. A graduate of the University of Brunei, he has Masters degrees from the universities of Hull and Reading, and received his PhD in politics from the University of Oxford. He has published works mainly on public policy and political economy with a special interest in Malaysia.

R. Santhiram (PhD) is a Professor and Dean of the School of Education, Languages and Communications, Wawasan Open University, Penang. His research interests are in education for ethnic minorities, educational policy analysis and history of education. He has written extensively on minority education in Malaysia, especially for the Indians.

Kuppusamy Singaravelloo is Senior Lecturer in the Department of Administrative Studies and Politics, Faculty of Economics and Administration, University of Malaya. He is Deputy Director (Academic) at the University of Malaya Centre for Continuing Education.

Jasbir S. Singh (PhD Malaya) is a former Professor of Sociological Studies, Faculty of Education, University of Malaya and Chief Programme Officer, Commonwealth Secretariat, London.

Tan Yao Sua holds a doctorate in History and Educational Development. He is currently a Senior Lecturer and Research Fellow at the Centre for Policy Research and International Studies, Universiti Sains Malaysia, Penang.

1 Introduction

*Suseela Malakolunthu and
Nagappan Rengasamy*

Education and national development

Conventional wisdom has it that education plays a crucial role in nation building. This is more distinctly promulgated in the histories of countries that have developed or are deeply engaged in the process of developing after they overcame imperial rule. All the countries in Southeast Asia sought their independence after the Second World War when the concepts and practices of nationhood and nation building were already in vogue in the western world. The immediate post-war years of 1945 and 1948 saw Indonesia, the Philippines and Burma (now Myanmar), along with India, Pakistan and Ceylon (now Sri Lanka) in South Asia, attaining freedom from colonial supremacy. Between the years 1949–1965, Cambodia, Laos, Vietnam, Malaya and the Borneo states of Sabah and Sarawak, and Singapore achieved their sovereignty. And Brunei was proclaimed a free state by the British in 1984 after about 13 years of the right of governance for internal affairs. Thailand, of course, was the only country in the region that was never under any form of foreign governance.

Today, all these countries are at different stages of nation building, while striving to attain the next. Singapore has for some time been recognised as a developed country, some even consider it as advanced, because of its strong open economic position in the world. Singapore reigns as the economic superpower in Southeast Asia. Malaysia (a confederation of Malaya, Sabah and Sarawak), Vietnam, Indonesia, Philippines, and Brunei along with Thailand have also been accounted for their status as developing countries despite the experiences of long lingering internal disturbances politically and ethnically; the rest of the states namely Myanmar, Cambodia and Laos continue to lag within the cornerstones of agrarian and commodity-based economies struggling to put their acts together to arise from the underdeveloped countries pool. These countries provide exemplary cases where education shows up remarkably as a major force with a correlational role in the economic, social and national development of a state (Brock & Symaco, 2011).

A unique feature among most of these Southeast Asian countries was, and is, their multi-ethnic and multicultural population that came about largely because of the inflow of immigrants historically, who in the past had come in as traders and stayed on, who were brought in large numbers by the colonial governments to serve their economic interests, and who left their homeland at their own free will in search of a better life. The immigrant peoples had also brought along their own tradition, culture, language, and religion which in the years forthcoming posed formidable challenges to nation building in the respective host countries. Besides developing the polity industrially, economically, and socially, these countries had to create the ethos and an amiable environment for the various ethnic and cultural groups to live in peace and harmony alongside the others, while at the same time taking care of the predominance of the nation's indigenous people.

In describing and characterising the role of education in nation building, scholars underscore that it generates a literate and enlightened society, a crucial precondition for the national development process. An educated society will be prudently civil and will listen, learn and reason. If at all there is going to be any social cohesion and unity among the diverse groups in society it was to be placated by a well nurtured and informed mind-set. Moreover, education is a direct contributor to human resource development, which in economic terms has come to be connoted as human capital denoting its criticality and relevance in establishing and managing institutions that support a democratic and meritocratic bureaucracy at the same time providing the multifarious resource needs of economic and industrial activities. Education also underlies the social stratification of a society which inherently falls in place according to individual urges, motivation, drive, capacity and opportunity. For example, it raises and determines the largeness of the middle-class of a country constituting professionals, doctors, lawyers, entrepreneurs, teachers and professors, technocrats, administrators, and so forth, which the economists say is an extremely important factor in national well-being and growth.

This book, "Policy Discourses in Malaysian Education: A Nation in the Making" emerged out of a project to capture and document the historical surge and strife of a confederation namely, Malaysia, in the course of its developmental crusade, and how education has been deployed and manoeuvred politically, as the two are deeply intertwined especially in developing countries, to harness national aspirations, ideas and goals as well as to regain and recoup from any shortfalls.

In a matter of fifty over years since independence Malaysia had progressed from a largely agricultural and commodity-based nation into an industrialised, technologically advanced, knowledge-based, and export oriented economy. Politically as well, it has evolved its own form of democracy, attaining new levels of maturity and functionality, while maintaining a monarchical system. However, this book by no means aims to theorise or arrive at any fundamentals of the correlation between education and nation building as it does not constitute adequate number of chapters on all the relevant aspects of education policies which contribution would bear a direct influence on the federation's total development. Nevertheless, it may be pointed out that the materials in the book do span over a reasonable space, time and facets of history of the country and offer opportunity for incidental triangulation and counter verification that readers may draw their own conclusions and assumptions about the nature and narrative of development in the country. The articles assembled present a critical analysis of select policies, of their objectives, implementation, and outcome and, in some cases, expropriated consequences.

The Malaysian experience may resemble those of certain other countries categorically in the region but may not necessarily hold a model to prescribe them. Individually, the manuscripts aim for policy-based discourses and cover several different aspects and perspectives as to how education has been used by those in power as a political protocol in developing the nation. Also, a careful reading of the materials will reveal that the form and state of education in the country may have carved their own courses of growth beyond those deliberately targeted, for the better or worse, along with national development. Additionally, the materials may also help to shed light on whether or not education has directly played a role in the country's growth, or it has been subjected to political expediency, aspirations and controversial stances thus to undermine otherwise a humanistic evolvement of the country and its populace.

By the standards of academic norms, the manuscripts do convincingly qualify as well researched productions supported by both primary and secondary data to deserve meaningful intellectual appeal. The authors are qualified personnel in their respective disciplines. However, none of the chapters on the policy discourses would make much sense independently to strangers lacking sufficient knowledge of the historical background of Malaysia. This chapter as an introduction to the book would serve to address the issue. It will essentially lay out the critical markers of the country's historical and educational development along with the progress directed at growth. In fact, the chapter would stand out as a framework to proffer the context and historical connectivity to all of the different educational policy discourses covered in the different chapters. It begins from the time when Malaya, Sabah and Sarawak parted ways with the colonial rulers, and reaches out to the current period.

Malaysia as it emerged

Malaysia became a national and political reality in 1963 as a confederation of three different countries geographically separated by the South China Sea, namely Malaya, Sarawak and Sabah. Singapore was a member of the organisation at the time of formation but opted out two years later because of political and ideological differences. Malaya or the Malay peninsula (also known as peninsular Malaysia) is an extended terrain of mainland Asia while Sarawak and Sabah are located along the northern shores of the Borneo island. The general history is that the three countries had been long time colonies of the British, Malaya for nearly two centuries, and Sarawak and Sabah since the mid-nineteenth century when they sought British intervention for protection and self-preservation. The three countries had their individual historical background and demographic makeup. Thomas (2007) cited that when independence was proclaimed, it was first for Malaya in 1957, the population was estimated at 6.3 million constituting 49.8% Malays, 37.2% Chinese, and 11.3% Indians. The formation of Malaysia automatically raised the population to a new norm of 9.3 million, and altered the demographic structure which, according to the 1964 census, was at 52.5% Malays and other *Bumiputras* (referring to the natives of Sabah and Sarawak), 36.7% Chinese, 9.6% Indians, and 2.2% Others. The departure of Singapore from the federation, of course, did not make a major difference in the overall population mix but for the Chinese. The new coalition of states had also increased the demographic multiplicity and multiplexity with the inclusion of the indigenous peoples of the two Borneo states with the already multiracial and multi-ethnic population of Malaya.

Economically, the federation had depended largely on agriculture and primary commodities such as rubber, rice and tin. In Malaya, the Malays lived largely in rural areas and relied on farming and fishing for their livelihood, while the Indians concentrated in the estate areas adjoining rubber plantations and provided the necessary labour, and the Chinese formed the majority of the urban population and occupied themselves with tin mining and commercial activities. The people of Sarawak and Sabah were known also to have been involved in agriculture and fishing; however they were not scaled at a comparative level with Peninsular Malaysia. Obviously, there was huge disparity in household income among the ethnic groups, which was coupled with a national poverty rate of 49.3% around the time Malaysia was formed. Data for Peninsular Malaysia revealed the Chinese, then, as the richer of the lot at a poverty incidence of 26%, followed by the Indians and Malays at 39% and 65% respectively (Yusoff, Abu Hasan & Abdul Jalil, 2000). This was legitimately reflected in the corporate ownership of the different groups: Chinese at 27.2%; Malays and *Bumiputras* with 2.4%; Indians with only 1.1%; and, foreigners holding 63.4% (Gomez & Jomo, 1997). However, related data on the economic status of the people could not be obtained for Sarawak and Sabah. Also noteworthy was the Gross National Product (GNP) which at the time of Malaysia formation was at USD 6362 million (Hirschman, 1974). And again, no statement could be produced about the contribution of Sarawak and Sabah to the Malaysian GNP at the time.

Educationally, independent Malaysia was still lingering with the colonial mould, which was designed to serve British political and economic interests rather than promote scholastic and social advancement of the locals. It was more in the form of public offering, often organised and sponsored by the various communities to safeguard their culture, language and tradition, than for institution building let alone national development. It was segregated and disjointed along linguistic-ethnic streams of English, Malay, Chinese and Tamil in the case of Malaya, and was immensely impoverished in terms of resources. Malakolunthu and Rengasamy (2006, p. 121) wrote about the Malayan education at the time of independence in 1957, in *Globalization, Modernization and Education in Muslim Countries*:

> By and large, the educational policy of the British in Malaya had a colonial orientation, exploitative, limited and constricted. There was no noble ideology or greater aspirations or concern for the country, its national development and integration of the ethnically divided population, all of which could have been attained through education. However, the British colonial government opened a number of English medium schools for creating a local educated workforce to fill the support staff positions in the administration. Some local

educated individuals seeking to profiteer from the prevalent situation as well as missionary societies also ventured into the provision of Western education especially for the mixed urban population. A key factor in all these schools was that education was not free hence could not reach out to the masses, especially those in the rural areas. Moreover, the thought of having to pay for education, which was beyond the means of many families, coupled with the desire to promote and retain the identity of home culture led the Chinese and Tamil communities to set up their own vernacular schools to cater for the educational needs of their children. For the Malay children, the colonial government set up Malay vernacular schools that provided free education.

During the pre-independent days secondary education was attributed with economic value: one could proceed to tertiary education that would lead to covetous positions in the government or be offered a better job placement. This was provided only by the British government and missionary schools. However, the Chinese, who were pro-active in their educational pursuits, set up their own independent Chinese secondary schools. The Malays and Tamils were deprived of secondary education because their vernacular schools were limited to primary education. Structurally, the Malays were also allowed the opportunity of secondary education after completion of four years of vernacular education and in attendance of transition classes in English. Technically, during the pre-independent days, English was the main medium of instruction.

A word of caution may be necessary to do academic justice to the narrative in this section especially with regard to facts in the areas of economy and education. More often than not, the historical data are more representative of Malaya than Sabah and Sarawak as such data were scanty or inaccessible for the latter two states. They seemed to have evaded academic scrutiny over the years. But, it may not mean that the two states were devoid of any economic, educational and other institutional development activities prior to their independence. The British government along with the local leadership in the Borneo states, after the Second World War that led to the end of Japanese occupation in the Southeast Asian region, and which left the two states war torn and in shambles, had indeed engaged in rebuilding them with basic infrastructure, amenities, educational system and medical facilities (Lee, 2011).

The context of independence

History has it that the British precluded offering independence to Malaya and, subsequently, the formation of Malaysia, without the assurance of a precondition for unity and harmony among the various ethnic groups (Thomas, 2007). Although the peoples of the land (Malaya) had long lived in a segregated environment culturally and institutionally each taking care of their own communal interests because of the British "divide and rule" policy for unscrupulous economic gains (Drakakis-Smith, 1992), the three major races including all the inherent ethnic groups had to be brought together to foster a common front for independence. The founding fathers who were leaders of the various racial groups thus convened an alliance which in due course emerged with a memorandum called the "Social Contract" which was duly enshrined in the Federal Constitution. Although the drafting of the Social Contract commenced prior to the independence of Malaya, the basic principles from it were adopted for a set of 20 and 18 points of common allegiance for Sabah and Sarawak respectively as the "Malaysia Agreement" to envisage the governance of Malaysia as a federation. Thomas (2007) reported on the nature and essence of the Social Contract in a paper presented at the 14th Malaysian Law Conference in 2007. Accordingly, the obligatory position of the non-Malays in exchange for full citizenship with a right to use their own language and practice their own religion was to accede to the special privileges of the Malays aimed at elevating their economic standing. The paper also highlighted as a crucial element of the memorandum that the multiracial composition of the Malayan population was to be recognized and encouraged, and no form of pressure asserted to integrate it through assimilation.

The readers may also take note that the Malaysia Agreement of the 20/18 points that was drawn between Sabah (previously known as North Borneo), Sarawak and Malaya was signed on the 9th of July 1963 with the British government for the formation of the new federal state before it was officially declared to the world. There may be a brief background on the history of the Malaysia Agreement; however, of relevance to this chapter is the fact that the 20 points for Sabah constituted brief commentaries or descriptions under separate sub-headings, which supposedly was to prescribe the safeguarding of the state's security and autonomy. For the 18 points of Sarawak, apparently, the same 20 points of Sabah but short of the last two were incorporated in the Malaysia Agreement. It seemed that in the case of Sarawak only the sub-headings of the Sabah 20 points were mentioned in the agreement, and the related texts or explanatory notes were not available to-date. Substantially, apart from the administration of the Federation and the States with regard to the new alliance, the Malaysia Agreement raised consensus on key areas such as religion, language, constitution and constitutional safeguards, immigration and citizenship, special position of the indigenous people, and education.

Essentially, the Social Contract in the case of Malaya and the Malaysia Agreement for Sabah and Sarawak with Malaya underscore the inherent diversity and the right of claim for self-identity and self-preservation as factors of allegiance by the three national entities. The key elements of these bonding documents, which were later enshrined in the Federal Constitution, laid the foundation for a multicultural model of governance that was not to be assimilative but accommodative. They were also to be cherished dearly by all future generations to determine the character of nation building for Malaysia.

Becoming a developing nation

While approaching the middle of the second decade of the 21st century Malaysia has just spanned a fifty year period and has made leaps and bounds in its national development. As of 2015, Malaysia may be at the last lap, about five years, of becoming a fully developed nation according to its Vision 2020 which was established in 1991 by the then prime minister Mahathir Mohamad (1991). Since independence, the rate of national development per the key indicators of industrial growth, economy, education, health and social welfare has been sturdy and rapid; and, as registered by many historians, one of the best in the developing world. It is acclaimed of a remarkable achievement of GDP growth at an average of 6.7% through the seventies and eighties (Ariff, 1998). The country had stabilized itself as an upper middle income member state with per capita income of more than USD 9000 as of 2011, which was a 24-fold growth over that of 1970; the national poverty level had been drastically reduced to below 4.0% and unemployment had been touted to remain around 3.0% (Department of Statistics Malaysia, 2011), which is often weighed against a couple of million foreign workers, officially about 12% of the total employment, providing professional and manual labour services in various industries (Economic Report, 2004/2005).

Industrially, Malaysia's growth also has been a telling story about its success. The infrastructure is of world-class; there is ample supply of a versatile, skilled and qualified workforce coupled with investor friendly business policies. Together, they have drawn up to USD 9.2 billion as of 2010 in terms of foreign direct investment (Rasiah & Govindaraju, 2011). The Companies Commission of Malaysia reported that as of 2010 there were about 4000 companies of various business interests from about 40 countries operating in Malaysia (CCM, 2010). According to the Malaysian Institute of Economic Research (MIER, 2012), the main drivers of industrial growth were sectors such as services, manufacturing, agriculture, mining, and construction. All in all, Malaysia has grown as a viable trading partner, holding the 25th position in the world. Moreover, the Global Competitiveness Report (2012–2013) ranked Malaysia as the second highest among the Southeast Asian countries and sixth in Asia after Singapore, Hong Kong, Japan, Taiwan and South Korea. Educationally as well, Malaysia has marked its potential as an educational hub in this part of the world claiming the 10th position as a preferred destination for international students. There are about 80,000 foreign students pursuing their education in local institutions (Tengku, 2011).

Policies and reforms in education

The official document that is often fallen back on to trace the history of Malaysian, or rather Malayan, education is the Razak Report, 1956, which is deemed to have laid the initial groundwork for education post-independence. However, it was the Rahman Talib Report, 1960, which served as the basis for the first Education Ordinance and the Education Act of 1961 for the Malayan peninsula. The Rahman Talib Report came up as an improvised version building on the perceived shortcoming of the Razak Report, which arose from a review of the latter. It also became the legal educational tool for the extension of the mainland Malaysian educational policies and practices over Sarawak and Sabah in the latter years and decades of the 1970s, thus paving the way for the fulfilment of a total National Education system.

Essentially, the policies under the first Education Act aimed at first the Malayanisation, then Malaysianisation, of education. It heralded a period of localisation of the Educational aims and objectives to be managed by the local politicians and policy makers. The National Language Act of 1963 ensued from it elevating the language of the indigenous people, Malay, as the official and national language of the country at the same time emphasising the need to make it the main medium of instruction in all schools, although the actual implementation was to take place in stages. Meanwhile, the English medium and vernacular schools of the Chinese and Indians were required to teach the Malay language as a compulsory subject. Additionally, efforts were undertaken to standardise the curriculum across all forms of schools to reflect the locality, history, economy and culture.

Then, there was the controversial but historical period of the New Economic Policy coupled with the Malay Affirmative Action Policy that lasted for about three decades between the 1970s and 1990s, which came about effectively after the 1969 racial riot that was claimed to have flared up because of the socioeconomic disparity and tension between the races especially the Malays and the Chinese. However, the riot was colour-blind and affected the people across race and ethnicity. The period of NEP (New Economic Policy), as it was popularly known, rolled out a series of educational policies and implementations accompanied by social restructuring and economic advancement strategies that served as the foundation for the dramatic transformation of the country to its current status in the world. However, these policies were not without repercussion or adverse consequences as they were seen by the non-Malay citizens to be lop-sided and Malay-centric. Historians and other scholars would unveil a large number of perspectives that were diverse and polarised on how the NEP had manifested in real terms, and its ramification in terms of socioeconomic and industrial development of the country. They would also tell that the foundation of modern Malaysia was laid during this period. At the same time, there is a prevalent view that the rapid growth of the country and expansive institutionalisation of education and other sectors without due regard for the multi-ethnic nature of the society have undermined the integrity and the nature and character of national development.

The NEP period also introduced the Hussein Onn Report and Mahathir Report in 1971 and 1979 respectively. The accentuation that came out from the Hussein Onn Report was the abolition of the English medium schools altogether and introduction of the English language as a compulsory subject in all primary and secondary schools. Even in the universities the medium of instruction was converted to Malay. But, it was the Mahathir report, also popularly known as the Cabinet Committee Report that stepped out of the context of the previous educational reports, ordinances and legal enactments of building a national education system that underpinned unity among the various races and localization of curriculum to focus on the more direct factors of national development. Rahimah (1998, p. 19) commented that the report "did not delineate a new education policy, the emphasis shifted towards building a truly Malaysian society of the future. To that effect, it emphasizes at all levels of schooling, a holistic (intellectual, spiritual, physical and emotional) approach to quality human development to ensure development from all domains – cognitive, affective, and psychomotor." As a matter of fact the shift in focus was in line with the National Education Philosophy, and set the platform for the declaration of Vision 2020 in 1991.

In 1996, the duo of the current Education Act and the Private Higher Education Institutions Act were passed. These Acts were geared toward internationalizing education and making Malaysia an education hub. Accordingly, they aimed at providing fast paced economic and human resource development by encouraging more liberal policies related to public and private higher education, science and technology, management, and information. As a result, there was a mushrooming of higher education institutions in the form of colleges, university colleges and public and private universities. As of 2011, there were 20 public universities, 4 foreign university branch campuses, 33 private universities, 500 private colleges, 24 polytechnic colleges, and 37 public community colleges (Malaysian Higher Education System, 2012).

On the domestic front, the Education Act 1996 also claimed to be more multiculturally attuned and assured the status quo of the school system with increased fiscal support for the non-Malay medium or vernacular primary schools (only the national or Malay medium secondary schools were endorsed by the government and received statutory financial aid, not the fifty odd Chinese or Mandarin secondary schools which were otherwise sponsored by the community itself; none existed for the Indians.) However, the claim and assurance did not seem to go well with the non-Malay observers. Additionally, there had been ten five-year Malaysia Plans and a couple of Education Blueprints including the latest that would span over 2013 and 2025 on the theme of transformation of education, all of which had given rise to more policies formulated and augmented thus elevating the role and contribution of education at all levels in preparation for making Malaysia a developed nation by 2020.

Chapter summaries

This volume comes with seven core chapters (excluding the Introduction and Concluding chapters) written by persons with relevant experience in the respective fields and necessary educational and professional background; while most are affiliated to universities, a few have held high office in government as well as local and international non-governmental agencies. Their contributions have been based on recent or on-going research, each covering a different aspect of policy intervention and its ramification. Because they come from different cultural and professional background the chapters present a range of multifaceted perspectives.

Also, the chapters have been screened and thematically selected to avoid repeat or redundancy of the same central theme. Besides, they cover the related policies in the context of current developments in the country and thus deal with issues of on-going interest and debate. As assured by the authors, all the chapters in the current format have been prepared for first-time publication. The chapters, in addition to documenting scholarly views and interpretations of the various educational policies and their ideological and systemic impact on national development, will be informational and illustrative to all those who are policy-inclined in Malaysian Education.

Coming next is a chapter on globalisation and the politics of education in Malaysia. It captures the whole of Malaysian historicity with regard to becoming an independent nation encompassing the eras of colonisation, Malaysianisation and globalisation. It categorically underscores and elucidates the constant strife of a newly independent and multiracial state for control, balance and stability between politics and education, even in territorial gains, in the face of an economically egregious status of the races toward nation building. The multiplicity and complexity of challenges and hardships, and the delicate nature of formulating and implementing policies that would appease and bring about harmony among the various sectors of a diverse multiracial society are cautiously dealt with. The topic taken up is rather multifarious in terms of issues covered which, in a number of cases, remain fundamentally unresolved to-date. Nevertheless, the author has done a fair amount of justice to it in an article of a given length. The chapter indeed raises a fundamental question on the relationship between politics and education as to whether it should be one over the other or set apart.

The third chapter is on education of ethnic minorities in Malaysia. It examines the phenomenon of the integrative and instrumental roles of education in the Malaysian context, how they have been handled and what their outcomes have been. The interplay between politics and education and how they affect one another in developing the education system and the delivery mechanism are discussed. It reflects upon the underpinning power struggle between the Malay majority and non-Malay minority groups, the former set for political and cultural supremacy, while the latter for maintenance of cultural identity and right of coexistence with social equanimity, all in the name of nation building. From the narrative, the underhand of a third element, namely economics, may also be perceived as a contributing factor in the discourse. The authors exemplify the integrative role through a number of desegregation and standardization measures undertaken by the government, which were disregarded by the minorities for the sake of upholding their traditional background. For the instrumental role, the authors produced evidence from the decades of a New Economic Policy which was introduced after a racial riot in 1969. The policy constituted largely Malay preferential practices and initiatives seemingly radical for educational mobility, and became a crucial turning point in the history of the country causing a dissentious memory for the minorities.

In the fourth chapter, the authors present a statistically viable narrative of how access and equity have played out in the impactful growth and development of higher education in Malaysia since independence to-date. The authors demonstrate and substantiate the nation building efforts of the government via human resource and educational infrastructure and institutional developments, and how they seem to have affected the various ethnic groups through a range of resultant numeric data that stretched over four decades between 1970 and 2010. The data have been drawn from authentic sources and verified by an independent study, mainly the World Bank (which sponsored the original study of the same title in the East Asia and Pacific region), the Ministry of Education (MOE), Ministry of Higher Education (MOHE), and Department of Statistics. The numbers seem to tell far more than what the narrative suggests. Erstwhile speculations about lopsided implementation of the New Economic Policy which was originally designated to eradicate national poverty and right the socioeconomic imbalance between the races are discussed. The wisdom and actual outcome of the Malay Affirmative Action policies especially in the areas of educational mobility and employment are also evaluated in relation to the ethnicity proportions and accomplishments. The chapter ends with a caution rather than a conclusion about the advanced nation status by 2020, when policy interventions would deeply entrench the differences among the various ethnic groups.

Chapter five refreshes an old issue, namely English language education in Malaysia. The authors attempt at a new diagnosis and perspective on handling of the nation's language policy which, apparently, is grounded in the native or Malay language dominance. They reassess the situation in the context of the English language becoming a lingua franca of the ASEAN region, and make their case against a backdrop of the historical and geopolitical perspectives of its own as well as the neighbouring countries in the region. National development in the face of fundamental changes in the regional and global arenas plays a crucial role in the analysis. The ancestry of the English language in the region and its pervasive nature are weighed in. Counter-productive policy stands taken against the language at the time of independence, and after, to the extent of involving the government in experiments of uncertainties are reassessed. Complications arose because of the multiracial population with the stronger ethnic groups such as the Chinese and Indians demanding their own vernacular rights, and the coping abilities of the urban and rural population which in the latter case constituted largely Malays. Reasons were also extracted from a socioeconomic point of view as the country was aiming to become a developed nation by 2020. The authors record that the foreign language is not only here to stay but has to be strengthened in administrative and communicative usage as well as in the education sector for maintaining Malaysia's global position and creating a globally competitive workforce. And, these have to be done without affecting or undermining the status and ambition of the National language, which is the indigenous people's native language.

In chapter six, the authors take up the development, maintenance, administration, and current status of the Technical Vocational Education and Training or TVET system in the country. Emerging from a World Bank project on Workforce Development, the chapter offers the collective insight of the strengths and weaknesses, and the administrative handling (or mishandling) of the system, along with a question if it would be able to sustain the country's aspiration of becoming a high-income based developed nation by 2020. An awful truth that overlays the system appears to be the delineation of the public and private sectors with the absence of a comprehensive monitoring and coordinating system especially in the case of the latter. Moreover, the authors reveal that the entire system is largely devolved. The genesis of the TVET system as a strategic national interest took shape with rapid expansion of the industrial development programme in the decades preceding the turn of the century coupled with factors of inadequate supply of labour requiring its import, the deceleration of GDP growth during the years of 2000, the populace's desire to belong to the higher rungs of the value chain, and declining quality of education. In the end, the authors raise concerns, seemingly operational in nature, with an earnest call for rethinking and reinventing the system notably in the areas of institutional coordination, funding, quality of education, public-private sector collaboration, programme administration and delivery, and aspects of centralisation and decentralisation.

Chapter seven focuses on the overall trend of the education policy and how it was aligned with human capital transformation over the years. The author writes about growth and development of the nation's education in terms of sophistication and modernisation along with the policies and strategies, and the institutional and infrastructure enactments, which empowered it, especially after the New Economic Policy period. Building on the shortfalls of the New Economic Policy, the chapter narrates the various manoeuvres by the government via education both to recoup and reinvent the nation building efforts toward becoming and sustaining as a developing country with a knowledge economy in a broadly globalising world. The author makes concerted effort to scope the narrative within the parameters of the relationship between education and human resource development, and creating a resilient economy in line with the national vision of a developed nation status by 2020. The author undertakes schematic analysis of the many divergent educational initiatives and elements in a whole range of policy and strategic instruments namely the Education Acts, 1996, the 9th and 10th Malaysia Plans for the periods 2006–2010 and 2011–2015 respectively, the National Economic Action Council (NEAC, 2010), Education Blueprints (2001–2010), the Long-Term Third Perspective Plan (RRJP3), National Key Results Areas (NKRA), and New Economic Model. Although the chapter takes an academic approach with less focus on evidential linkages on the ground on the degree of effectiveness qualitatively of the various policy and strategic enactments, it contributes in providing a holistic perspective of the ideology of establishing the Malaysian education system.

Finally, in the last of the core chapters the author deals not with any particular education policy but a specific issue namely graduate employability. In the past couple of decades, there has been an increasing trend of graduate unemployment, not only among local but foreign university graduates as well. The issue has challenged the government to reposition and reshape its policy stand on higher education planning and administration. Instead of a retrospective or introspective examination of policy effects the chapter investigates the government's mind-making process in policy formulation. The author adopts Critical Discourse Analysis approach, by anchoring on extracts from the "Malaysia and the Knowledge Economy: Building a World-Class Higher Education System" publication and the Graduate Employability Blueprint. The respective roles of the higher education institutions, employment market, and students are arbitrated and redefined. The reasoning on the part of the government seems to orchestrate more, at least from viewpoint of the Graduate Employability Blueprint, towards accentuating the economic value of higher education both to the individual graduates and the nation in the form of a knowledge economy. The chapter raises certain fundamental questions: Has the government's new policy stance toward higher education been arrived after a thorough and comprehensive analysis and understanding of the problem in graduate employability, or has it been overblown to deflect attention from other important aims and objectives? Are the recent higher education reforms consistent with existing policies and strengths as well as the national vision of becoming an advanced country by 2020?

Of course, many more aspects and perspectives could be tapped from the educational and national development of Malaysia. For this volume, substantially, only these eight chapters were made available covering separate areas of interest from an abundance of policy matters in Malaysian education. In the concluding chapter, an attempt is made to weave through the main ideas of the core chapters to bring out a holistic picture of how education has played its role in nation building in Malaysia. It is hoped that there is on-going endeavour on the part of scholars to build on this volume with more chapters to unravel the facts and myths about the Making of Malaysia especially in the education aspect so that the real history of the nation may be made comprehensible for the future generation.

References

Ariff, M. (1998). The Malaysian economic experience and its relevance for the OIC member countries. *Islamic Economic Studies, 6*(1), 1–31.
Brock, C., & Symaco, L. P. (2011). *Education in South-East Asia*. Oxford: Symposium Books.
CCM Companies Commission of Malaysia. (2010). Retrieved from http://www.ssm.com.my/statistic-total-business-companies
Department of Statistics Malaysia. (2011). Retrieved from http://www.statistics.gov.my/main/main.php
Drakakis-Smith, D. (1992). *Pacific Asia*. London: Routledge.
Economic Report (2004/2005). Retrieved from http://www.treasury.gov.my/index.php?option=com_content&view=category&id=73&Itemid=174&lang=en
Global Competitiveness Report (2012–2013). Retrieved from http://www3.weforum.org/docs/WEF_GlobalCompetitivenessReport_2012–13.pdf
Gomez, E. T., & Jomo, K. S. (1997). *Malaysia's political economy: Politics, patronage and profits*. Cambridge, UK: Cambridge University Press.
Hirschman, C. (1974). Economic progress in Malaysia: How widely has it been shared? *UMBC Economic Review* (United Malayan Banking Corporation) (Kuala Lumpur), *10*(2), 35–44.
Lee, C. (2011). 17 missing years in Sabah's history. Retrieved from http://www.freemalaysiatoday.com/category/nation/
Mahathir, Mohamad. (1991). *Malaysia: The way forward. (Vision 2020)*. Retrieved from http://www.isis.org.my/attachments/Vision%202020%20complete.pdf

Malakolunthu, S., & Rengasamy, N. (2006). Elementary and secondary education in Malaysia. In Rukhsana Zia (Ed.), *Globalization, modernization and education in Muslim countries* (pp. 119–134). New York, NY: Novo Science Publications.

Malaysian Higher Education System. (2012). Retrieved from http://www.studymalaysia.com/education/MIER. (2012). Retrieved from http://www.mier.org.my/outlook/

Rahimah, Haji Ahmad. (1998). Educational development and reformation in Malaysia: Past, present and future. *Journal of Educational Administration, 36*(5), 462–475.

Rasiah, R., & Govindaraju, C. (2011). Inward FDI in Malaysia and its policy context Columbia FDI Profiles. Country profiles of inward and outward foreign direct investment issued by the Vale Columbia Center on Sustainable International Investment (pp. 1–16). Retrieved from http://www.vcc.columbia.edu/files/vale/documents/Malaysia_IFDI_Profile_FINAL_FOR_WEBSITE.pdf

Tengku, S. B. (2011). Private higher education in transition: A personal perspective. In Institute of International & Strategic Studies (Ed.), *Malaysia: Policy issues in economic development* (pp. 323–328). Kuala Lumpur: ISIS Malaysia.

Thomas, T. (2007). *The social contract: Malaysia's constitutional covenant.* Paper presented at the 14th Malaysian Law Conference 2007. Kuala Lumpur Convention Centre, Kuala Lumpur. Malaysia. 29–31 October 2007.

Yusoff, M., Abu Hasan, F., & Abdul Jalil, S. (2000). *Globalisation, economic policy, and equity: The case of Malaysia.* Paper presented at the "Poverty and Income Inequality in Developing Countries: A Policy Dialogue on the Effects of Globalisation" Conference, 30 November – 1 December 2011. OECD Development Centre, Paris.

2 Globalisation and the politics of education in Malaysia
Some past and contemporary policy issues

K. S. Balakrishnan

Introduction

Globalisation is challenging the government of the day in various ways, bringing about improvements in the delivery system for the people. It is indeed crucial to remain competitive in attracting foreign investment and international visitors in numerous service sectors. Education too has become an important sector in this light of internationalisation and competitiveness that hold political implications. Malaysia is a developing country with an evolving democratic system of government. It has a relatively stable and strong government. Democracy is growing from the old style single dominant coalition party to one that is challenged by a strong opposition coalition. The issue of good governance has become politically an important theme in recent years; there is no doubt that the activities of state and society as a whole are highly inter-related and closely connected. This chapter will address the nexus of politics and globalisation within the context of Malaysia's education policies and politics.

While the population has great expectation on the government of the day to perform, the state often looks for guidance from the government to do what is necessary for the societal advancement of a plural and multi-ethnic society. Each sector of society is being scrutinised in one way or another with a political mindset. Education and politics in Malaysia are inseparable. The government of the day sometime uses the platform to assert its role in order to capture the political audience in the process of political contestation within the system. This is done in order to overcome political challenges from various parties and to demonstrate a strong sense of nationalism so that the existing regime remains strong. Education is an important sector which becomes the platform for this type of political battle.

Politics and the role of a state from the Aristotelian perspective emphasises that it "must work towards goals which have value, affecting a synthesis between mechanism and ethos, between survival and meaning." Another important principle of Aristotelian thinking is that it includes the "art of finding a proper equilibrium for the forces in the state" (Lerner, 1943). Whether we like it or not, every democratic state or society generally focuses on the search for an equilibrium or balance and meaning of what is good for societal development. The education sector driven by governmental policy too sometimes moves toward such pattern of thinking about equilibrium and balance. There is always an attempt to be comprehensive in addressing the problems of community and state.

Malaysia is no exception in this context. It has not fully, whether we like it or not, come out of its colonial legacy and the dilemma of nation building from the early decades of its nationhood. As a result, this can affect the educational policies and the existing mechanisms put in place. The country's education policy has yet to capture the imagination of a truly liberal education, very much reflecting the nature of its statehood that is still parochial in mindset amidst the claim of liberalisation. This chapter will address some of the political and policy issues connected to education in Malaysia in the age of globalisation. It will focus on how and in what ways communal politics and issues of education are intertwined. Secondly, this survey will offer a critical perspective of the ongoing political progress and expose that globalisation is pushing educational policies beyond communalism. Issues on access, quality, competitiveness and international recognition are also becoming equally important in this transformative stage of the national educational policy in line with the state goals of Vision 2020 aimed at making Malaysia a developed nation by 2020.

Colonial history, communal politics and challenges to educational rights

The theme of colonisation and education is inseparable in the Malaysian context. Colonisation by Portugal, the Netherlands and Britain since 1511 till the time of independence in 1957, had shaped the national political ethos in one way or another, especially when it comes to the desire to view progress and modernisation from a western perspective. Malaya was also temporarily occupied by Japan during World War II which also spurred nationalism and the anti-West sentiment. This painful colonial history brings with it the historical baggage of ethnic politics whereby the Chinese and Indians were once brought into colonial Malaya as tin mine workers and indentured labourers. The granting of independence by Britain was also conditional till ethnic cooperation, peace and stability was more visible. Ethnic based political parties were established before independence, especially after World War II. UMNO (United Malays National Organisation), MCA (Malaysian Chinese Association) and MIC (Malaysian Indian Congress) worked as a coalition party that was known as Alliance Party (*Parti Perikatan*) which later became the National Front (*Barisan Nasional*). National unity and ethnic bargaining was crucial during the constitutional process, granting of citizenship and in seat allocation during elections held when Britain was still in charge till 1957. Singapore, Sabah and Sarawak joined Malaya on 16 September 1963 to form Malaysia. Singapore then broke away in 1965 also due to communal reasons because of the demands of the PAP (Peoples' Action Party) for a Malaysian Malaysia which was basically about equal status and rights for all races.

Anything that challenges Malay political dominance and leadership was closely watched by the state. The Malays as indigenous community were fully aware of their political rights as far before independence as part of the whole idea of nationalism. Nationalism of both the right and leftist origin was spreading worldwide in the age of globalisation, especially toward the end of the World War and the colonial era in Asia. Colonial powers such as Britain were also not all that generous when it came to education and also in managing ethnic communities during colonial Malaya. British rule was seen as conspicuously adopting the politics of "divide and rule." Malays generally lived in the villages, while some of them were employed in the government sectors in lower administrative positions. The Chinese were working in the tin mines. They were located nearer to the urban areas which also gave them an advantage in commerce. Indians were predominantly in the estates or in the plantation sector. Divide and rule was obvious during British colonisation, as efforts to integrate were not encouraged, except when the idea of independence was mooted and negotiations were underway. Britain had lost India in 1947. The Dutch were also ousted in Indonesia. The French were also defeated in Indochina. These events had a significant impact on political change in Southeast Asia and on Malaya and the Borneo states.

The desire of Britain to leave the Southeast Asian region on a positive note was high. It was also important for Britain to protect all her economic and strategic interests for long-term gains in Malaya, Borneo and Singapore. Brunei remained a protectorate until 1984. Prior to leaving Malaya, Britain was also not all that firm in establishing a single education system although there were plans to improve the education sector and reports were produced to suggest a better educational system. Politically and socially, the colonial system permitted for the institutionalisation of Malay Schools, English Schools, Chinese Schools and Tamil Schools. By 1937, Malay schools had 90,436 students. The Chinese vernacular schools had 86,289 students. Tamil schools already recorded some 22,691 students. Some 57,615 students were already enrolled in the better established English schools. This is a clear indication that the divisions were already sown during the British era. Even though Britain later suggested the plan for a single education system through the Barnes Report in 1950, it was already too late (Ahmad, 2003). Overall, the attempt to create a national education system during the colonial era was unsuccessful. Various schools, modes of delivery and languages flourished and became well established under the colonial administrative structure and private sector initiatives. Protecting educational rights became a political issue given the structural social and political system of that era. Later it became a problem because it was difficult to talk about education without touching on politics and political sensitivities of ethnic communities.

Consociational model and Malay political supremacy in the post-colonial era: Implications for the education sector

Ethnic politics, the policy of "divide and rule" by the British, and the manner in which polarisation shaped the very fabric of Malaysian society in the post-colonial era is an important aspect for understanding educational rights and the challenges faced by the multi-ethnic society in Malaysia today. Malaysia was in many ways fortunate that ethnic accommodation was forced upon it indirectly by the British in granting independence, whereby each group has to learn to respect one another and think of ways to collaborate in the nation-building process. The model of cooperation and accommodation can be explained in many ways. The greatest success is of course the victory in elections before and after independence using an ethnic cooperation model.

Scholars have explained and elaborated Malaysia's politics of ethnic accommodation in various ways. One popular model explaining this political process is often known as consociational politics. Forming of consociation and cooperation by sharing power and seats allowed ethnic accommodation in a quite civilised manner. Scholars see this approach as consociational democracy and a system that provides guarantee for the various groups involved in political contests. Its effectiveness can be naturally debated. The consociational approach is about "proportional representation of ethnic based party in legislature" in Malaysia. Parties represented are also allocated seats in the Cabinet. This can allow for a grand coalition. There is also what can be called cultural autonomy on education, religion, language and other elements (Horowitz, 2007, pp. 20–37).

Besides Horowitz's concept of consociation, others such as Harold Crouch, Means and Milne and K J Ratnam had all explained Malaysian politics this way in many of their scholarly works on Malaysian politics. What is important here, however, is that we have to understand the politics of the formation of the alliance party (*Parti Perikatan*) and later the National Front (*Barisan Nasional*) after 1974 in explaining consociational politics in Malaysia. Ethnic bargaining has had a significant impact on the constitutional process and politics in general. Leaders of the various ethnic communities have had a great share of contribution by taking a highly accommodative approach in the political process. The entire process toward constitution making was politically known as social contract and it strives by way of compromise. However, this may not explain well the internal political dynamics without understanding the concept of Malay political supremacy or *ketuanan Melayu* as the indigenous group having different political struggle than that of the non-indigenous community such as the Chinese and the Indians. Article 153(1) of the Federal Constitution enshrines the special position of Malays and their rights and privileges as the sons of the soil and Article 152(1) focuses on the Malay language and Article 3(1) on Islam as the official religion. Numerous other articles and provisions and amendments have been made over the years on quota, civil service, scholarships and reserve land issues (Cheah, 2007, pp. 40–56) Overall, the position of the Malays and other bumiputras were enhanced in every area, while the cultural rights and economic interests of other communities are also protected. This so called liberal approach of inter-ethnic political compromise has allowed peace and stability to prevail for decades now.

It is also important to understand the political dynamics of the colonial era in order to explain the politics of education and the educational system in Malaysia. Creating the education system in post-colonial Malaysia was rather difficult because of this past historical baggage and challenges of the colonial era. For the Malays, the need for creating national identity and nation building without compromising their political supremacy became an important agenda of politicking. Political bargaining in Malaysia after independence too was all about ethnic communities and the struggle for political interest along that line. The introduction of the New Economic Policy (NEP) in 1970 after racial riots was also aimed at creating unity and addressing the challenges of the past, which delineated the social fabric of Malaysian society along ethnic lines. But its success in closing the developmental gaps and distribution of wealth is commendable. Creating a single unified education system, however, remains a challenge. In many ways, the delivery and evaluation system had been more or less unified. But other issues of ethnic bargaining were not all that simple in a post-colonial society.

Ethnic communities in Malaya were conscious of their cultural and language rights via the educational system. Education, like economic rights, became an important platform for politicians and political parties after independence. The Malay community led the struggle against colonial rule to protest the introduction of the Malayan Union in 1946 which was about to give more citizenship for the Chinese and Indians. The process for securing independence was done in stages where an inter-ethnic accommodative political model was adopted with elections in 1955. The right to education was part of the political bargaining and struggle between ethnic communities after independence in 1957. The constitutional process was favouring the Malays and *bumiputra* from the context of the political bargaining or what was then known as the social contract. The Malays who always wanted to ensure their ethnic political dominance and rights were not challenged on issues of their special rights, had also always ensured the use of language, especially Malay language as the national language of the entire nation was well entrenched. Islam was given the status of official religion while other religions and cultural rights were allowed to be part of the system.

While English, Chinese and Tamil education were allowed, support from the government of the day was not very strong for vernacular schools. National schools with Malay education had better support. The introduction of the New Economic Policy after the communal riots in Malaysia in 1969 brought about another important dimension to education and the status of Malay language. By the second half of the 1970s, almost all the subjects began to be taught in Malay. The use of Malay language was even further pushed at the tertiary level for both arts and sciences fields. All government correspondence and reports were to be produced in Malay language as well. Scholarship and quota system for the *bumiputra* were substantive in comparative terms in order to protect the political, economic and cultural rights of the Malays and other *bumiputras*. After the NEP was established, the call for greater use of Bahasa Malaysia became an issue.

The setting up of higher educational institutions such as Universiti Kebangsaan Malaysia (National University of Malaysia) and MARA institutions strengthened the role of the *bumiputra* and expanded the opportunities for the Malays in education. Federal scholarships, state government foundations and other financial facilities were developed to help more students acquire higher education. The aim of uplifting the Malays and *bumiputras* of Sabah and Sarawak became ingrained as part of the national education agenda. The use of Malay language was further strengthened via a massive translation project undertaken by a national literary agency called Dewan Bahasa dan Pustaka (DBP), which also played a vital role in ensuring the supremacy of the Malay language. The entire tertiary education system was channeled into the usage of Bahasa Malaysia, except in the case of certain sciences. But toward the year 2000, the government decided to reverse the policy by introducing the use of English in mathematics and science at all school levels because of the fear that the Malays will be left out in the knowledge economy propelled by the IT revolution. This policy too was altered recently prior to the 13th General Election by the Najib administration because of internal politics and grievances expressed among the teachers and parents in the Malay or national schools. The Iranian revolution too had impact on Malaysia via the means of Islamisation. The rise of fundamentalism had an impact via movements such as ABIM (Angkatan Belia Islam Malaysia), a powerful non-governmental organisation (NGO) led by Anwar Ibrahim who was included into the government by Dr Mahathir. Since then, Islamic values swept into the education system via courses such as religious studies, moral studies for the non-Muslims, and civilisation studies at the tertiary level made compulsory for students.

Globalisation and political change: Educational policy changes beyond communalism

With globalisation, policy liberalisation and changes are imminent in every field. Globalisation as a phenomenon affects many sectors. Changes in the world outside have implications for the domestic scene. Education is definitely not an exception in this regard in the Malaysian context. To explain globalisation as a new phenomenon can be a grave mistake. One could trace globalisation from the times of early civilisations, rivalry between empires, and to that of the creation of new nation-states in Europe. This was later followed by industrialisation, modernisation and without doubt the colonial empires were also dominated from the West. Asia's domination was not well recorded. Throughout ancient and modern history, people, goods, religions and the ideas of science and technology have travelled across the various continents. Conquest and slavery have influenced cultures in an unimaginable way. In line with this, contemporary globalisation is perceived rather differently within the context of a borderless world.

Nobel prize winner Joseph Stiglitz (2002) explains in his famous work on *Globalisation and Its Discontents* that the process of globalisation has a lot more to do with removing barriers to free trade and closer integration which can enrich everyone in the world. The emphasis on good governance, transparency or openness is also given due attention. The focus also is about the planet we share as a single community, social justice, and democratisation. The role of institutions, governments and policies to address the challenge of globalisation is seen as vital (Stiglitz, 2002). Stiglitz is an economist and it is obvious that his perspectives are on managing and straddling globalisation effectively from a material perspective. A nation such as Malaysia has no choice but to somewhat succumb and adjust to the influence of globalisation in order to stay competitive in the global economy. Education of the country can be under scrutiny as well. Globalisation in the contemporary world is also more than that. It is about harmonising rules and regulations and ways of doing things internationally, not just to suit the local scene.

Education is also influenced in various ways by the forces of globalisation. It is as if we are living in a borderless global village and have no choice but to receive the influences of global norms and standards that are spreading widely. Who are setting the standards in the field of education is another issue altogether. With the rapid advancement in information technology, everything is shrinking and appears to have become one, amidst all the inequalities that exist in the global arena. It is inevitable that politics too will be affected by globalisation.

Malaysia is a plural and multi-ethnic society where politics affect practically every aspect of the social and economic dimensions. The impact on education is unimaginable in magnitude because of the way national politics and education are inter-related. Just as the sharing of the nation's economic wealth is often known as a vital issue in national politics of a multi-ethnic Malaysian society, education too is inescapable from undergoing such scrutiny. One can argue that the politics of globalisation and politics of education in Malaysia do have some vital inter-linkages. This is related with the way democratic values and knowledge systems are transferred globally via various means.

Among the areas affected on education in Malaysia is the history of identity politics. This can be analysed from the perspective of a developmental state and the identity of the nation. Identity politics in Malaysia is without doubt based on ethnic politics in a multi-ethnic environment. Political scientists often used the term known as plural society. Ethnicity is still alive in contemporary politics of Malaysia despite all forms of global influences and increased level of democratisation. This is also placed in the aim of positioning Malaysia as a developed country by 2020 from one that has been always seen as a developing country. The aim is also geared toward creating a Bangsa Malaysia or a single Malaysian race or nation as stipulated in the Vision 2020 policy document of 1991 during the Mahathir era. Ultimately, it is for the creation of a single, united and progressive community that is far more secure and intellectually robust.

National politics and education are naturally intertwined. The recently concluded UMNO General Assembly hailed the Malaysia Education Blueprint 2013–2025 in a positive manner. The new educational Blueprint has been developed over more than a year through consultation. It involved, for the first time in the history of education in the country, an inclusive document. The Education Ministry under the leadership of the Deputy Prime Minister Muhyiddin Yassin managed to receive feedback from the whole nation and specifically from important civil society organisations. People at all levels were encouraged to provide input to the ministry's website. Various political parties took the opportunity to champion their political and ethnic interest so that no one feels excluded. This inclusive approach might not have occurred if not for the kind of political liberalisation that had taken place after the Mahathir era. Today UMNO and the government as a whole are responsive on many issues and engage civil society organisations in policy making. It fits well with the slogan of the ruling BN government which advocates a motto of "people first, performance now."

The making of the Malaysia Education Blueprint in 2012 was totally unique compared with the political history of the educational policy document developed before because of the kind political liberalisation in the age of globalisation, influencing Malaysia. Every vote counts where the government of the day is concerned. Therefore, listening and empathy is the rule of the game. Government is responsive in a positive way to help not just the *bumiputra* education but also the vernacular schools. Since independence, education has been an important part of politics. The ruling National Front or Barisan Nasional (BN) coalition had always used education as a political tool. It was an important political agenda for nation building and national unity. Malaysia has yet to come out strongly and sturdily on the educational objective even after almost six decades of independence. In the early years, UMNO politics was also strongly capitalised by teachers and educators. Schools were a vital ground for campaigning. This can be said of the MIC (Malaysian Indian Congress) and MCA (Malaysian Chinese Association) as well.

Language issues and the status of the vernacular schools and their upgrading have always been a political concern. Language is often used by the government as a political tool for nation building. All ethnic communities are constantly vigilant if their language, educational rights and culture are affected or marginalised in any manner. However, the policies of education in the old politics were more protective rather than liberal. The above political concerns over economic interest, culture and education are better addressed in recent years in Malaysia, after more than five decades. The result of the 2008 General Election and the pressure from certain ethnic groups by going to the streets have altered the attitude of UMNO leaders and the ruling BN government as a whole toward greater liberalisation. The revisiting of the idea of *ketuanan Melayu* or Malay political supremacy reveals there is an obvious mind-set change to be more considerate and progressive. Malay leaders are now receptive and were openly talking about being the government for all Malaysians during the 13th General Election in May 2013. UMNO leaders had gone as far as stating that they protect not only the Malays but the rights of all Malaysians while the special rights of one ethnic group is given due attention. This has changed somewhat the political landscape in Malaysia and resulted in much more liberal policies in addressing educational issues of a plural society.

While on the one side the motive of nation building using education is good, there is also pressure faced by ethnic communities about the status of the vernacular schools. This dilemma is not over even today although the government of the day has loudly claimed that vernacular education will remain as it is. Given many of the Chinese and Tamils schools are very much dependent on government approval and assistance, the fear and political bargaining continue to persist even today. Interestingly, even in the recent 13th General Election, one could easily notice how UMNO and its coalition BN used educational issues as part of the campaigning process prior to and during the elections. For example, funds were distributed for upgrading Tamil Schools and Chinese Schools by the incumbent.

Promises were made for continuous support for all the communities. Tamil and Chinese schools have been rewarded with millions of dollars for renovation, repair, upgrading of facilities and procurement of educational tools. Salaries of teachers nationwide were increased prior to the 13th General Election to show the ruling government is serious about the education sector.

Chinese and Indians have also gained in this political promotion of education by the ruling government in order to retain power. Prime Minister Najib decided at the very last month near election to upgrade the status of the New Era College in Kajang to the level of University College. This is actually the location of Dong Jiao Zong, headquarters of the Chinese community's educational pressure group that is politically vocal and sometime associated with the opposition parties. Dong Jiao Zong often puts pressure on the MCA (Malaysian Chinese Association) party and the BN government. While the decision was a good one, it nonetheless did not result in bringing the Chinese votes to the BN during the 13th General Election. However, the government's decision is commendable in trying to please the various ethnic groups. During a book launch ceremony at University of Malaya on 1 December, 2013, Deputy Prime Minister Tan Sri Muhyiddin Yassin who is also Minister of Education stated that the Education Blueprint 2013–2025 guarantees and had already cemented the rights of vernacular education, that include both Chinese and the Tamil schools. The government now seems to be more committed to give aid (Yunus, 2013). However, Dong Jiao Zong's remarks in December, 2013 were not positive of the Education Blueprint 2013–2015. It argued that the blueprint did not provide clear policy and measures for developing vernacular schools. Instead, the gist of the Education Blueprint is about implementing a monolingual education system (Are vernacular schools in jeopardy? 2013).

While many political issues of education have been positively treated in recent years, Malaysia still has a long way to go in attaining the goals of Vision 2020 pertaining to a unified developed nation that is psychologically liberated from the old identity based issues. Ethnic and religious issues will crop up from time to time. For example, after the 13th General Election, another issue emerged where one of the schools under renovation was severely attacked in the media for making students have their meals not in the canteen but in the changing room which is also closer to the washroom. The public were furious and the school headmaster and the Education Ministry were severely criticised by the public for being insensitive. Somehow ethnic and religious issues rear their ugly heads in a multi-racial society because of the certain irresponsible acts committed by the few.

One of the educational issues in Malaysia most heavily discussed and criticised since 2007 was the course to be introduced in all public universities known as Ethnic Relations Module. Initially the module was attacked and brought up in parliament for being biased and having factual inaccuracy. It was later pulled back and the government set up a five member panel, led by a professor from Universiti Kebangsaan Malaysia to sort out the problem (Syed Hussin Ali, 2008, pp. 139–145). While the problem was solved amicably, issues of this nature tend to create negative image for the ruling government that has been in power since

1957. In the past, books used in teaching certain modules were questioned for representing ethnic communities in a negative manner with factual errors and prejudice. Malaysia's history books too are sometimes being questioned for distorting historical facts.

Access, quality, competiveness in education: Challenges in the age of globalisation

Malaysia is a developing country with a vision to become a developed or high income economy by 2020. Its concerns are an array of issues in order to attain this goal and become a modern society while sustaining its own cultural, religious and traditional good values and identity. Attaining Vision 2020 in itself is a significant challenge for the nation. Whether Malaysia can achieve the goal of a truly developed society in every aspect is questionable. The possibilities are that Malaysia can develop parallel to some developed countries in certain areas if proper policies, actions and amenities are put in place in the educational sector. Basic access to education and literacy is a vital part of the educational and national political agenda. Malaysia has in many ways developed its basic educational facilities, infrastructure and access for its citizens regardless of ethnic background. But this may not be enough.

In line with the United Nations Millennium Development Goals (MDG), Malaysia recently highlighted its progress in literacy. The report pointed out that the enrolment ratio in primary education in 1990 was 96% and reached 98% in 2009. The proportion of students reaching from grade 1 to last grade was 98.1% in 1990 and 99% in 2009. Literacy rate for those between the age of 15–24 which included men and women stood above 95% in 1990 and 97% in 2009 (Millennium Development Goals, 2011). During a ceremony in November, 2013, while presenting to the UNESCO (United Nations Educational, Scientific and Cultural Organisation) the Malaysia Education Blueprint 2013–2025, Deputy Prime Minister and Education Minister Tan Sri Muhyiddin Yassin highlighted the country's achievement in the educational field and its outreach. In his view, Malaysia has currently achieved the near-universal primary and secondary school enrolment rates at 96 per cent and 91 per cent respectively (DPM, We can be in the world's top 3, 2013). This is indeed a remarkable achievement for a nation that is still at times grappling with issues of nation building and ethnic challenges. It is important to highlight that Malaysia has been able to achieve this even though not all schools in this category are fully government-funded.

The above indicates generally a positive trend. However, the method used to gauge literacy can be questioned. The UN Resident Coordinator, Kamal Malhotra in his remarks in the 2010 report argued that some indigenous groups are still left behind (MDG, 2011). Obviously, there are many more issues to look at, in the case of literacy and access. While literacy and access to education in Malaysia overall can be said to be high, the quality of the overall education for the school going children needs further scrutiny. Malaysia still ranks poorly in the PISA (Program of International Students Assessment) assessment test in comparison with other

Asian nations. It was reported that Shanghai, Singapore, Hong Kong, Taiwan and South Korea appeared among the top five in ranking. While the global average score for reading was 496, for mathematics, 494 and for science, 501, Malaysia's score for reading remained at 398, for mathematics 421, and for science 420. Some 5700 students aged above 14 years participated in the study conducted in 2012 (Arumugam, 2013). Malaysia ranked 52 out of 65 countries which participated in the PISA survey. This is not a positive sign at all.

Overall, it is obvious Malaysia is still far behind in comparative terms on quality of education and competitiveness. International rankings by various organisations have put Malaysia in a not so comfortable position. This is the same in the case of ranking the tertiary education institutions. So far, only University of Malaya has been ranked in the top 200 universities of the world in the QS World University Ranking. Other Malaysian universities are far behind UM, even though there are now about 20 public universities funded by the government with good infrastructure and facilities for quality education. The adherence on ranking and research competitiveness is currently on the radar of the government in power. By looking at these issues, it is quite obvious how both globalisation and politics affect the educational policies in Malaysia. The government is pushing but many local universities are resisting this global trend by not participating. The reasons are always both lack of performance and politics.

The development of social and educational capital in Malaysia is without doubt in line with the competitive needs of the country's economic demand and geared toward attaining high quality human resource goals. This is naturally in line with the politics of globalisation. The development of credible human resources or social capital has pushed the national educational agenda to emphasise science and technology. Malaysia currently focuses on science and technology education for enhancing the workers' skills and human resource development for the long term. There is an attempt to cap at 60:40 the ratio for science and technology versus the arts and social sciences education. The degree programs in the universities throughout the nation are all tailored to fulfill this national policy. But the reality on the ground can be different and can range at a ratio of 30:70 between science and arts. Research is heavily encouraged at the higher learning institutions. For the 2013 budget alone, some RM$600 millions was allocated by the government. While this is important, Malaysia still stands far behind the developed countries in the 2013 allocation for research and development. Only 1.07% in the gross domestic product (GDP) was allocated for such purpose, which is still far behind many developed nations in the West (Povera, 2013).

Overall, the policies established thus far in view of obtaining global competitiveness for education in Malaysia have yet to bring about solid results. While Malaysia ranked very well on the global competitiveness index in the economic field, hovering between 18 and 23 positions in the recent decades, it is still unable to correct its ranking on the quality of education. Visits and exchanges are regularly held by Ministers and ministry officials to developed countries such as Australia, United Kingdom, United States of America, Canada, New Zealand and Singapore for study and benchmarking standards. Educational policies too are altered to ensure Malaysia is not left behind and is able to compete in the global education sector. Ulrich Zachau, World Bank Country Director for Southeast Asia observed that Malaysia's education system is excessively centralized, thus affecting responsiveness and adaptability to local needs. Information fragmentation on actual performances and shortage of qualified teachers were also pointed out by him (Zachau, 2013); many issues remained unresolved.

While Malaysia can improve, it is important to highlight the country is among the most resourceful on education. Billions of dollars are allocated annually to uplift education. New approaches with greater autonomy are needed. Changes in this light are slow, but indications are there. For example, the University of Malaya is given more autonomy on research, curriculum and fund raising. More universities will be moving in that direction if such policies can be implemented. Support for developing a high quality teaching staff is encouraged via government scholarship and grants for expanding the pool of PhD qualified lecturers. Teachers in schools are currently encouraged to pursue postgraduate studies.

It is hoped that policy and program autonomy will also slowly move into the school system. But this can take some time given the traditional structural problems of the education system as a whole which must be overcome. More activities of benchmarking with best foreign learning institutions are also taking place in line with internationalisation. Students are given more courses for enhancing their soft skills and thinking skills. International student exchange programs have been growing rapidly in recent years. Overall, one could see that Malaysia is adapting to the changes and challenges of globalisation in order to improve its reputation in education moving beyond the old agenda of communal politics, to one that promotes quality and competitiveness. But this is not an easy task ahead as communal politics often hamper policy implementations towards adopting multiculturalism and educational freedom. Ethnic issues and doubt about the so called meritocracy adopted in the selection process for universities for certain courses are sometime raised by NGOs and others. Politicians too sometime raise issues during party conventions; these are widely reported, particularly on the status of ethnic based education. These developments can frustrate all the other positive dimensions of educational policies.

Education as commodity

Malaysia has also been promoting itself as a regional education hub so that many in the developing countries can benefit and enjoy quality education at a lower cost and to prevent student exodus to costly places such as the United Kingdom, USA, Australia, New Zealand, Canada and Singapore. Education is also viewed as a competitive commodity and is seen as vital to the economic interest for attracting foreign investment. Emulating the government's success of promoting the tourism sector can be used as a model. Many twinning programmes with foreign western universities are found in Malaysia. Foreign university campuses and brands such as Monash University, Nottingham University, Swinburne University, RMIT Melbourne, Warwick, Heriot-Watt and many more are becoming part of Malaysia's promotion strategy of private education. Malaysia's very own top private universities such as HELP, LimKokWing and many more are also going global by setting up branch campuses and extended programmes abroad. University of Malaya has also set up its own private university by partnering with the University of Wales. Malaysia is currently hosting more than 80,000 foreign students (Tengku, 2011). It is aiming at doubling the intake in the decades to come. Malaysia's free investment zone such as Iskandar in Johor, which is not far from Singapore, is also drawing billions of dollars in terms of foreign direct investment. Education and health sectors are also promoted as a vital component for luring top foreign universities in this type of free economic zone. Even China's top universities are showing interest in this investment zone.

Conclusion

The educational policy and facilities in Malaysia are growing in an unprecedented manner, moving beyond the politics of communalism and striving for competitiveness. This is definitely in line with the national goal of attaining a developed nation status and a high-income society. More changes can be witnessed in the coming years as education remains a priority sector. There is speed and realisation in implementing good policies. However, it can be frustrating to see how the political forces of globalisation can affect educational policy in a developing country such as Malaysia without much deeper thinking and analysis. There is some lack in implementing a liberal sense of education and philosophy as a whole. The challenge is always about how domestic politics is managed so that liberal education does not suffer. Obsession with science, technology and development may not always bring about the expected social and societal advancement if the social and political forces are not well addressed. Political liberalisation is still an ongoing process in Malaysia. Ultimately, it is not the material advancement desired but the mental liberation and mindset change which will be the real game changer for total educational and national advancement.

The aims of Vision 2020 for creating a developed society are certainly good for Malaysia, but the dynamics of policy changes, infrastructure and autonomy are still a work in progress. If Malaysia is not careful, it will not become truly competitive in education. While policy changes are put in place by the top level, change in the local mindset at lower level of the education system is also highly desired when it comes to implementing credible policies. Local ideology and tradition can be frustrating in the knowledge age. Certain ideological barriers must be overcome in order to pursue true advancement, quality and competitiveness. Traditional values sometimes can be a major hindrance to progress. Balancing all the forces at play in a developing nation such as Malaysia is also not that simple politically. Ethnic dominance over values and educational culture can affect noble policies. Transformation takes real courage and leadership. How Malaysia regressed in implementing the use of English in teaching mathematics and sciences after the Mahathir era offers a good lesson in understanding the political psyche of the nation on educational policies. It is obvious that Malaysia is suffering from an identity crisis in making the necessary changes in a globalised world. The overall results are also indicating that Malaysia is still far behind in comparative terms with many countries in Asia. This is a common problem among the advanced developing states in balancing material progress and mental liberation.

Malaysia is slowly but surely maturing on the right path in doing its soul searching and in trying to be accommodative of all views. Democracy and political liberalisation in the age of globalisation seems to be pushing the boundaries and opening up the minds of the leaders to be consultative in orientation. The school system and tertiary education must be geared to attaining this inclusive noble goal and move beyond the past limited approaches. Policy issues such as language or medium of instruction, type of education whether arts or science, educational values and cultural and religious issues are inescapable from being politicised. Political bargaining and its effect on ethnic interest can sometimes complicate basic educational issues. Whether Malaysia likes it or not, technological advancement and its implications will affect the future trends in education. Information sharing and the debate on educational policy to move beyond communalism are gaining momentum. But one cannot expect immediate results given the inherent problems such as ethnicity, traditional values and political realities continue to be a challenge.

References

Ahmad, R. M. (2003). Education in Malaysia. In R. B. Abdul & P. Schier (Eds.), *Education in Malaysia: Unifying or divisive?* (pp. 11–31). Kuala Lumpur: Malaysian Strategic Research Centre and Konrad-Adenauer-Foundation.
Are vernacular schools in jeopardy? (2013, December 20), *Malaysian Insider*.
Arumugam, T. (2013, December 15). Aiming to be among the top education systems. *New Straits Times*.
Cheah, B. K. (2007). Malaysia: Envisioning the nation at the time of independence. In R. E. Abdul (Ed.), *Rethinking ethnicity and nation building* (pp. 40–56). Puchong: Malaysian Social Science Association.
DPM: We can be in world's top 3. (2013, November 10). *New Straits Times*.
Horowitz, D. (2007). Approaches to inter-ethnic accommodation: A comparative perspective. In R. E. Abdul (Ed.), *Rethinking ethnicity and nation building* (pp. 20–37). Puchong: Malaysian Social Science Association.
Lerner, M. (1943). *The politics of Aristotle*. New York, NY: The Modern Library.
Povera, A. (2013, December 18). PM: Science will create wealth, jobs for people. *New Straits Times*.
Stiglitz, J. (2002). *Globalisation and its discontents*. New York, NY: Penguin Books.
Syed, H. A. (2008). *Ethnic relations in Malaysia: Harmony and conflict*. Petaling Jaya: Strategic Information Research Development Centre.
Tengku, S. B. (2011). Private higher education in transition: A personal perspective. In Institute of International and Strategic Studies (Ed.), *Malaysia: Policy issues in economic development* (pp. 323–328). Kuala Lumpur: ISIS Malaysia.
Yunus, A. (2013, December 2). Vernacular schools will remain, says Muhyiddin. *New Strait Times*.
Zachau, U. (2013, December 21). Spend better on learning, not more. *New Straits Times*.

3 Education of ethnic minorities in Malaysia

Contesting issues in a multiethnic society

R. Santhiram and Tan Yao Sua

Introduction

Education of ethnic minorities is a much debated subject in multiethnic societies when it involves the integrative and instrumental roles of educational delivery among the different ethnic groups. The integrative role of education in multiethnic societies is compounded by opposing stands from the assimilationists (generally from the majority group) and the pluralists (generally from the minority groups). The former argues for a common language policy and a common schooling process to bring about value consensus and social cohesion, while the latter argues for pluralism to ensure the coexistence of diverse languages and cultures (see, for example, Edwards, 1981, 1994). It is within a specific socio-cultural context that the integrative role of education takes on relevance in one direction or the other. Alternatively, policy makers may opt for a middle course by adopting some form of combination between assimilation and pluralism. All in all, policy intervention to facilitate the integrative role of education in multiethnic societies has often become a "pluralist dilemma" (Bullivant, 1981) to policy makers. Meanwhile, the instrumental role of education is most crucial in helping disadvantaged ethnic groups to narrow the socioeconomic gap through educational advancement. This is often aided by preferential policies that offer special treatments to disadvantaged groups. But preferential policies along ethnic lines have become contentious given their built-in propensity to perpetuate ethnic animosity, despite the dire need for educational institutions to uphold social equity and social equality among the various ethnic groups.

Viewed against this backdrop, the education of ethnic minorities in Malaysia (Malaya before 1963) provides an interesting case study as far as the integrative and instrumental roles of education are concerned. This is primarily because of its demographic structure that results in competing ethnic groups. Malaysia is a multiethnic society comprising three main ethnic groups, namely Malays, Chinese and Indians. The Malays are the indigenous group, whereas the Chinese and Indians are originally migrants who came to Malaya in large numbers beginning in the mid-nineteenth century. The influx of these migrants was largely drawn by economic opportunities created by the British in Malaya. The Chinese were mainly involved in tin mining activities, while the Indians were mainly engaged in the opening up of land for large scale planting of rubber. These diasporas of migrant workers, who were transient in nature in the beginning but later developed roots into settled communities, have transformed the demographic structure of the Malay Peninsula, which was until then, a predominantly Malay enclave. By the time of independence in 1957, the ethnic composition of the population was 49.8 per cent Malays, 37.2 per cent Chinese, 11.7 per cent Indians and 1.8 per cent other ethnic groups (Hirschman, 1974). Going by this demographic structure, the Malays are the dominant majority group, while the Chinese and Indians are significant minority groups. Over the years, the Malay population has grown steadily, constituting 53.2 per cent in 1970 (Malaysia, 1972), 57.3 per cent in 1987 (Malaysia, 1987) and 58.2 per cent in 1996 (Malaysia, 1997). This has strengthened their status as the dominant majority group. By contrast, the population of the Chinese and Indians has shown marked decline over the years. They respectively constituted 30 per cent and 8 per cent of the total population in 1996 (Malaysia, 1997). In 2000, their population further declined to 24.5 per cent and 7.2 per cent respectively (Tey, 2006). Nevertheless, the Chinese and Indians are not relegated to marginal status, more so the Chinese who still constitute a sizeable group to challenge the Malays.

Given this demographic structure, it is inevitable that education has become a contested terrain for the various ethnic groups in Malaysia, especially in relation to its integrative and instrumental roles. In fact, prior to independence, the integrative role of education has been largely compromised to accommodate the strong linguistic and cultural assertions of ethnic minorities for mother tongue education, resulting in a segregated multilingual primary school system comprising the Malay primary school, the English primary school and the vernacular primary schools: the Chinese primary school and the Tamil primary school. There is nothing much that the post-colonial government could do to revamp such a system of primary education given the strong support of the Chinese and Indians for mother tongue education in the formative years of schooling, except for desegregation measures to foster greater ethnic interaction within the existing primary school structure. Although these desegregation measures were not opposed by the Tamil community, the Chinese community, led by the Chinese educationists affiliated to the United Chinese School Teachers' Association (UCSTA or Jiao Zong) and the United Chinese School Committees' Association (UCSCA or Dong Zong), had adopted a strong stand against these measures. However, it was a different scenario at the post-primary levels where the government was determined to push for a common language policy from early on to strengthen the integrative role of education. It was felt that a common language not only could provide the means of communication across ethnic boundaries, but also a common dominator for the various ethnic groups in the country (Ibrahim, 1981). The Chinese secondary schools (the Tamil primary school was terminal in nature as there was no Tamil secondary school in the country) were the main casualty of this intervening measure, resulting in their conversion to the national medium (initially English medium and subsequently Malay medium), despite the strong opposition of the Chinese educationists. Meanwhile, the instrumental role of education in Malaysia is compounded by the divide and rule policy of the British which deprived the Malays of the much needed educational mobility during the colonial period. This problem of educational mobility was addressed by the post-colonial government through the implementation of preferential policies in favour of the Malays, culminating in much discontent among the Chinese and Indians.

This chapter begins by tracing the emergence of a multilingual primary school system and discusses subsequent government attempts to desegregate this system of education. It then goes on to examine the elevation of Malay, the majority language, as a main medium of instruction and how this measure has impeded the development of Chinese secondary schools in Malaysia. Finally, it examines the implementation of preferential policies in favour of the Malays and the implications of these policies.

Attempts at desegregating the multilingual primary school system

Since independence, the Malaysian educational system has allowed for the vernacular primary schools of ethnic minorities, partly financed by the respective communities, to coexist with the Malay primary school (officially known as the national school) and the English primary school (converted to Malay medium of instruction in the 1970s). This multilingual primary school system has its historical roots in the British colonial era. The influx of the Chinese and Indian migrants to Malaya, the *laissez faire* educational policy adopted by the British and the political intent of the British to divide and rule Malaya led to the emergence of this multilingual primary school system. But during the period of decolonisation in the 1950s, this multilingual primary school system was deemed malintegrative by the British as it had resulted in ethnic segregation. However, efforts by the British to replace this malintegrative primary school system with an English-Malay bilingual school system were opposed by the Chinese and Indian communities and failed to bring about the desired outcome (Haris, 1983). Prior to independence, out of political exigencies, the Razak Report retained the multilingual primary school system amidst an overarching measure to impose a uniform school curriculum for all the primary schools regardless of medium of instruction. It was hoped that this overarching measure would bring about a common process of enculturation (see Federation of Malaya, 1956). The promulgation of the Razak Report was the fulfillment of promises made by the Alliance during the 1955 Federal Legislative Election – the first ever election held by the British to elect an interim local government. The Alliance was a tripartite political coalition comprising the United Malays National Organisation (UMNO), the Malayan/Malaysian Chinese Association (MCA) and the Malayan/Malaysian Indian Congress (MIC). It won the 1955 Federal Legislative Election and formed the interim local government. It went on to rule the country until now but was transformed into the National Front to include more coalition members in 1974.

Subsequent developments showed that this segregated system of primary education was regarded by some quarters of the Malays as the root cause of ethnic polarisation in the country, though strongly disputed by Chinese and Indian educationists who are staunch advocates of cultural pluralism. There were even repeated calls by these Malays to abolish the vernacular primary school system. Thus far, the government has not succumbed to this pressure. But since the mid-1980s, the government has resorted to several intervening measures to desegregate the primary school system to foster greater ethnic integration among the primary school students. As we shall see, these measures were strongly contested by the Chinese educationists.

The first desegregation measure undertaken by the government came in 1985 when it pushed for implementation of the integrated school project to bring the three different streams of primary schools under the same building (Haque, 2003). This project involved relocation of three different streams of primary schools to newly built integrated school complexes. Alternatively, the three different streams of primary schools found to be located adjacent to one another were combined to become integrated schools. A coordinating committee comprising school administrators and teachers from the participating schools would be tasked to oversee the integrated school project. It was hoped that establishing integrated schools would enable joint participation of students in co-curricular activities, thereby promoting better ethnic interaction, understanding, cooperation and tolerance among them (Sia, 2005). There was not much resistance to the project from Indian educationists. But it was different for the Chinese educationists who feared that being part of the integrated school project would make Chinese primary schools lose their character. Their main concern was directed at the dominant use of Malay in the integrated school project which would diminish the use of Chinese as a language of wider communication within the school domain. This concern was raised by the Chinese educationists following their visit to the first integrated school established by the government, the Teluk Sengat Integrated School located in Kota Tinggi, Johor, which comprised the Nan Ya Chinese Primary School, the Ladang Teluk Sengat Tamil Primary School and the Teluk Sengat National School. The opposition by the Chinese educationists put paid to the integrated school project (Tan & Santhiram, 2010).

Despite the failure of the integrated school project, the government has not given up hope to desegregate the primary schools. In the mid-1990s, it mooted the vision school project (Haque, 2003). The underlying concept of this project was quite similar to that of the integrated school project. But in contrast to the integrated schools, participating schools were given the autonomy to administer their schools to maintain their original identity or character (Ministry of Education, 2001). Apparently, this was an attempt to win over the support of the Chinese educationists who had rejected the integrated school project on the grounds that the Chinese primary schools would lose their character upon participating in the project (Kementerian Pelajaran Malaysia [KPM], 1995). But, like the integrated school project, the vision school project also did not find favour with the Chinese educationists. By 2005, the government could only establish five vision schools: the Pekan Baru Vision School, Parit Buntar (Perak), the Taman Aman Vision School, Alor Setar (Kedah), the Tasik Permai Vision School (Penang), the

USJ 15 Vision School, Subang Jaya (Selangor) and the Pundut Vision School, Seri Manjung (Perak) (Ng, 2009). Of the five vision schools, only one, the USJ 15 Vision School, involved the Chinese primary school. But the Tun Tan Cheng Lock Chinese Primary School participating in this particular vision school was not an existing Chinese primary school but a new Chinese primary school established by the government (Tan & Santhiram, 2010). It appears that the government was forced to resort to this deliberate measure to realise the vision school project. Since the establishment of the five vision schools, the government had not made any significant breakthrough in the vision school project.

It was perhaps because of the lack of support for the integrated and vision school projects, especially from the Chinese educationists, that the government was forced to come out with a new measure to integrate the primary school students. This new strategy was implemented in 2006 following the launching of the Ninth Malaysia Plan (2006–2010). Among other things, the Ninth Malaysia Plan aimed at making the national school (the Malay primary school) the school of choice for all races (Malaysia, 2006). This aim was subsequently incorporated into the Education Blueprint (2006–2010) prepared by the Ministry of Education (KPM, 2006). Indeed, as mainstream primary schools, the national schools have not lived up to government expectations to become a common platform to foster ethnic interaction. For instance, from a population of 2,211,971 students enrolled in the national schools in 2002, the number of Chinese students was a mere 46,670 (2.1 per cent) and Indians 95,180 (4.3 per cent) (Abdul Rafie, 2005).

A host of strategies were adopted by the Education Blueprint to ensure that the national school would become the school of choice for all races. These strategies included upgrading of infrastructural facilities, offering of Chinese and Tamil languages as elective subjects, inculcating academic excellence, promoting a positive school culture and climate, providing strong support systems, strengthening the basic reading, writing and arithmetic (3Rs) skills, producing students with high aspirations and moral values, implementing an effective curriculum, and ensuring quality and effectiveness of administrators and teachers (KPM, 2006). Among these strategies, the offering of Chinese and Tamil languages as elective subjects deserve our attention primarily because it provides the extra impetus and incentive to attract more non-Malay students to the national schools. Prior to this, the learning of Chinese and Tamil was not given such an emphasis and position. Traditionally, Chinese and Tamil are being taught as language subjects in an ad hoc manner through the Pupils' Own Language (POL) classes which are dysfunctional in most cases. Although, in 1996, some national schools started offering Chinese and Tamil as Additional Language subjects within the formal school curriculum for students from Primary Year Three to Year Six with an allocation of four periods per week, these classes were not purportedly targeted at the non-Malay students; they also catered for Malay students who aspired to pick up an extra language or the basic skills of Chinese and Tamil. The same goes for the introduction of Chinese and Tamil for Communication classes in 2003 with an allocation of two periods per week for students from Primary Year One to Year Six (Ong, 2009).

This new measure was viewed with much mistrust by the Chinese educationists who cautioned the government of the need to provide equal treatment to all primary schools (*Nanyang Siang Pau*, 23 April 2006). This note of caution was targeted at the government's neglect of the development of Chinese primary schools (and also the Tamil primary schools) over the years. It is a well-acknowledged fact that the vernacular primary schools had not been provided with adequate development funds as well as sufficient trained teachers to strengthen their development. Other problems arising from demographic changes also resulted in overcrowding of classrooms in urban areas and declining enrolments in rural areas. These problems required government interventions as they involved land acquisition for building new schools to ease overcrowding and to relocate under-enrolled schools to prospective areas (Tan, 2002).

It is still too early to say with certainty that the measure to make the national school the school of choice for all races will bring about the desired outcome. For one thing, more Indian students would be attracted to the national schools given the generally deplorable state of Tamil primary schools in the country (Marimuthu, 1984). Prior to adopting this measure, a large number of Indian parents (about 50 percent) had already shown their preference for the national schools over the Tamil primary schools (Yong, 2003). This is most alarming as it appears that these Indians are forced to abandon their mother tongue education not because they do not value their own language and culture but more because they reject the poor quality of education provided by the Tamil primary schools. But it is a different case for the Chinese. The Chinese primary schools have evolved strongly to become the preferred schooling choice of Chinese parents. For instance, in 2003, it was estimated that about 80–90 per cent of Chinese parents enrolled their children in the Chinese primary schools (Yong, 2003). This strong preference for the Chinese primary schools could be attributed to the fact that they are well run, enforce strict discipline and achieve good academic results (Tan, 2002). Thus, it will be an arduous task for the national schools to outbid the Chinese primary schools. Also, the teaching of Chinese as an elective subject may not be a viable replacement for mother tongue education. More importantly, the government has not addressed the strong Islamic element embedded within the national schools that deters many Chinese parents from sending their children there. It appears that the latest government move to integrate the primary school students may suffer the same fate as the earlier moves due to its failures to involve the Chinese.

From the foregoing, it is clear that the main detractor of the government's desegregation measures comes from the Chinese educationists. This is primarily because of their desire to maintain the Chinese primary schools as providers of Chinese mother tongue education as well as their firm stand for equality of educational development across ethnic boundaries. To be fair, the Chinese educationists are not totally against fostering greater ethnic interaction among the primary school students as long as the character of the Chinese primary schools remains intact. They did support the Integration Plan for Unity among Students or *Rancangan Integrasi Murid-Murid untuk Perpaduan* (RIMUP) mooted by the government in 1985. This Plan did not involve the merger of the three different streams of primary schools. It only involved joint participation of students in sporting activities as well as other co-curricular activities. But for some reason, this Plan has not been rigorously implemented by the government.

Malay as the main medium of instruction and the Chinese secondary schools

The promulgation of the Razak Report in 1956 marked the beginning of attempts by the government to implement a common language policy at the secondary level. As mentioned, the Razak Report had retained the multilingual primary school system that had existed since the colonial period. But beyond this level of education, the Razak Report had no intention to allow for other languages to be used as the medium of instruction. Instead, it opted for Malay as the main medium of instruction. This was declared as the ultimate objective of the national educational policy (see Federation of Malaya, 1956). The main target of this ultimate objective was the Chinese secondary schools which had developed strongly alongside the Chinese primary schools. The aim was to convert these schools to the national medium to strengthen the integrative role of education via Malay as the language of national integration – these schools would be initially converted to English medium and subsequently Malay medium when the position of English as the official language of the country was reviewed ten years after independence as prescribed by the constitution. The Razak Report attempted to convert the Chinese secondary schools through the provision of public examinations. This was reflected by its intention to establish a single-type of National Secondary School (NSS) in which the students sat for a common public examination (Federation of Malaya, 1956).

The attempt to convert the Chinese secondary schools to the national medium came barely a week after the promulgation of the Razak Report via a directive from the Department of Education. This directive notified the Chinese secondary schools that the Lower Certificate of Education (LCE) examination (taken at the end of Secondary Year Three) would be conducted in English and they had a week to register their students for the examination. The Chinese secondary schools were caught off-guard by the directive and the Chinese educationists immediately came out in the open to accuse the government of attempting to force the Chinese secondary schools to switch their medium of instruction to English in order to allow their students to sit for the LCE examination (Jiao Zong Jiaoyu Yanjiu Zhongxin, 1986). However, the government was determined to stick to the directive. Much to the relief of the Chinese educationists, no Chinese secondary school had taken the drastic measure to switch to the English medium of instruction in compliance with the directive. Although the Chinese secondary school students were deprived of an important means of social mobility that the public examinations would provide them, their qualifications obtained through the Chinese school internal examinations, especially Senior Middle III Examination (equivalent to grade 11), remained sufficient for them to seek employment in the Chinese commercial and industrial sectors.

However, subsequent developments showed that the Chinese secondary schools were unable to hold their ground against the promulgation of a new educational policy (i.e., the Rahman Talib Report), which upheld the ultimate objective of the Razak Report. In an obvious reference to the Chinese secondary schools, the Rahman Talib Report felt that it would be unwise to publicly finance schools that used a non-official language as the medium of instruction and more so when they had also perpetuated ethnic differences within the national educational system (Federation of Malaya, 1960). The Report went on to recommend the conversion of all Chinese secondary schools to national-medium secondary schools, failing which state funding (grants-in-aid) would be withdrawn and they had to exist as Independent Chinese Secondary Schools (ICSSs) or Duli Zhongxue (Duzhong) outside the ambit of the national educational system. This was a devastating blow to the Chinese educationists who had not expected the government would take such a drastic action against the Chinese secondary schools.

Despite the strong opposition by the Chinese educationists who argued for a multilingual and multicultural approach to foster national integration in multi-ethnic societies, the 1961 Education Act incorporated the recommendations of the Rahman Talib Report by allowing only two types of fully-assisted secondary schools: the NSS that used Malay as a medium of instruction with English being taught as a compulsory subject and the National-Type Secondary School (NTSS) that used English as a medium of instruction with Malay being taught as a compulsory subject. Both types of schools would provide facilities for teaching Chinese and Tamil as language subjects at the request of parents of 15 children from any school (Federation of Malaya, 1961). The Chinese secondary schools were given an ultimatum to decide on their future status by 1 January 1962. In a desperate attempt to safeguard the Chinese secondary schools, the Chinese educationists reminded the management committees of the Chinese secondary schools that they had to uphold their schools as bastions of Chinese culture in accordance with the *historical raison d'être* that underpinned the establishment of their schools. But much to their disappointment, 55 of the existing 71 Chinese secondary schools decided to conform to state policy and became the National-Type Chinese Secondary Schools (NTCSSs) or popularly known as the Conforming Chinese Secondary Schools (Gaizhi Huawen Zhongxue). The remaining 16 became the ICSSs (Tay, 2003). This decision was taken out of the dire need for state funding, though other reasons such as the provision of more teaching periods for Chinese and the establishment of ICSSs as private branches of the NTCSSs were also contributing factors. The NTCSSs were supposed to switch their medium of instruction to Malay in 1967 (ten years after independence). But this switch of medium of instruction was delayed until the early 1970s. By the early 1980s, all secondary schools in Malaysia used Malay as the main medium of instruction. The switch of medium of instruction was subsequently extended to the tertiary level.

The conversion of Chinese secondary schools to NTCSSs was a huge blow to the Chinese educationists. The ICSSs were left in the doldrums for a decade before a revival movement was launched in the 1970s to strengthen their position as an alternative avenue of secondary education for the Chinese. This revival movement had helped many ICSSs to upgrade their infrastructural facilities through charitable financial contributions from the Chinese community. It had also reaffirmed the commitment of the ICSSs to the provision of Chinese mother tongue education. However, the main stumbling block to a more vigorous development of the ICSSs was the refusal by the government to recognise academic qualifications acquired through the Unified Examination (Tongkao) conducted in Chinese by the ICSSs, despite repeated appeals by the Chinese educationists (Tan, 1988). This had resulted in a lack of breakthrough in enrolment rates – only about 10 per cent of Chinese primary school students opted to join the ICSSs. But the Chinese educationists did not give up hope. The emergence of China as an economic power was regarded by them as an impetus that would provide the comparative advantage to an education acquired through the ICSSs. Along with other efforts to enhance the quality of education offered by the ICSSs, there was, of late, a surge of enrolment in some schools to the extent that students had to be turned away because of limited capacity to cope with this surge in enrolment.

It is clear that the Malaysian government felt that six years of primary education in the mother tongue is sufficient for the Chinese to uphold their language and culture, and beyond that, they have to comply with a common process of schooling based on Malay as the main medium of instruction to foster national integration. Such a nature of educational provision is apparently aimed at achieving language maintenance within a larger context of language switch, though at the expense of Chinese mother tongue education at the secondary level. Despite a large number of Chinese secondary schools switching to the national medium in the early 1960s, the Chinese educationists had not abandoned the ICSSs as an alternative avenue of secondary education to the Chinese in the country, indicating their strong commitment to Chinese mother tongue education beyond the primary level.

Preferential policies for the Malays and implications

The implementation of the divide and rule policy by the British had resulted in socioeconomic disparity between the Malays and the non-Malays, especially the Chinese. In the case of the Malays, the British implemented a two-pronged strategy to ensure that they were confined to rural areas. First, they were encouraged to engage in the peasant economy of rice cultivation and fishing. This semi-subsistence economy could not help to improve the economic position of the Malays. Second, they were provided with a rudimentary primary education that had a strong manual and agricultural bias (Chelliah, 1960[1947]; Shaharuddin, 1988; Stevenson, 1975). The lack of educational mobility among the Malay masses was quite evident given that up until 1959, there were no Malay secondary schools to cater for their educational needs (Ramanathan, 1985). It was the Chinese who benefited most from the British colonial rule. They were encouraged by the British to get involved in the tin mining sector which had spurred the development of urban centres in the west coast states of the Malay Peninsula

(Lim, 1978). These urban centres generated a host of commercial activities and the Chinese were able to fully exploit these activities. The educational mobility of the Chinese was also much better than the Malays as they had the opportunity to attend either Chinese or English secondary schools located in urban areas.

The Malays had not made significant inroads in the economy despite the enormous opportunities emerging after the departure of the British. Instead, the Chinese had seized on these opportunities leading to the emergence of a dominant Chinese merchant class (Jesudason, 1989). The government's failure to improve the socioeconomic position of the Malays was one of the root causes of the May 13 race riots in the aftermath of the hotly contested 1969 General Election (see Comber, 1986; Goh, 1971; National Operations Council, 1969). Following the race riots, the government implemented the New Economic Policy (NEP), a social engineering policy, in 1971, to narrow the socioeconomic disparity between the Malays and non-Malays, in particular the Chinese, within a stipulated period of 20 years. The narrowing of this disparity was supposed to transcend ethnicity (see Institut Tadbiran Awam Negara [INTAN], 1988). But subsequent developments showed that preferential policies implemented under the aegis of the NEP had largely favoured the Malays, resulting in much discontent among the non-Malays. In fact, this was driven by drastic changes in the political orientations of the country following the race riots. Prior to the riots, the Alliance government was guided by the true spirit of consociational democracy in which UMNO, despite being the dominant component party, was willing to accommodate the interests of the non-Malays mediated by the MCA and the MIC. But in the aftermath of the race riots, the UMNO leadership was determined to safeguard Malay interests by invoking Malay political dominance (see Means, 1991). By the 1980s, Malay political dominance had become entrenched in Malaysian politics to the extent that the Malaysian state was dubbed "semi-authoritarian" (Crouch, 1992), "quasi democratic" (Zakaria, 1989) and "semi-democratic" (Case, 1993). Among other things, such a change of political orientations was manifested by the implementation of the NEP which largely favoured the Malays.

One of the measures through which the NEP attempted to narrow the socioeconomic disparity between the Malays and the non-Malays was by enhancing Malay educational mobility; education was seen as a key medium for correcting the socioeconomic backwardness of the Malays (Brown, 2007). This intervention was mainly targeted at the provision of science and technical education. At the secondary level, for instance, the government established fully residential science secondary schools for the Malays. Meanwhile, *Majlis Amanah Rakyat* (MARA) or the Council of Trust for the Indigenous People, a government agency, also played a key role in advancing Malay educational mobility in science and technology education at the secondary level under the aegis of the NEP. MARA established fully residential MARA Junior Science Colleges for the Malays (Santhiram & Tan, 2010). These two types of fully residential schools are premier schools attended by elite Malay students who have to undergo a stringent selection process prior to admission. Upon admission, they are provided with the best facilities and teaching staff to ensure that they excel in their secondary education. These schools even allow instruction in English to facilitate movement into higher education overseas, giving rise to accusations that there are two standards, one for the Malays and another for the others (Jasbir & Mukherjee, 1990).

At the tertiary level, MARA was tasked by the government to provide more tertiary opportunities through the injection of development funds. It established the MARA Institute of Technology (transformed from the MARA College) that offered certificate and diploma courses. Branch campuses of the MARA Institute of Technology were established in almost every state in the country to ensure wider access to the Malays (Mok, 2000). In 1999, the MARA Institute of Technology was upgraded to the MARA University of Technology to allow for the offering of degree courses. In 2001, it became the largest university in the country with a student population of 79,274 (Lee, 2004b).

Meanwhile, an ethnic quota system of admission to public universities in favour of the Malays (on a ratio of 55:45 for Malay and non-Malay students) was also implemented by the government under the aegis of the NEP. As a result of this ethnic quota system, the number of Malay students in public universities had increased steadily. Up until the early 1970s, these universities were mainly dominated by the non-Malay students, especially the Chinese. For instance, from 1963 to 1964, only 20.6 per cent of Malay students were enrolled in public universities as compared to 60 per cent of Chinese students (Mauzy, 1985). By the time of the introduction of this ethnic quota system, the enrolment rate of Malay students surged to 49.7 per cent at the expense of Chinese students whose enrolment rate dropped significantly to 42.7 per cent. In 1975, the enrolment rate of Malay students increased further to 65.1 per cent, while the enrolment rate of Chinese students continued to decline to a level of 31.1 per cent. Besides enrolment in general, the implementation of the ethnic quota system also had a significant impact on enrolments in critical courses such as science, engineering and medicine which were previously dominated by non-Malay students. For instance, the respective enrolment rates of Malay and non-Malay students at the University of Malaya (UM) (the premier university of the country) in the 1966–1967 academic year were 7.5 per cent and 81.5 per cent for science, 1.6 per cent and 90 per cent for engineering and 15.9 per cent and 73.6 per cent for medicine. But in the 1976–1977 academic year, the Malay student enrolment rate in these courses had increased significantly to 21.6 per cent for science, 13.4 per cent for engineering and 33.6 per cent for medicine (Watson, 1980).

The implementation of the ethnic quota system was strongly contested by the non-Malays, leading to its replacement by a merit-based system (meritocracy) in 2002. What has become an issue is that despite this replacement, the percentage of Malay admission had risen to 69 per cent, exceeding the previous 55 per cent under the ethnic quota system of admission (Lee, 2004a). Admittedly, this has created much discontent among non-Malay students who have failed to secure places in their preferred courses at the public universities. There is no doubt that the pre-university matriculation colleges established by the government have played a big part in this increased percentage. These colleges were established mainly for the Malay students. Before the establishment of matriculation colleges, matriculation programmes were managed by public universities. The government treats these one-year matriculation programmes as equivalent to a two-year Sixth Form pre-university education that leads to the *Sijil Tinggi Pelajaran Malaysia* (STPM) examination or the Malaysian Higher School Certificate (HSC) examination (equivalent to the A-level) (Lee, 2004a). But beginning in 1983, due to a lack of standardisation across these matriculation programmes, the Ministry of Education decided to establish 12 matriculation colleges throughout the country to take over the matriculation programmes from the public universities. Clearly, the establishment of matriculation colleges provided a shorter and easier alternative route than the existing two-year Sixth Form classes to Malay students seeking admission to public universities. There is a general perception that the STPM examination is of higher standard than the matriculation examination because students have to undergo an extra year before they can sit for the STPM examination and this is indicated by the better performances of the STPM students in the university examinations. In spite of this, a large number of STPM applicants (mainly Chinese) have failed to obtain places in public universities, whereas virtually every matriculation student is given a place in the university regardless of performance. While the matriculation colleges were originally established to ensure that Malay students could take up the places reserved for them in public universities under the ethnic quota system, the government, for some reason, did not close down these colleges when the ethnic quota system of admission to public universities was replaced by a merit-based system. Instead, more matriculation colleges were established since then. This was the main reason for the percentage of Malay students in public universities exceeding the previous 55 per cent under the ethnic quota system.

Indeed, preferential policies that favour the Malays have become a source of deep frustration among the non-Malays, especially the Chinese, who see themselves as being relegated to an underprivileged position and deprived of equal access to educational opportunities. This ethnic based dichotomy between privileged and underprivileged groups has created so much mistrust among the different ethnic groups in Malaysia that it has, in many ways, led to ethnic polarisation that impedes the nation building process. While the government has allowed non-Malays admission to the science secondary schools and the matriculation colleges, their numbers (about 10 per cent), could not offset the predominance of Malays in these privileged educational institutions. Meanwhile, the MARA educational institutions remain a purely Malay enclave – there is a strong resistance to allowing non-Malay admission to these institutions to uphold Malay interests.

Conclusion

The education of ethnic minorities in multiethnic societies has always invoked strongly felt emotions among the various ethnic groups. The integrative and instrumental roles of education are perhaps among the most contested issues in multiethnic societies. As far as Malaysia is concerned, the integrative role of education is impeded by the coexistence of different streams of primary schools resulting from an accommodative policy to redress ethnic assertions for language and cultural maintenance. This multilingual primary school system is instituted out of political exigencies but subsequently has become malintegrative, forcing the government to adopt desegregating measures. However, these desegregation measures are strongly opposed by the Chinese educationists who are determined to maintain the character of the Chinese primary schools. This is especially true with regard to the integrated and vision school projects, which involve the merging of three different streams of primary schools. The latest move by the government to make the national school the school of choice for all races is certainly a better thought-out strategy, though strongly contested by the Chinese educationists who argued for equitable development across the different streams of primary schools. It remains to be seen whether the Chinese parents will be attracted to these schools given the impressive performance of the Chinese primary schools in the country.

The implementation of a common language policy at the secondary level is also driven by the government's intention to strengthen the integrative role of education in a multiethnic society. Such a language policy is strongly challenged by the Chinese educationists who have developed a strong system of Chinese secondary education. But the Chinese educationists could not block the policy implementation, leading to the conversion of a substantial number of Chinese secondary schools to the national medium. Nevertheless, this is not the end of Chinese secondary education in Malaysia because the remaining private Chinese secondary schools are able to survive despite initial hiccups to become an alternative educational pathway for the Chinese in Malaysia, though their development is largely circumscribed by government refusal to recognise academic qualifications awarded by them.

The instrumental value of education in Malaysia has been the main concern of the Malays. This concern could be traced to the colonial period where the Malays had been disadvantaged by the political intent of the British to divide and rule Malaya, depriving them of the much needed educational mobility. This was meant to subvert them into a docile population. The implementation of preferential policies under the aegis of the NEP beginning in the 1970s was a concerted move to address this long-standing problem. The general feeling of the non-Malays with regard to the preferential policies was one of frustration and resentment and they saw this as the whittling away of what they believed to be their legitimate educational rights within the context of equal educational opportunity. Thus, the NEP was viewed by the non-Malays, especially the Chinese, as an open and blatant form of racial discrimination. Although Connell (2012[2001]) notes that "the legitimacy of educational competitions depends on some belief in level playing fields" (p. 471), this legitimacy should not be pursued along ethnic lines that have serious ramifications on the normative role of educational delivery in multiethnic societies.

In the final analysis, the integrative and instrumental roles of education in Malaysia have been largely challenged by the Chinese who are, in many ways, a pluralistic minority in Malaysia. By pluralistic minority is meant one which seeks tolerance for its differences by the dominant group based on the idea that disparate cultures can flourish peacefully in the same society (see Wirth, 1970). However, as far as the instrumental role of education in Malaysia is concerned, it is also compounded by the position of the Malays as an underprivileged majority. By underprivileged majority is meant one that despite its numerical strength is lagging behind the minorities in terms of socioeconomic mobility. As Rothermund (1986) puts it, this type of majority group will resort to deliberate policy to put the minorities in their deserved place. As for the Indians in Malaysia, they can be regarded as an underprivileged minority who do not have the resources to cater for their educational needs.

References

Abdul Rafie, Mahat. (2005). Education in a multicultural and multireligious society: Divisive or unifying? In Abdul Razak Baginda & P. Schier (Eds.), *Education in multicultural societies: Perspectives on education in Malaysia* (pp. 13–33). London: ASEAN Academic Press.

Brown, G. K. (2007). Making ethnic citizens: The politics and practice of education in Malaysia. *International Journal of Educational Development, 27*, 318–330.

Bullivant, B. M. (1981). *The pluralist dilemma in education: Six case studies.* Sydney, Australia: Allen & Unwin.

Case, W. (1993). Semi-democracy in Malaysia: Withstanding the pressure for regime change. *Pacific Affairs, 66*(2), 183–205.

Chelliah, D. D. (1960 [1947]). *A history of educational policy of the straits settlements with recommendations for a new system based on vernaculars.* Reprint. Singapore: G. H. Kiat.

Comber, L. (1986). *13 May 1969: A historical survey of Sino-Malay relations.* Kuala Lumpur: Heinemann Asia.

Connell, R. W. (2012 [2001]). Poverty and education. In J. H. Ballantine & J. Z. Spade (Eds.), *Schools and society: A sociological approach to education* (pp. 469–478). Belmont, CA: Wadsworth/Thomson Learning.

Crouch, H. (1992). Authoritarian trends, the UMNO split and limits to state power. In J. S. Kahn & Francis Loh Kok Wah (Eds.), *Fragmented vision: Culture and politics in contemporary Malaysia* (pp. 21–43). St. Leonard's: Allen & Unwin for Asian Studies Association of Australia.

Edwards, J. (1994). *Multilingualism.* New York, NY: Routledge.

Edwards, J. (Ed.) (1981). *Linguistic minorities, policies and pluralism.* London: Academic Press. Federation of Malaya. (1956). *Report of the education committee 1956.* Kuala Lumpur: Government Press.

Federation of Malaya. (1960). *Report of the education review committee, 1960.* Kuala Lumpur: Government Press.

Federation of Malaya. (1961). *Education Act, 1961.* Kuala Lumpur: Acting Government Printer.

Goh, Cheng Teik. (1971). *The May Thirteenth incident and democracy in Malaysia.* Kuala Lumpur: Oxford University Press.

Haque, M. S. (2003). The role of the state in managing ethnic tensions in Malaysia. *American Behavioral Scientist, 47*(3), 240–266.

Haris, bin Md. Jadi (1983). *Ethnicity, politics and education: A study in the development of Malayan education and its policy implementation process.* PhD. dissertation, University of Keele, United Kingdom.

Hirschman, C. (1974). *Ethnic and social stratification in peninsular Malaysia.* Washington, DC: American Sociological Association.

Ibrahim, Saad. (1981). The national culture policy in a plural society: The Malaysian case. *Negara, 5*(2), 7–13.

Institut Tadbiran Awam Negara. (INTAN) (1988). *Dasar-dasar utama kerajaan Malaysia* (Key Policies of the Malaysian Government). Ampang Jaya: INTAN.

Jasbir, Sarjit Singh, & Mukherjee, H. (1990). *Education and national integration in Malaysia: Stocktaking thirty years after independence.* (Occasional Paper). Kuala Lumpur: Pengajian Pembangunan Manusia, Institut Pengajian Tinggi, UM.

Jesudason, J. V. (1989). *Ethnicity and the economy: The state, Chinese business, and multinationals in Malaysia.* Singapore: Oxford University Press.

Kementerian Pelajaran Malaysia. (2006). *Rancangan Malaysia Ke-9: Pelan Induk Pembangunan Pendidikan 2006–2010* (Ninth Malaysia Plan: Education Development Master Plan 2006–2010). Putrajaya: Bahagian Perancangan dan Penyelidikan Dasar Pendidikan, Kementerian Pelajaran Malaysia.

Kementerian Pelajaran Malaysia (KPM) (Ministry of Education Malaysia) (1995). *Sekolah wawasan: Konsep dan pelaksanaan* (Vision school: Concept and implementation). Kuala Lumpur: Bahagian Perancangan dan Penyelidikan Pendidikan, Kementerian Pelajaran Malaysia.

Lee, N. N. Molly. (2004a). *Higher education in Malaysia.* Monograph Series No: 4/2004. Penang: School of Educational Studies, Universiti Sains Malaysia.

Lee, N. N. Molly. (2004b). Malaysian universities: Toward equality, accessibility, and equality. In P. G. Altbach & T. Umakoshi (Eds.), *Asian universities: Historical perspectives and contemporary issues* (pp. 221–246). Baltimore, MD: The Johns Hopkins University Press.

Lim, Heng Kow. (1978). *The evolution of the urban system in Malaya.* Kuala Lumpur: Penerbit UM.

Malaysia. (1972). *Population and housing census of Malaysia: Community and groups.* Kuala Lumpur: Government Printers.

Malaysia. (1987). *Perangkaan penting Semenanjung Malaysia* (Vital statistics Peninsular Malaysia). Kuala Lumpur: Jabatan Perangkaan Malaysia.

Malaysia. (1997). *Vital statistics Malaysia.* Kuala Lumpur: Department of Statistics Malaysia.

Malaysia. (2006). *Ninth Malaysia Plan 2006–2010.* Putrajaya: The Economic Planning Unit, Prime Minister's Department.

Marimuthu, T. (1984). Schooling as a dead end: Education for the poor especially the estate children. In S. Husin Ali (Ed.), *Ethnicity, class and development: Malaysia* (pp. 265–273). Kuala Lumpur: Malaysian Social Science Association.

Mauzy, D. K. (1985). Language and language policy in Malaysia. In W. R. Beer & J. E. Jacob (Eds.), *Language policy and national unity* (pp. 151–177). Totowa, NJ: Rowman & Allanheld.

Means, G. P. (1991). *Malaysian politics: The second generation.* Singapore: Oxford University Press.

Ministry of Education. (2001). *Education in Malaysia: A journey to excellence.* Kuala Lumpur: Educational Planning and Research Division, Ministry of Education.

Mok, Soon Sang (2000). *Malaixiaya jiaoyushi* (A History of the Malaysian Education). Kuala Lumpur: UCSTA.

Nanyang Siang Pau (Nanyang Daily). 23 April 2006.

National Operations Council. (1969). *The May 13 tragedy: A report of the National Operations Council*. Kuala Lumpur: Government Press.

Ng, Swee Huat. (2009). *Isu dan kontroversi sekolah wawasan di Semenanjung Malaysia: Masalah pelaksanaan dalam masyarakat Cina* (Issues and Controversy of the Vision Schools in Peninsular Malaysia: Problems of Implementation within the Chinese Community). MA dissertation, University of Malaya, Kuala Lumpur.

Ramanathan, K. (1985). *Politik dalam pendidikan bahasa 1930–1971* (Politics in language education 1930–1971). Kuala Lumpur: Fajar Bakti.

Rothermund, D. (1986). Introduction. In D. Rothermund & J. Simon (Eds.), *Education and the integration of ethnic minorities* (pp. 1–11). London: Frances Pinter.

Santhiram, R. Raman, & Tan, Yao Sua. (2010). Ethnic segregation in Malaysia's education system: Enrolment choices, preferential policies and desegregation. *Paedagogica Historica, 46*(1&2), 117–131.

Shaharuddin, Maaruf. (1988). *Malay ideas on development: From feudal lord to capitalist*. Singapore: Times.

Sia, Keng Yek. (2005). *SJK(Cina) dalam sistem pendidikan kebangsaan* (National-type Chinese primary schools in the national educational system). Kuala Lumpur: Penerbit UM.

Stevenson, R. (1975). *Cultivators and administrators: British educational policy towards the Malays 1875–1906*. Kuala Lumpur: Oxford University Press.

Tan, Liok Ee. (1988). Chinese independent schools in West Malaysia: Varying responses to changing demands. In J. W. Cushman & Wang Gungwu (Eds.), *Changing identities of the Southeast Asian Chinese since World War II* (pp. 61–74). Hong Kong: Hong Kong University Press.

Tan, Liok Ee. (2002). Baggage from the past, eye on the future: Chinese education in Malaysia today. In Leo Suryadinata (Ed.), *Ethnic Chinese in Singapore and Malaysia: A dialogue between tradition and modernity* (pp. 155–171). Singapore: Times Academic Press.

Tan, Yao Sua, & Santhiram, R. (2010). *The education of ethnic minorities: The case of the Malaysian Chinese*. Petaling Jaya: Strategic Information and Research Development Centre.

Tay, Lian Soo. (2003). *Malaixiya huawen jiaoyu fazhanshi* (Historical development of Chinese education in Malaysia). Vol. IV. Kuala Lumpur: UCSTA.

Tey, Nai Peng. (2006). Population and development trends. In Wong Yut Lin & Tey Nai Peng (Eds.), *Our people our future: Malaysian population in perspective* (pp. 7–28). Kuala Lumpur: University of Malaya Press.

Watson, J. K. P. (1980). Education and cultural pluralism in South East Asia, with special reference to peninsular Malaysia. *Comparative Education, 16*(2), 139–158.

Wirth, L. (1970). The problem of minority groups. In M. Kurokawa (Ed.), *Minority responses: Comparative views of reaction to subordination* (pp. 34–42). New York, NY: Random House.

Yong, T. K. (2003, February 23). Daunting task to check polarization in national schools. *New Straits Times*.

Zakaria, Haji Ahmad. (1989). Malaysia: Quasi democracy in a divided society? In L. Diamond, J. J. Linz & S. M. Lipset (Eds.), *Democracy in developing countries: Asia* (pp. 347–381). Boulder, CO: Lynne Rienner.

4 Access and equity issues in Malaysian higher education

Hena Mukherjee, Jasbir S. Singh, Rozilini M. Fernandez-Chung and T. Marimuthu

Malaysia is one of the smaller countries in the Asia Pacific region, comprising Peninsular Malaysia and the Borneo states of Sabah and Sarawak, with a population of about 28.2 million as of the first quarter of 2008. The multiracial and multicultural country consists of Malays, Chinese, Indians and other indigenous groups such as the Orang Asli in Peninsular Malaysia, Kadazans in Sabah and the Ibans in Sarawak. On obtaining independence from the British in 1957, Malaysia established a constitutional monarchy with a political system based on the UK's parliamentary democracy. Politically, Malaysia has enjoyed stability since independence. The Malaysian constitution provided the basis for the social contract among the various races which gave special privileges for Malays and other Bumiputera (indigenous) groups while preserving the languages and culture of the other races.

After race riots following the general elections in 1969 in Kuala Lumpur, the Malaysian leadership determined that economic balance among Malaysia's three major ethnic groups – Malays, Chinese and Indians – was the only road to communal peace. The result was the New Economic Policy (NEP) which was designed to create national unity through two prongs: firstly, to reduce and eventually eradicate poverty by raising income levels and increasing employment opportunities for all Malaysians, irrespective of race; and secondly to restructure Malaysian society to correct the economic imbalance, through income distribution, employment, ownership of wealth between Malays and non-Malays. To achieve the second objective, the government encouraged greater Malay urbanisation, privileged access to education and training, employment and economic ventures, so as to control 30 percent ownership of capital in commerce and industry by 1990. It is widely acknowledged that the NEP has had an important role in reducing poverty in the country which was at 50 percent in 1970 to less than 4 percent in 2010.

At Higher Education (HE) level, the NEP set quotas for students from the different ethnic groups to reflect their proportions in the population as a whole. The distribution of student enrolment in public HE institutions was to be fixed at 55 percent for Malays and 45 percent for the Chinese and Indian ethnic groups. Although the NEP ended in 1990, the objectives of the NEP, particularly the preferential treatment for Malays in education, employment and economic ventures, continued in the subsequent national policy statements such as the recent New Economic Model (NEM, 2010) which is premised on high income, inclusiveness and sustainability. The policy was aimed at creating more opportunities for Bumiputeras through ethnic quotas in university admissions and providing scholarships and loans for studying in local and foreign universities. Malaysia's pro-Bumiputera affirmative action and redistributive policies were seen widely as successful in creating a prosperous, harmonious, multiethnic society in the 1980s and 1990s and in reducing poverty among Bumiputeras.

Malaysian policy-makers recognised soon after independence that HE was a critical instrument in bringing about national development and social change. The government had invested substantially in education ". . . But compared to other countries – both in the region and developed countries worldwide – the quality of students being produced . . . continues to be inadequate. Education policies have stymied the national objective of producing the best talent to meet the country's needs" (NEM, 2010, p. 55). Up for debate are the status of HE in Malaysia, the utilisation of public funds for its citizens, and the impact upon the country of "modern history's greatest experiments in social engineering and possibly the world's most extensive attempt at affirmative action" (Schuman, 2010).

The data, spanning the period 1970 and 2008, and findings discussed in this chapter are drawn from a World Bank-financed study "Affirmative Action Policies in Malaysian Higher Education" (2010) which is part of a larger World Bank analysis of HE access and equity in the East Asia and Pacific region.

Affirmative action policies for the Malays had its origin in the Federal Constitution's Article 153(1) enacted to safeguard the special position of the Malays and the legitimate interests of the other communities in accordance with the provisions of that Article, ensuring that a reasonable proportion of public service positions, scholarships and other educational privileges accorded by the Federal Government is reserved for Malays. An amendment of the constitution in 1971 'empowered the Yang di-Pertuan Agong (King) to give directions to any university, college or other educational institution providing education at post-secondary level where the number of places for any course of study is less than the number of candidates qualified for such places, to reserve for Malays (and natives of the Borneo States) such proportion of such places as the Yang di-Pertuan Agong deems reasonable. The intention of the amendments is to reserve places in those selected areas of study . . . where the numbers of Malays and natives of the Borneo States are disproportionately small (Suffian, Lee & Trindade, 1978, pp. 114–115)'.

The Ministry of Education (MOE) definition of HE covers certificate, diploma, undergraduate as well as postgraduate levels. The providers of HE in Malaysia are universities, university colleges, polytechnics and community colleges. This chapter reviews the issues of HE access and equity in terms of the implementation impact of the Malaysian Government's affirmative action policy on the country's major ethnic groups, gender, geographical regions and the socioeconomically disadvantaged.

Methodology and data

The study draws heavily on government documentation issued by the MOE and Ministry of Higher Education (MOHE), Department of Statistics, particularly its

Census Reports and Labour Force Surveys. Data provided by officials and politicians to the press have been included as have information from stakeholders met in individual interviews and focus group discussions. To triangulate and supplement existing published and documented data, a survey to ascertain information on student respondents' socioeconomic background was conducted using a sample of 13 public and private institutions with the assistance of the Malaysian Qualifications Agency.

Difficulties dogged the study process in accessing reliable data. These included changing definitions, shifting of age cohort bands in different years, inconsistent reporting and a general view that data could not be shared readily. The inconsistencies identified in published data proved to be one of the more intractable of the data collection problems encountered during the study.

Education and national development

In March 2010, the Prime Minister presented the NEM, which pledged to revise and roll back affirmative action policies. After three decades of NEP (previous New Economic Policy) implementation, the NEM linked Malaysia's economic structural woes with affirmative action policies, providing grist for many an economist's mill that such policies were inefficient, unjust and too entrenched in the system to be mended. The NEM also identified the loss of talented and qualified human resources, citing the large numbers of tertiary-educated non-Bumiputera Malaysians who have sought more non-discriminatory, financially and socially attractive environments in developed countries. Intertwined with national growth and development and HE are the issues of access and equity.

Growth and expansion of higher education

The growth in HE in Malaysia may be traced from the early days of independence with the establishment of Universiti Malaya in 1962, the only degree granting institution in the country until the establishment of Universiti Kebangsaan Malaysia (UKM) in 1970. By 2007, the number of HE institutions (HEIs) had grown to 606 in various categories. Table 4.1 provides a breakdown by category of institution. It is estimated that about 25 percent of the total population aged 18–24 were in HE in 2007.

The seventies and eighties saw the effects of school-level education policies in lower drop-out rates, and universalisation of primary and secondary education, resulting in rising numbers of school leavers eligible for university admissions. Coupled with the demand for appropriately educated workers for an expanding economy, the government response was to double intakes of public HEIs, and diversify programme offerings from private HEIs. Important pieces of legislation such as the Private Higher Education Institutions Act were put in place chiefly to regulate the burgeoning private HE sector and also to help stem outflow of currency to foreign institutions. The 1986/87 economic downturn etched a permanent mark in the HE industry with many seeking local alternatives as the rising costs of overseas education became unaffordable.

Table 4.1 Expansion of Public Higher Education Institutions in Malaysia: A Comparison, 1967 and 2007

Item	1967	2007
Public Universities	1	20
Private Universities And University-Colleges	0	33[a]
Foreign Branch Campuses	0	4
Private Colleges	2	488[b]
Polytechnics	0	24
Community Colleges	0	37
Students (Postgraduates)	4,560 (398)	873,238 (45,888)
Malaysian Students Studying Abroad	N/A	54,915
Population Age 18–24	N/A	3,474,200

Source: 1997 Data: Interim Report to The Higher Education Advisory Council, 1974. 2007 Data – Ministry Of Higher Education, www.mohe.gov.my.

Notes
a Excluding Local Branch Campuses
b Including Local Branch Campuses

Access to higher education

The period 1985 to 2008 saw great improvement in access to HE in Malaysia. All levels of education, primary, secondary and tertiary, increased their enrolment during this period but HE enrolment showed the most dramatic increase. While primary enrolment increased by 43.9 percent over this period and secondary school enrolment increased by 84.6 percent, tertiary education enrolment increased by 1339.4 percent. This represented an annual increase of 1.9 percent for primary schools, 3.7 percent for secondary schools and 58.2 percent for tertiary education institutions (see Table 4.2).

Increased access to HE is reflected in the percentage of the population aged 19–24 enrolled in HE. Table 4.3 shows that in 1970 only 0.6 percent of the age group 19–24 was enrolled in HE. By 1990, 2.9 percent of this age group was enrolled in HE and by 2000, 8.1 percent of the age group was enrolled in HE. A huge leap in enrolment took place after 2000 so that by 2007, 24.4 percent of the 19–24 age group was placed in HE institutions (see Table 4.3).

Significant improvement in increasing opportunities for HE took place during the 1980s, 1990s and the first decade of the 21st century. In this respect public universities have played a major role. Intake increased from 48,004 in 1995 to 175,106 in 2008, an annual average increase of 22.1 percent. Enrolment improved significantly in the public HE institutions from 109,918 in 1987 to 511,224 in 2008. Enrolment in degree courses took a sharp uptrend from 43,430 in 1987 to 274,349 in 2008. Masters and doctoral student enrolment also saw major increases. Keeping pace with increased

Table 4.2 Expansion in Enrolment by Educational Level, 1985–2008

	1985	1990	1995	2000	2005	2008	Increase in enrolment (%) 1985–2008	Annual Rate Increase (%) 1985–2008
Primary	2,191,676	2,447,206	2,827,627	2,907,123	3,137,280	3,154,090	43.9	1.9
Secondary*	1,251,447	1,366,068	1,589,584	1,950,746	2,217,749	2,310,660	84.6	3.7
Tertiary**	64,025	99,687	146,581	363,949	463,482	921,548	1,339.4	58.2
Total	3,507,148	3,912,961	4,563,792	5,221,818	5,818,611	6,386,298	82.1	3.6

Source: MOE 1985–2008, Secondary Education Regional Information Base: Country Profile, Malaysia (UNESCO)

Table 4.3 Percentage Population Age 19–24 enrolled in Tertiary Education

Year	Population	Enrolment	%
1970	1,420,687	8,633	0.6
1980	1,624,274	26,410	1.6
1990	2,028,100	58,286	2.9
2000	2,626,900	211,484	8.1
2005*	3,353,600	649,653	19.4
2007*	3,474,200	847485	24.4

Sources: 1970–2000 data adapted from Pembangunan Pendidikan 2001–2010, MOE Kuala Lumpur. 2005 and 2007 18–24 age group data adapted from Department of Statistics, and Enrolment data adapted from Educational Statistics/MOHE website.

intake and enrolment, output of graduates from public universities rose from 18,529 in 1987 to 126,317 in 2008 indicating an annual increase of 48.5 percent (see Table 4.4).

The story is once again of rapid increase in enrolment in private institutions. In 2002 there were 294,600 students in private institutions in Malaysia but by 2008 the number had increased to 399,852 recording an increase of 35.7 percent or an annual increase of 4.5 percent. The trend is for more students to enrol for diploma and degree courses than certificate courses. In 2002, of the total enrolment in private institutions, 31.7 percent were enrolled in certificate courses, 44.1 percent in diploma courses, 22.2 percent in degree courses, 1.3 percent in masters' courses and 0.1 percent in doctoral courses. However, in 2008, 15.2 percent were enrolled in certificate courses, 44.5 percent in diploma courses, 38.0 percent in degree courses, 2.1 percent in masters courses and 0.2 percent in doctoral courses. While intake and enrolment in private institutions increased considerably between 2002 and 2008, graduate output decreased possibly due to students moving to overseas institutions as part of twinning programs (see Table 4.5).

Opportunities for HE are also available in public polytechnics and community colleges. Again reliable data are available for 2002–2007. In 2002 52,898 students were enrolled in polytechnics and 3,207 were enrolled in community colleges. By 2007 polytechnics had an enrolment of 84,250 and community colleges an enrolment of 14,438.

The overall situation pertaining to enrolment in the HE sector for 2008 is portrayed in Table 4.16 (see Appendix). Enrolment included 408,862 in public universities, 399,852 in private institutions, 85,280 in polytechnics and 17,082 in community colleges, a total of 911, 076. Graduate output has kept pace with intake and enrolment.

Given the expansion of public and private systems, there would appear to be places for all seeking HE. Large numbers are accommodated in the public sector which is heavily subsidised, and the rest have to seek places at a cost in the private sector, or at an even greater cost in HE institutions overseas.

Table 4.4 Graduates of Public Higher Education Institutions, 1987–2008

Date	Certificate		Diploma		Degree		Masters		Doctoral		Total	
	N	%	N	%	N	%	N	%	N	%	N	%
1987	2,469	13.3	6,227	33.6	8,420	45.4	1,388	7.5	25	0.1	18,529	100.0
1990	3,154	13.2	8,101	33.9	10,932	45.7	1,710	7.1	27	0.1	23,924	100.0
1995	5,017	13.8	11,678	33.2	16,432	45.3	3,084	8.5	73	0.2	36,284	100.0
2000	8,792	12.6	23,364	33.6	33,095	47.6	4,199	6.0	148	0.2	69,598	100.0
2005	7,848	6.7	56,010	48.0	45,618	39.1	6,309	5.4	857	0.7	116,642	100.0
2008	19,176	15.2	37,660	29.8	60,040	47.5	8,656	6.9	785	0.6	126,317	100.0

Source: 1987–2005 Ministry of Education: Educational Statistics of Malaysia. Data Include public universities, teacher training colleges. MARA Institute of Technology, polytechnics, Tunku Abdul Rahman College and Community Colleges. 2008 MOE-excludes teacher training colleges.

Table 4.5 Graduates in Private Higher Education, 2002–2008

Year	Certificate		Diploma		Degree		Master's		Doctoral		Grand total	
	No. of students	%	No. of students	%	No. of students	%	No. of students	%	No. of students	%	No. of students	%
2002	62,332	44.8	55,988	40.2	20,255	14.6	571	0.4	4	0	139,150	100
2004	60,073	44.5	56,060	41.5	18,385	13.6	423	0.3	46	0.1	134,987	100
2006	18,046	21.7	36,321	43.7	27,176	32.7	1592	1.8	51	0.1	83,186	100
2008	18,269	23.3	32,685	41.6	26,590	33.8	962	1.2	55	0.1	78,561	100

Source: Ministry of Higher Education, Malaysia

However, the success in access comes at a cost. The system has not managed to channel more students into science and technology, an important platform for home-grown knowledge generation. Increasingly worrisome in terms of national development is the loss of graduates in high demand disciplines to other countries including OECD countries (Docquier & Marfouk, 2010). Recruitment of talent has not kept pace with expansion with the sector overall suffering from a lack of qualified academic staff. In 2008 only 17.8% of the total number of academic staff in public and private HE institutions possessed doctoral degrees with public HEI profiles faring better than the private. As a corollary, publications and citations compared unfavourably with other HEIs in the region (Mukherjee & Wong, 2011).

There are also grave concerns about graduate quality as demonstrated by a recent study which looked at employer perception of graduates from the various HEIs. The study revealed that employers were most satisfied with graduates from foreign universities outside Malaysia with a satisfaction rate of 79.0%. This was followed by graduates from foreign branch campuses in Malaysia with a satisfaction rate of 63.0%, from local private universities at 62.0%, from private colleges at 52.0% and from local private university colleges at 45.0%. The lowest level of satisfaction of 39.0% was reserved for graduates from the local public universities. It appears that employers are most likely to employ graduates from foreign providers outside Malaysia, and least likely from local public universities (Fernandez-Chung, Cheong & Hill, 2014).

Impact of national policies on equity

Participation in higher education

The democratization and universalization of primary and secondary education since Independence in 1957 built up the social demand for tertiary education in Malaysia. The enrolment by ethnicity for the year 1959 at the Universiti Malaya was 60 percent Chinese, 20 percent Malay and 20 percent Indians and Others. The enrolment of Malay students was far below their proportion in the population of Peninsular Malaysia in 1957 where the ethnic composition was 49.8 percent Malays, 37.2 percent Chinese, 11.3 percent Indians and 1.8 percent Others. There was an urgent need to increase the participation rate of Malay students, in line with the proportion in the population.

Student admissions and ethnic quotas

Prior to 1971, enrolment figures both in the upper secondary classes and in the tertiary institutions show a rapid increase. The participation rate of Malay students in the year 1971, when the NEP was launched, was already equal to that of Chinese students at about 44 percent at the Universiti Malaya. The seeds of the affirmative action policy were embedded in the Federal Constitution of

1957, prepared when the Federation of Malaya obtained its independence from the British.

The NEP broadened the initial statements and made its coverage more comprehensive. After 1971 and on the wave of the watershed event of the 1969 race riots, a committee formed by the National Operations Council (NOC) to study student development at Universiti Malaya, recommended an ethnic quota system in the proportion of 55:45 percent for Bumiputera and non-Bumiputera students as the basis for admission to universities, reflecting the ethnic composition of the country, and on a faculty by faculty basis (Malaysia, 1971). It had found that Malay students were enrolled predominantly in the Arts and Humanities courses, while non-Malays were in the Science and Technology programmes.

This ethnic quota system remained until the meritocracy system was introduced in 2002. The preferential ethnic quota policy, framed and implemented for Universiti Malaya, was extended to Universiti Sains Malaysia and Universiti Putra Malaysia. The proportional distribution of quotas was not maintained, however, as newer universities were established.

The NEP provided the impetus to recruit more Bumiputera students especially for science and technology courses through the establishment of junior science colleges, residential secondary schools, matriculation programmes and provision of university scholarships exclusively for Bumiputera students. The universities themselves started pre-university science centres (Pusat Asasi Sains) exclusively for Bumiputera students to prepare them for science and technology courses. All these programmes served to increase the number of Bumiputera students enrolled in the universities.

Implementation of the Higher Education Planning Committee's recommendations (Malaysia, 1967), in terms of expansion of universities and conversion of existing colleges to university status, brought about positive results in terms of greater participation of Malay students in public tertiary institutions. By 1973/74, the combined enrolment for degree, diploma and certificate courses for the five universities showed 66.0 percent Malay, 28.4 percent Chinese, 4.8 percent Indians and 0.8 percent Others. The low enrolment of Malays had reversed demonstrating the success of Government affirmative action policies.

A similar view is also expressed by Charles Hirschman who analysed census data to assess the proportion of males with Malaysian Certificate of Education/ Sijil Pelajaran Malaysia (MCE/SPM) or HE qualifications by birth cohort and ethnicity. Hirschman's analysis showed the educationally disadvantaged position of the Malay and other Bumiputera students in the first half of the 20th century. By the 1970s "Malay students reached educational parity and then surpassed Chinese and Indian rates of MCE completion" (Hirschman, 2013). The author states that the gains made by Malay students in the 1970's and 1980's were not only "phenomenal" but also a significant national achievement. However, "the very slow pace of educational gains of other Bumiputera and Indian youth is a cause for concern" (Hirschman, ibid.) Our analysis of enrolment data (Table 4.6) in HEIs shows a similar pattern.

Table 4.6 Enrolment in Public Universities by Ethnic Group-1980

Institution	Race	Malay	Chinese	Indian	Others	Total
Universiti Malaya (UM) (%)		4,045 (50.3)	3,162 (39.3)	676 (8.4)	162 (2.0)	8,045 (100.0)
Universiti Sains Malaysia (USM) (%)		1,956 (54.4)	1,354 (37.6)	270 (7.5)	17 (0.5)	3,597 (100.0)
Universiti Kebangsaan Malaysia (UKM) (%)		4,997 (86.1)	621 (10.7)	180 (3.1)	9 (0.1)	5,807 (100.0)
Universiti Putra Malaysia (UPM) (%)		3,025 (87.3)	294 (8.5)	130 (3.8)	14 (0.4)	3,463 (100.0)
Universiti Teknologi Malaysia (UTM) (%)		3,669 (88.2)	348 (8.4)	108 (2.6)	34 (0.8)	4,159 (100.0)
Total Number (%)		17,692 (70.6)	5,779 (23.1)	1,364 (5.4)	236 (0.9)	25,071 (100.0)

Source: Fourth Malaysian Plan, 1981–1985. Kuala Lumpur

In 1980, except for Universiti Malaya and Universiti Sains Malaysia, the enrolment for Bumiputera students shows a disproportionately higher percentage compared with the population distribution at the time. The total enrolment for the five universities in 1980 were as follows : Malays 70.6 percent, Chinese 23.1 percent, Indians 5.4 percent and Others 0.9 percent, whereas Malays constituted only 58.6 percent, Chinese 32.1 percent, Indians 8.6 percent and Others 0.7 percent in the population in 1980 (Table 4.6).

Student admissions based on meritocracy

In 2002, the student admission policy changed from the ethnic quota system to meritocracy where the minimum entry requirement is a Cumulative Grade Point Average (CGPA) based on STPM or Matriculation examinations of 2.0 with the four research universities of Universiti Sains Malaysia (USM), Universiti Malaya (UM), UPM, and Universiti Kebangsaan (UKM) requiring a higher CGPA for entry.

Under the meritocracy policy the intake of ethnic groups into universities seems to have more or less normalized with the Bumiputera intake maintained at an average of 64.3 percent, the Chinese at 30.1 percent and Indians at about 6.5 percent over the eight year period (see Table 4.6). The composition of the population in 2009 was 66.1 percent Bumiputera, 25.2 percent Chinese, 7.5 percent Indians and 1.2 percent Others, with the 2009 intake reflecting the proportion in the population except for the Indians. (A 2013 update showed a disproportionately higher percentage for Bumiputera students (74.3 percent) than for the Chinese (19.0 percent) and Indians (4.4 percent).

A key prong in the strategy of Bumiputera enrolment expansion was the establishment of Bumiputera-only educational institutions with Universiti Teknologi

Table 4.7 Intake in UiTM (2007–2009) According to Level of Study

Year	Doctoral	Masters	PG Diploma	Bachelors	Diploma	Others	Total
2007	138	1,198	151	18,983	21,661	2,743	44,874
2008	189	1,768	117	20,023	22,640	3,309	48,046
2009	307	2,699	233	26,590	29,822	4,558	64,209

Source: MOE, 2010

MARA (UiTM) at the pinnacle. The current enrolment figure is 180,000 (2013 figure) which is expected to increase to 250,000 students by 2020 (NST, 15 Sept 2013 p. 6).

Table 4.7 shows the student intake for 2007, 2008 and 2009 into UiTM. The intake figures for undergraduate degree courses for every year between 2007–2009 shows an almost equal number of Bumiputera students compared with the total intake of Bumiputera students into 19 public universities particularly for the years 2007 and 2008. However, data for 2009 show that the total intake into UiTM is about 50 percent more than the total intake into all 19 public HEIs which was 40,416 (MOHE, 2010).

The cumulative impact of the NEP affirmative action policy implementation on HE institutions in Malaysia is clearly shown in Table 4.8. The average Bumiputera enrolment for the four-year period between 2005–2008 in public universities which includes UiTM has been over 80 percent, Chinese about 12 percent, Indians 3 percent and Others 2.7 percent. In 2008 the enrolment for Others was higher at 3.0 percent than the Indians at 2.7 percent. The same enrolment pattern is evident for Polytechnics and Community Colleges. At these institutions, Bumiputera enrolment has been maintained above 90 percent, whereas the Chinese enrolment has varied between 2 percent – 4 percent, the Indians between 3 percent – 4 percent and Others between 1 percent – 2 percent.

As for the total enrolment in public institutions of HE which includes community colleges and polytechnics between 2005 to 2008, Bumiputera enrolment has been maintained consistently around 84 percent; the Chinese at 10 percent; Indians at 3 percent; and Others at 2.4 percent. These enrolment figures do not reflect the ethnic composition in the population, where in 2008 66.0 percent were Bumiputera, 25.2 percent Chinese, 7.6 percent Indians and 1.2 percent Others.

In the period of the NEP and its subsequent policies under various names, and based on the data collected from government sources, HE affirmative action policies of the government have benefitted the Bumiputera students more than other ethnic groups.

The affirmative action policy approach of NEP will continue as Malaysia moves forward to implement the 10th Malaysia Plan (2011–2015).

Table 4.8 Enrolment in Public Higher Education Institutions by Ethnicity, 2005–2008

Year & Race	Universities		Polytechnics		Community Colleges		Total	
	N	%	N	%	N	%	N	%
2005								
Bumiputera	207021	81.8	68264	92.5	9205	92.7	284490	84.4
Chinese	33484	13.2	2656	3.6	172	1.75	36312	10.8
Indian	7838	3.1	2169	2.9	373	3.86	10380	3.1
Other	4675	1.9	745	1.0	179	1.82	5599	1.7
Total	253018	100.0	73834	100.0	9929	100.0	336781	100.0
2006								
Bumiputera	237886	80.8	75901	92.1	10363	91.9	324150	83.5
Chinese	38430	13.0	3307	4.0	231	2.0	41968	10.8
Indian	9073	3.1	2405	2.9	457	4.1	11935	3.1
Other	9132	3.1	799	1.0	222	2.0	10153	2.6
Total	294521	100.0	82412	100.0	11273	100.0	388206	100.0
2007								
Bumiputera	304719	82.9	77542	92.0	12860	91.8	395121	84.8
Chinese	41863	11.5	3591	4.3	287	2.0	45741	9.8
Indian	10422	2.8	2357	2.8	557	4.0	13336	2.9
Other	10448	2.8	760	0.9	307	2.2	11515	2.5
Total	367452	100.0	84250	100.0	14011	100.0	465713	100.0
2008								
Bumiputera	333235	83.1	78123	91.6	15706	91.9	427064	84.8
Chinese	45062	11.2	3645	4.3	323	1.9	49030	9.7
Indian	10901	2.7	2678	3.1	675	4.0	14254	2.8
Other	11975	3.0	834	1.0	378	2.2	13187	2.6
Total	401173	100.0	85280	100.0	17082	100.0	503535	100.0

Source: Ministry of Higher Education – information provided MOHE in November 2009

National policies and gender

This section examines the impact the NEP and subsequent national education policies have had on access and equity for women in the HE sector. While HE policies were not gender specific, did the policies directed to increasing access to HE benefit all women equally or did these policies benefit unequally women from different ethnic and regional groups?

Between 1985 and 2008 women took advantage of the expanding educational opportunities and made significant advances in obtaining HE. At nearly every level both in the public and private HE institutions women overtook their male counterparts in accessing HE. However, this did not guarantee equitable access to the different ethnic and regional groups.

Enrolment

Overall, women's enrolment at all levels of HE increased significantly between 1987 and 2008. Women overtook men at all levels of HE except at the certificate and doctoral level. In the public sector universities and colleges women's enrolment increased from 44.4 percent in 1987 to 56.6 percent in 2008. At the certificate level women's enrolment increased from 22 percent in 1987 to 39.8 percent in 2008, at the diploma level women increased their share from 50.1 percent in 1987 to 53.8 percent in 2008, at the degree level women's enrolment moved up from 44.6 percent in 1987 to 62.4 percent in 2008; at masters level from 43.5 percent in 1987 to 52.7 percent in 2008, and at doctoral level from 29.9 percent in 1987 to 38.5 percent in 2008.

Women were beginning to represent a significant proportion in universities and HE institutions offering professional and technical courses. Women's enrolment at the Universiti Teknologi Malaysia (UTM) increased from 382 (20.5 percent) in 1975 to 17,188 women out of a total enrolment of 38,842, that is, 44.2 percent women while at Universiti Putra Malaysia (UPM) female enrolment increased from 90 (15.4 percent) in 1970 to 18,580 women out of a total enrolment of 29,063, that is, 63.9 percent women. In 2008, 35,375 women were enrolled in technical fields out of a total of 83,326, that is, women constituted 42.5 percent of enrolments in non-traditional technical fields. In information technology and communication studies more women (13,361 of 20,936 or 63.8 percent) than men were enrolled in public institutions. Similarly, in science disciplines women outnumbered men with 47,729 women of 69,786 or 68.4 percent women enrolled in science disciplines (Malaysia, 2008, p. 12).

With their focus on market oriented courses, private sector institutions have opened up greater opportunities for Malaysian women to enter varied technical and vocational courses not offered by the public institutions. In 2008, 19,408 of 38,331 (50.6 percent) students enrolled in first degree science and technological disciplines were women. In technical and vocational courses 6,415 of 23,728 (27.0 percent) students enrolled were women (Malaysia, 2008, pp. 58–59). At the diploma level 49,729 of 71,159 (69.9 percent) women enrolled in science and technological courses while 5,217 of 26,226 (19.9 percent) enrolled in technical and vocational courses (Malaysia, 2008, pp. 56–57).

Detailed information provided in the MOHE statistical handbook (MOHE, 2008) reveals that in public universities women had overtaken men at all levels of HE, ranging between 63.0 percent (degree courses) and 54.6 percent (masters courses) except at the doctoral level (40.8 percent). However, women were under-represented in polytechnics and community colleges, ranging between 36.7 percent and 43.2 percent in their certificate and diploma courses.

Reliable data for private HE institutions are only available for the period 2002–2008. Private sector enrolments follow a similar pattern as the public sector with women overtaking their male colleagues by 2008. The data for 2008 show that intake of women into private institutions was 56.5 percent, enrolment was 55.4 percent and women graduates made up 56.5 percent of all graduates from private HE institutions. Women also overtook men at all levels of HE for intake, enrolment and output except at masters and doctoral levels.

Breakdown of enrolment by ethnicity and region by gender is unavailable from the Ministry of Higher Education/Education. However it is realistic to assume that women in all social groups benefitted significantly from the overall increased access to HE. However the question remains whether different social groups benefitted equally.

Women in the labour force

Impact of national policies on women's access to HE participation by ethnicity and regions is assessed through labour force data. On the whole women's participation in the country's economy has been on an upward trend, from 27 percent in 1957 to between 44.7 percent and 47.2 percent. Presently women's participation rate in the labour force is 45.7 percent.

Tertiary education improved chances of participation in the labour force for all women. Table 4.9 demonstrates that of those employed with diplomas the percentage of women had increased from 40.5 percent in 1985 to 49.9 percent in 2008 while among those employed with degrees the percentage of women in the labour force had dramatically doubled from 23.8 percent in 1985 to

Table 4.9 Number of Employed Persons by Highest Certificate Obtained by Gender (1985–2008)

		Diploma		Degree	
		N	%	N	%
1985	Male	89.7	59.5	91.7	76.2
	Female	61.1	40.5	28.5	23.8
	Total	150.8	100.0	120.2	100.0
1990	Male	120.6	55.6	114.8	69.2
	Female	96.2	44.4	51.0	30.8
	Total	216.8	100.0	165.8	100.0
2000	Male	288.3	53.9	300.9	63.8
	Female	246.8	46.1	170.4	36.2
	Total	535.1	100.0	471.3	100.0

(*Continued*)

Table 4.9 (Continued)

		Diploma		Degree	
		N	%	N	%
2005	Male	460.2	54.7	421.1	57.4
	Female	380.5	45.3	312.4	42,6
	Total	840.7	100.0	733.5	100.0
2008	Male	394.5	50.1	470.9	53.8
	Female	391.6	49.9	403.2	46.2
	Total	786.1	100.0	874.1	100.0

Source: Department of Statistics, Putrajaya

46.2 percent in 2008. In comparison, men's share of the employed for the same levels of education had decreased.

However, chances for women from different ethnic, geographical and social backgrounds were unequal.

Differences by ethnicity

Data on percentage distribution of persons in the labour market by ethnicity (see Table 4.10) show that between 1990 and 2008 women of all ethnic groups with tertiary education revealed a significant increase of their share in the workforce. However, Bumiputera women with tertiary education showed the greatest increase of their share in the labour force and Indian women the least. Among Bumiputera women in the labour market, 30.9 percent in 2008 possessed tertiary education compared with 6.30 percent in 1990, marking an increase of 24.6 percent over the period 1990 to 2008. Chinese women with tertiary education increased from 5.9 percent in 1990 to 28.3 percent in 2008, an increase of 22.4 percent. Over the same period Indian women with tertiary education increased from 4.1 percent in 1990 to 22.4 percent in 2008, an improvement of 18.3 percent.

Regional differences by gender

Data on employed persons in the labour force by stratum (urban and rural) and gender demonstrate the strides women have made in achieving HE (see Table 4.11). Of females in urban areas, percentage of women with HE increased from 16.7 percent in 1995 to 30.3 percent in 2008, an increase of 13.6 percent. Over the same period, of women in rural areas, the proportion with HE increased from 7.4 percent to 18.9 percent in 2008, an increase of 11.5 percent. However, the gap in achieving HE between rural and urban areas remains considerable. In 1995, a

Table 4.10 Percentage Distribution of Persons with Tertiary Education in the Labour Force by Gender and Ethnic Group, 1990 to 2004

	Bumiputera		Chinese		Indian		Others	
	Male	Female	Male	Female	Male	Female	Male	Female
1990	5.1	6.3	5.4	5.9	4.6	4.1	23.4	13.8
1995	10.3	13.6	11.0	13.6	9.3	9.7	6.7	8.1
2000	13.0	18.1	15.0	19.7	11.2	13.8	4.3	8.9
2004	15.8	24.2	18.0	26.7	15.0	20.4	8.0	12.7
2008	19.4	30.9	19.8	28.3	17.2	22.4	10.6	9.2

Source: Malaysia. Department of Statistics. *Labor Force Survey Reports 1990–2008*

Table 4.11 Percentage Distribution of Employed Persons with Tertiary Education in the Labour Force by Stratum and Gender, 1995–2008

Year	Gender	Male %	Female %	Total
1995	Urban	14.3	16.7	15.0
	Rural	5.8	7.4	6.3
2000	Urban	17.0	20.5	18.3
	Rural	7.8	11.4	8.9
2004	Urban	20.3	27.4	22.9
	Rural	8.0	13.2	9.7
2008	Urban	21.0	30.3	25.0
	Rural	10.1	18.9	12.9

Source: Malaysia. Department of Statistics. Labour Force Survey Reports. 1995–2008

gap of 8.5 percent existed between urban and rural women; in 2008, a gap of 11.7 existed between the percentage of women with HE in urban and rural areas. Thus, it would seem that while women in both urban and rural areas have increased access to tertiary education, the gap in accessing tertiary education between urban and rural women has in fact increased over the period 1995 to 2008.

Thus, data on women's presence in the labour force clearly show that while women may still lag behind men in terms of their participation rates in the labour force, women, with their improved educational achievements, have made significant leaps in entering the labour force. Furthermore, the groups targeted by the NEP, that is the Bumiputera and those in the less developed areas, benefitted greatly through obtaining HE. However, in the rural areas women have still failed to match their urban counterparts. Furthermore, while all women have increased their access to HE and participation in the labour force, the gap in labour force participation between urban and rural women has increased over time

Student financing

HE in Malaysia is constitutionally a Federal responsibility. In a system where public HE is heavily subsidised by the government, financial support for students in both public and private institutions becomes a critical area for ensuring equity for all. With close to 50 percent of students enrolled in the for-profit private HE sector, the pertinent question is equitability of access given the disparity in fees between the public and the private HE sectors. Given that average private sector fees are much greater than in local publicly-funded institutions, the impact of policies on access for private sector students, and government support to approximately 50 percent of the total number of students in the tertiary subsector, warrants in-depth study.

Study findings indicate that while access to HE may be abundant, insufficient attention has been paid to the equality of access mechanisms. Table 4.12 summarises the fees payable for five fields of study in the public and private HE sectors, showing significant disparity between them. The percentage range of variation for fees payable in the private sector in comparison to the public sector is between 78 percent and 2511.4 percent, explained by the large subsidies – between 88.2 to 2511.4 percent – for the public sector.

HE funding for students in this discussion incorporates all forms of funding, scholarships/sponsorship and loans. As in many emerging economies, a

Table 4.12 Tuition Fees and Total Government Subsidies for Five Fields of Studies in the Public and Private Sectors

Type of Study	Public Sector		Private Sector	Range of fees variation between public and private sector
	Tuition Fee	Government Subsidy	Tuition Fee Range	
Business & Social Science	1,865	13,915 (88.2%)	9,091–25,455	79.5–1364.9
Engineering	2,851	24,382 (89.5%)	13,939–30,909	79.5–1084.1
ICT	2,065	18,645 (90.0%)	9,697–25,455	78.7–1232.7
Medicine	4,018	47,788 (92.2%)	75,758–100,909	94.7–2511.4
Hospitality & Tourism	2,065	18,645 (90.0%)	9,394–16,667	78.0–807.1

Source: Malaysian Qualifications Agency (MQA). Report to MoHE on Private Sector Higher Education Fees: 2008 & University Putra Malaysia – information downloaded July 15, 2010

Notes
1 Private sector fee include the range for home grown, 3+0 and branch campus
2 Tuition fees for the complete programme
3 Fees are given in USD at the exchange rate of USD1.00 to RM3.30

substantial proportion of HE expenditure is from the central government budget through the MOHE. In 2006, for instance, expenditure for HE was 36.03 percent of current education expenditure for the year. A range of organisations provide financial assistance to students by various means such as scholarship, sponsorship and loans. These include foreign agencies, local communities, families and individuals, non-governmental organisations (NGOs), private enterprises and corporations as well as foreign aid.

Two major government agencies, the biggest players in awarding scholarships and loans nationally, are reviewed here to illustrate the existing scenario in public fund allocation. The Public Services Department (or its Malaysian acronym JPA) provides scholarships, tenable in local and foreign universities; and the National Higher Education Fund Corporation (or its Malaysian acronym PTPTN) provides loans to students in public and private institutions. Family socioeconomic status is the major criterion in awarding financial aid, coupled with students' academic achievement. As the number of students qualifying for university admission increases and becomes more competitive, the chances of obtaining full education financing are reduced. Many students resort to PTPTN loans, leading to the issue of students graduating with debts.

The JPA scholarship story

The government of Malaysia, through the Public Services Department (JPA), provides scholarships based on academic merit to students studying in foreign and local institutions. In 2008, the MOHE reported that out of a total of 59,107 students overseas, 21,517 were sponsored. Less than 10 percent of these were under JPA scholarship, largely due to the higher cost in sending students overseas. A large proportion of awards under the JPA Overseas Scholarship Program are allocated for disciplines deemed critical such as medicine and pharmacy. Under this program, students excelling in secondary school leaving examinations are placed in local preparatory colleges for about one to two years. On successful completion, they are placed in overseas universities of good repute, generally in Australia, the UK and USA. Placements are subject to their passing the preparatory program with distinction; being offered a place by the universities listed by JPA; and being certified medically fit. Given the usefulness of internationally recognised certification, the demand for overseas scholarships far outstrips their availability.

There has been gradual growth in the number of scholarships provided overall and the increase is significant particularly for study in the local HEIs as shown in Table 4.13. The smaller increase in foreign scholarships may be attributed to the higher cost of overseas study and the increase in the local provision of foreign programmes through twinning and 3+0 and branch campuses. The distribution of awards (Table 4.13) shows that between 2000 and 2008, of the total number of 58,506 recipients, 87.3 percent were Bumiputera while 12.7 percent were non-Bumiputera students. However the overall pattern shows a healthy sign over the years as the proportion awarded to non Bumiputeras moved from 8.5 percent in 2000 to 21.7 percent in 2008.

Table 4.13 Public Sector Department Scholarships for Studies at Domestic HEIs according to Bumiputera and non-Bumiputera – 2000–2008

	2000	2001	2002	2003	2004	2005	2006	2007	2008	*Total*
Ethnic Cluster										
Bumiputera	3,444 *(91.5)*	8,723 *(90.0)*	6,643 *(91.4)*	4,340 *(91.4)*	3,994 *(90.3)*	4,693 *(88.8)*	4,727 *(82.2)*	6,682 *(88.2)*	7,826 *(78.3)*	51,072 *(87.3)*
Non-Bumiputera	319 *(8.5)*	969 *(10.0)*	623 *(8.6)*	407 *(8.6)*	430 *(9.7)*	593 *(11.2)*	1,026 *(17.8)*	893 *(11.8)*	2,174 *(21.7)*	7,434 *(12.7)*
Total	3,763	9,692	7,266	4,741	4,424	5,286	5,753	7,575	10,000	58,506

Source: Public Services Department November 2009

Table 4.14 Bumiputera and non-Bumiputera Comparison in Enrolment and Scholarship Awards for the Year 2000

Ethnic Group	Enrolment*		Scholarship	
	No	%	No	%
Bumiputera	827,593	59.9	3,444	91.5
Non-Bumiputera	553,570	40.1	319	8.5
Total	1,381,163	100.0	3,763	100.0

Source: JPA and Ministry of Higher Education, www.mohe.gov.my

The JPA scholarship awards for overseas study show a different story over the same period. For the years 2000 to 2008, a total of 12,485 scholarships were awarded under this scheme, of which 73.4 percent or 9,160 were awarded to Bumiputera students and the remainder 26.6 percent or 3,325 to non Bumiputera students. The earlier years (2000–2005) had shown an apportioning of 80 percent Bumiputera to 20 percent non Bumiputera awards. JPA scholarship data showed a more equitable distribution of public funds in 2008, when for the first time distribution was 55 percent Bumiputera and 45 percent non Bumiputera, showing improved trends for overseas study awards compared with local. This is certainly more equitable than the distribution in scholarships for study locally.

Yet the JPA scholarship is not the only publicly funded scholarship scheme for students studying locally or abroad. Other scholarship schemes such as the individual state scholarships and the Yayasan Mara scholarships, to name a few, sponsor significant numbers of students. Unfortunately, data for these are unavailable. However, the general understanding is that the vast majority of students under state scholarships and certainly a 100 percent under the latter are Malays and other Bumiputera students.

When student scholarships were compared with student enrolment at local HEIs, inter-ethnic disparity was evident in the number of students from the non Bumiputera group obtaining scholarships as shown in Table 4.14. As enrolment figures disaggregated by ethnicity for public and private sectors are available only for 2000, the figure is compared with the JPA scholarship data for the same year. The total enrolment was about 1.4 million in 2000, of which about 59.9 percent were Bumiputera and the remainder non Bumiputera. The scholarship data for local institutions however show that 91.5 percent of scholarships were awarded to Bumiputera students and only 8.5 percent to non Bumiputera students, showing a dramatic imbalance in the distribution of awards between Bumiputera and non Bumiputera.

The PTPTN story

In keeping with the government aspiration that no Malaysian with the required admissions qualifications should be denied access to HE, Perbadanan Tabung

Pendidikan Tinggi Nasional (PTPTN), was established under the National Higher Education Fund Act 1997 (Act 566), beginning operations on 1st November 1997. Its objective is to ensure efficient management of low interest loan financing, using public funds, for eligible students in institutions of higher learning. The most recent development (Budget 2010) saw an extension of this function where loan holders with a first class honors degree will now be able to convert their loan retroactively into a scholarship, without any repayment obligations.

PTPTN loans were initially available only to students from the public sector HE institutions with eligibility based on monthly family income. Since 1999, it became available to students from both public and private sector HEIs, with loans provided in three categories:

i full loan for students from families with incomes below RM3,000 a month (or less than approximately USD 900 per month);
ii partial loan 1 for students from families with incomes between RM3,001 and RM 5,000 a month (or USD 1,001 and 1,380 per annum) to cover tuition fees and a portion for subsistence; and
iii partial loan 2 for students from families with monthly incomes of above RM 5,001 (or USD 1,381 and above) only for loans up to the maximum of *their tuition fees*.

In the last 10 years PTPTN has provided HE loans to the amount of RM 26.2 billion (US$8 billion) benefitting about 1.3 million students. In 1997, PTPTN had approved 12,000 applications and in 2008 the number of approvals increased to 97,000, an eight-fold increase. This is a remarkable achievement by the government of Malaysia, resulting in substantial increase in access for different categories of students. The availability of study loans had increased enrolment in the private HE sector, now totaling almost 50 percent of the student enrolment in the country.

As the main HE loan provider in the country, PTPTN has two pressing concerns. The first is the low loan recovery rate. As of 2009, it had recovered only 48 percent out of RM 36.8 million (US$11 million) paid out since its inception in 1997. Parliamentary recommendations for their recovery are awaited. The second is the issue of leakage of funds. The Auditor General's Report 2009 stated that a total of RM 23.78 million (USD7.2 million) were disbursed in loans to persons who had not applied and this involved 16,013 students. An audit analysis of 3,852 recipients from this category shows that payment could not be collected from 3,793 (98.4 percent). Planned actions to be taken by PTPTN are not known.

However, there are some variations in relation to the ethnic composition of students who had obtained PTPTN loans. The data can only be tabulated for the year 2000 as enrolment data for other years are not available by ethnic group. Table 4.15 shows the variation that while there were 60 percent Bumiputera students in HE for the year 2000, 75.4 percent had obtained loans from PTPTN. Non-Bumiputera students constituted 40 percent of total enrolment but only 24.6 percent obtained loans. The same table also shows that 44 percent

Table 4.15 Bumiputera and Non Bumiputera Comparison of Loan and Enrolment for the Year 2000

Ethnic Cluster	2000			
	Enrolment		Loan	
	No	%	No	%
Bumiputera	827,593	59.9	66,613	75.4
Non-Bumiputera	553,570	40.1	21,759	24.6
Total	1,381,163	100.0	88,372	100.0

Source: PTPTN and Ministry of Higher Education, www.mohe.gov.my

of Chinese students and 54.5 percent of Indian students received educational loans. As the loan process utilises a means-based test, one could conclude that Bumiputera students are in the lower income band and therefore are more eligible than non-Bumiputera students.

Increased access has not come with equitable patterns of participation particularly given the binary divide in the ethnicity of students in the public and the private sector institutions, the disparities in tuition fees and provision of scholarships. Government scholarships have financed a small segment of Chinese and Indian students but again not in proportion to their population. Over the last decade, loans have been of assistance to these two groups, helping to support their studies in private HEIs. The liberalisation of the HE system in private HE for qualified entrants has provided important avenues to qualified non-Bumiputra entrants for pursuing programs inaccessible through the public HE system, albeit at high cost to families. The issue of equity arises when well-qualified non-Bumiputera students, particularly from disadvantaged backgrounds, cannot access public HE and may never participate in HE because private HE is beyond their means. The equity objective is not *free* HE, but a system in which "no bright person is denied a place because he or she comes from a disadvantaged background" (Barr, 2004). The provision of scholarships can ameliorate the situation if they are distributed to all groups based on socio-economic disadvantages and performance in university entrance qualifying exams.

Study findings show that while government overseas scholarships have moved toward proportional ethnic representation after four decades of implementation, the overall sources and numbers of overseas and locally-held scholarships at federal, state and Government Linked Company (GLC)-levels remain a closed book with no documented information readily available in the public domain. The existence of Bumiputera-only or Bumiputera predominant HE institutions in the public sector bears testimony to the fact that equitable provision of student financing for all groups is still a goal to seek in the HE landscape. The establishment of PTPTN and the opening up of education loans to students enrolled in the private HEIs had progressively offered greater access to loans for non-Bumiputeras, albeit at much higher fee levels than in public HEIs. The highly-subsidised fees for public institutions becomes a relevant area of review in terms of equitable use of public funds given that 2008 figures show that Bumiputera students constitute 84 percent of all students in public HE institutions and the reverse is true in the private education sector.

In a system where public HE is heavily subsidised by the government, financial support for students in both public and private institutions becomes a critical area for ensuring equity for all. Given that the average private sector fee is much greater than that of local public institutions, the impact of policies on access for private sector students, and government support to approximately 50 percent of the total number of students in the tertiary subsector, warrants in-depth study. Study findings indicate that while access to HE may be abundant, insufficient attention has been paid to the equality of access mechanisms. The critical aspect of inequality in access lies chiefly in the variation of fees between the public and private sectors.

What lies ahead?

The HE sector in Malaysia has grown remarkably becoming by 2008 a multi-level, diversified system. The period 1985 to 2008 saw tremendous expansion of public and private HE with dramatic improvement in access. Contributing factors for the increase have been high secondary enrolment and completion; liberalisation of HE leading to a burgeoning private sector; diversified institutional structure (public and private universities, colleges, polytechnics, community colleges) providing destinations for varied groups; the establishment of the Higher Education Loan Fund; and a creative mix of private, public and foreign funds in financing HEIs. The increased participation has been in step with growing demand for a qualified and skilled workforce as the economy grew. Every group included in the study enjoyed better access over the last three decades: all the ethnic groups, women, and those from more inaccessible and less developed regions in the country.

Equitable treatment for all groups is not just an issue related to numbers although that is important as those who receive HE can look forward to better opportunities for upward mobility and therefore improved life chances for themselves and their families. A major goal of the country is integration among its various ethnic groups. Affirmative action policy implementation has served to compartmentalise Bumiputeras in education, training and employment. This has led to social and cultural silos as well as a loss of the healthy competition which is the hallmark of a vibrant, modern HE system. HE institutions need to review their missions in terms of their primary academic functions of teaching, learning and research.

The economic goals of Malaysia include that of becoming a high income country by 2020. The journey to achieving that goal is thwarted by the scarcity of experienced and technically-qualified personnel required by a modern, knowledge-based economy. The lack of inclusiveness, the need for greater competition right through the school and university system, the preponderance of subsidies, allocations and economic advantages to one group, have raised Hydra-headed issues which lie squarely on the table of policy-makers, strategists, and institutional decision-makers. These issues and their possible solutions have been laid out in a variety of ways but sustained political will and action are urgently required.

As the Malaysian Government puts it (NEM Concluding Part, 2010, p. 4) in a discussion of the nation as a high income, inclusive and sustainable economy by 2020 ". . . Malaysia cannot be an advanced country without social cohesion and stability . . . (which) means that the benefits of growth and prosperity must be shared by all . . ." In short, "The future challenge for Malaysians of all ethnic communities is to create a more integrated and compassionate society where ethnic diversity can be celebrated as a national resource and not as a point of division" (Hirschman, 2013).

References

Barr, N. (2004). Higher education funding. *Oxford Review of Economic Policy, 20*(2), 264–283.

Docquier, Frederic, & Marfouk, Abdesiam. (2010, May 16). *Brain Drain Database*, World Bank. Quoted by Fong Chan Onn in the *Sunday Star*.

Fernandez-Chung, R. M., Cheong, K. C., & Hill, C. (2014). A Report: TNE Graduate Employment Study: An Analysis of Graduate Employment Trends in Malaysia (A Research Study in Three Phases), Phase 1: Employability of Graduates in Malaysia: The Perception of Selected Employers. The British Council, UK.

Hirschman, C. (2013, September 11). Rapid Malay education trend but slow pace for Indians. *New Straits Times*, 19.

Malaysia. (1967). *Report of the Higher Education Planning Committee*. Kuala Lumpur: Government Printers.

Malaysia. (1971). *Report of the Committee Appointed by the National Operations Council to Study Campus Life of Students in Universiti Malaya*. [Also known as the *Majid Report*] Kuala Lumpur: Government Printers.

Malaysia. (1980, 1991, 2000). *Population census reports*. Kuala Lumpur: Department of Statistics.

Malaysia. (2008). *Perangkaan Pengajian Tinggi Malaysia*. Kuala Lumpur: Bahagian Perancangan dan Penyelidikan, Kementerian Pengajian Tinggi, Malaysia.

Malaysia. (2010). *The New Economic Model (NEM) Part I* and *The New Economic Model (NEM) concluding part*. Economic Planning Unit. Putrajaya: Government of Malaysia.

MOHE. (2008). Perangkaan Pengajian Tinngi Malaysia. Terbitan oleh Bahagian perancangan dan Penyelidikan. Kementerian Pengajian Tinggi: Malaysia.

Mukherjee, Hena, & Wong, Poh Kam. (2011). The national university of Singapore and the university of Malaya: Common roots and different paths. In P. G. Altbach & Jamil Salmi (Eds.), *The road to academic excellence: The making of world – class research universities* (pp. 129–166). Washington, DC: The World Bank.

Schuman, M. (2010, September 6). To modernize, can Malaysians move beyond race? *Time Asia*.

Suffian, Tun Mohammed, Lee, H. P., & Trindade, F. A. (Eds). (1978). *The constitution of Malaysia, its development: 1957–1977*. Kuala Lumpur: Oxford University Press.

World Bank. (2010). *Affirmative action policies in Malaysian higher education: A report for the World Bank*. H Mukherjee, Jasbir S Singh, Rozalini M. Fernandez-Chung and T. Marimuthu. Washington, DC: The World Bank.

Appendix

Table 4.16 Enrolment in All Higher Education Institutions in 2008

	Certificate			Diploma			Degree			Masters			Doctoral		
	Male	Female	Total	Male	Female	Total	Male	Female	Total	Male	Female	Total	Male	Female	Total
IPTA	571	778	1349	34,940	49,887	84,827	103,183	171,166	274,349	17,063	19,031	36,094	7,526	4,717	12,243
IPTS	29,318	31,299	60,617	73,112	104,661	177,773	70,736	80,855	151,591	4,398	4,142	8,540	799	532	1,331
Polytech	19,315	11,546	30,861	29,250	25,169	54419									
Community Colleges	9,333	6,956	16,289	466	327	793									

Source: MOHE. Buku Perangkaan 2008

5 English as a Malaysian and ASEAN language
Implications for language policy and planning

Azirah Hashim and Gerhard Leitner

Education institutions are regarded as agents for consolidating national identity and societal cohesion and also for producing a talent pool for the country. Malaysia, like most of the ASEAN states is a multiethnic society; therefore, the role of education in national identity construction and in facilitating societal integration has become intertwined with ensuring ethnic diversity. At the same time, regional policies and global challenges have impacted on national perceptions and policies, and countries like Malaysia have realised that their economic growth and competitiveness will be hampered unless they invest in this area. Countries have realised that students have to be empowered through English to participate in higher education and in the job market and that language policies need to identify the needs of education, English language teaching and the role of other regional languages. Furthermore, it is recognised that English will be the language of the ASEAN Economic Community once it is introduced at the end of 2015. With all this will come a communicative network in ASEAN and beyond with rapidly expanding regional and global tourism, economy, media, education and research networks, as well as cross-border university training networks and these will generate a new dimension of English. At the same time, the government continues to recognise that education should also play a role in creating a national identity and social cohesion amongst the different ethnic groups. Malay, English and other languages have a role to play there.

This chapter addresses the many English language situations in Malaysia focusing on regional and international developments that are taking place especially in the ASEAN context. It discusses what should be done in the face of what is happening in ASEAN and beyond without jeopardising the integrative function of the Malay language and the continued usage of the other languages in Malaysia. This chapter therefore begins by describing the national, regional and international language ecology. It then turns to English-medium teaching in schools and in higher education in relation to other languages. Finally, it seeks to explore future trends and to develop views on what should be done to manage the language ecology given the changes taking place at the regional and global level.

Introduction: Socio-political history of English

The geo-political, demographic, linguistic and cultural space of Malaysia and Southeast Asia has ensured that language contact has always been pervasive. Britain's colonial period has added a major reshuffling of the demographic and linguistic make-up of the Malayan Peninsula and its archipelago. The contact scenario of which Malaya was a part was being integrated into the wider Asian colonial empire of Great Britain. English slowly carved out for itself a considerable space at the expense of other languages in Asia's national and regional languages habitats. Inheriting colonial outcomes at independence, Malaysia and other former colonies in the region have formulated national policies of their own with regard to English and their (now) other national languages. The more contemporary geo-political changes brought about by the creation of regional organizations such as ASEAN, pan-regional such as APEC and globalisation have further challenged national language policies.

English was first brought to the region by the British East India Company during the 17th century (Tan, 2013, p. 24). But the relevant period that was the cause of policy responses began by the middle of the 19th century when English slowly replaced Malay as the language of communication between the British and Malay rulers and when schools were set up that included English so as to create an English-speaking elite. Unlike in India during the 19th century, there were no debates between what were referred to as the *Anglicists* and *Orientalists* there. The former had argued for the introduction of English as the language that should be imposed by the colonisers; the latter pointed to the value of India's classical languages, Sanskrit and Arabic, and their potential of winning the elite for the British cause. The situation in the wider region where Malay was used was different. British colonial power did not deal with a political entity like India's but with a cluster of independent sultanates that were united by religion. That did not warrant policies. Linguistically, there was a prestige form of Malay that was used between the British and the Malays (Asmah, 2012; Lim & Poedjosoedarmo, 2016). At lower levels such as the ports or bazaars Malay regional dialects and Bazaar Malaya, social dialect, were used. By the 1860s all European colonial powers strengthened their native languages like French in Indo-China, Dutch in Indonesia and English in British possessions, followed by American English in the Philippines. English was thus introduced as a signal of political power. English now spread as a school language under the control of the British East India Company until 1867, then under the control of the Empire. A second way English had already been spreading was its use as a trade language in the ports of Singapore, Penang and Malacca. To the extent that there was a considered language policy during the colonial era at all, Britain did not interfere with existing schools of the Malay, Chinese and Indian communities but added its own state and missionary schools. But English was promoted through education to create an Anglophone elite in trade, the economy and the public domain. Thus, British colonisers brought about major change to the demographic, settlement, and linguistic make-up of the Malay region as labourers were brought in from India and China. The Chinese tended to work in the tin mines, the south Indians in the rubber plantations, and the Malays remained largely rural. This division of labour was paired with settlements in different regions, the adherence to different religions and languages. The Chinese were mainly in the growing small towns where they also set up small shops and became influential traders. Today they form a strong urban middle class component, a fact that will be pertinent to the formulation and uptake of educational language policies. As the East India Company and Britain were mainly interested in trade up to the 20th century it was natural that they did not see it as their task to assimilate or integrate ethnic groups; nor did they consider it essential to facilitate a common identity. This might have been detrimental as the united group might eventually have been hostile to British interests. The two world wars last century had war theatres in South-East and East Asia nation-building and the freedom movements that followed required a consideration of the nature of the linguistic space. English turned out to be a strong element in this context.

This chapter addresses the many English language situations in Malaysia that focus on regional and international developments in the ASEAN context. It discusses what should be done in the face of what is happening in ASEAN and beyond without jeopardising the integrative function of the Malay language and the continued use of the other languages of the nation. This chapter therefore begins by describing the national, regional and international language ecology. It then turns to English-medium teaching in schools and in higher education in relation to other languages. Finally, it seeks to explore future trends and to develop views on what should be done to manage the language ecology given the changes now occurring at the regional and global level.

Malaysia's early language policy responses in nation-building

When the Federation of Malaya, i.e., Malaysia's former name for Peninsular Malaysia, acquired independence in 1957, there were hardly any structured language usage patterns in the Federated and the Non-Federated States. Malay with its dialects as well as Chinese languages and dialects, and the languages and dialects of the Indians and other languages in Peninsular Malaysia were distributed according to geography and ethnicity as developed through colonisation. The move to combine the two states, Sabah and Sarawak, in 1963, to form contemporary Malaysia added to this language complexity. The population today is about 28.31 million with the main ethnic groups being Malay (65.9%), Chinese (25.3%) and Tamil (7.3%) (Department of Statistics Malaysia, 2010). Its ethnic complexity has always been a part of the Malayan region with each ethnic group retaining their languages, cultures and education systems. In addition, the Islamic history of the country made nation-building perhaps a bigger issue than for other nations in the region. There was some reluctance to accept work migrants as citizens, which has remained an issue that surfaces on and off. Nation-building clearly required decisions on a number of linguistic and educational issues (Asmah, 2012; Azirah, 2009). The major ones included these:

a   the choice of a national and official language
b   the implementation of Malay along with its modernisation and a consideration of the distance to the Malay in Indonesia
c   the decision on what to do with English
d   the choice of representative ethnic languages of the Chinese and Indians
e   the decision on how best to deal with the other languages in Malaysia

A number of factors such as religion (Islam), settlement, economic status, gender, national benefit, and so on had to be taken into account when deciding on these and other issues. Malaysia needed to balance the rights of citizens with the aim of presenting an Islamic and Malay image. Malay was the natural choice as the majority and official language of the new nation at independence.

But if Malay was to replace English in all domains such as administration, parliament, law, education, and so forth, in which it had been used, it had to be modernised on a broad scale. The shift to Malay had to be gradual to ensure a high level of competence in these domains. An alignment with Indonesia would have been useful but co-operation was not achieved at the time. The shift to Malay was uncontroversial, but the question was what to do with English, the former colonial language. That question had been discussed widely before independence. India might have presented a model case at first sight when it stipulated in 1947 that English would disappear as de jure official language and be replaced by Hindi. That did not happen but in the Malaysia of 1957 that may not have been foreseeable. Malaysia took a similar step and English was to be phased out after ten years but was retained as a second important language. The abolition of English took longer in some domains such as the higher courts but it did lose ground.

As for the languages of the people from India and China, stipulations had to be written into the constitution which guaranteed the rights of these communities. Article 152 made the Malay language, now referred to as Bahasa Malaysia, the official and sole language of Malaysia with the provision that English would be maintained for ten years and then phased out unless the government made a different ruling. This function refers to the safeguarding of "the legitimate interests of other communities" without mentioning other languages explicitly except in Sarawak and Sabah. Though there was (and is) a multitude of Chinese dialects and Indian languages , Mandarin and Tamil were foregrounded as representative of the communities who were allowed to have their own schools where the vernacular languages were used as the medium of instruction. That state-of-affairs and the language rights of Chinese and Indians with their national-type schools and the use of Mandarin and Tamil as media-of-instruction had thus been guaranteed and maintained ever since. That was consensual and amounted to the continuation of a well-established tradition from colonial times. But the details and the alignment with the parameters mentioned earlier provided space enough for controversial debates, as can be seen in the long list of educational policy reports and policy acts up to the Malaysia Education Blueprint (MoE, 2013). Any real or apparent attack on these ethnic languages has always met with immediate responses from the communities' political organisations. When Malaysia drafted a new, long-term education policy in the recent Malaysia Education Blueprint 2013–2025 (MoE, 2013) that status quo was therefore maintained. In fact there is a mention that Mandarin and Tamil were to be strengthened. The fate of the many other dialects and languages was left to the activities of the communities themselves and no government intervention was stipulated. Arabic, the language of Islam, was not discussed widely either and only deserved a passing remark in the *Blueprint*. It continues to be taught to all Malay students and more intensively in Islamic schools. The indigenous languages continue to receive some support but are only mentioned as a part of the national heritage.

The educational challenges in nation-building can be seen in some of the key reports in the post-independence era (1957–1970) that are summed up in the *Blueprint* (2013, A1-A2). The Razak Report of 1956, for example, stipulated the establishment of an education system that incorporated national characteristics and guaranteed a place in schools for all children regardless of ethnicity or religion. The education policies outlined in the Razak Report were the foundation of a national education system that placed high emphasis on national unity. The Rahman Talib Report of 1960 confirmed the educational policy in the Razak Report and its general acceptance by the public. The recommendations of these two reports became the integral components of the Education Act 1961. In January 1976, the Act was extended to Sabah and Sarawak which had been incorporated into the formulation of Malaysia in 1963.

The aim of achieving unity through the policy of using the national language as the medium of instruction in all primary and secondary schools began in 1970 and was implemented in stages. The implementation of the New Economic Policy (1971–1990) (NEP) was shaped by social and economic issues, and the argument that racial harmony and efforts to curb economic imbalances and to establish equity in society were crucial for sustaining stability and progress. The NEP was a socio-economic policy aimed at achieving unity and development with a focus on eradicating poverty and on restructuring Malaysian society to eliminate the identification of race with economic function and geographical location. It also resulted in significant changes in the national education system as it stipulated that all students should follow the same curriculum and sit for the same examinations.

Implementation of the constitutional stipulation that English was (only) an important second language has, of course, been interpreted in a variety of ways. But along with the implementation of the shift to Bahasa Malaysia, English competency of school leavers and university students has significantly declined. The older generation had largely been taught in English by native speakers before independence and was more prolific. Each younger generation suffered a loss of competency.

A growing educational deficiency was widely visible and the government under Prime Minister Dr. Mahatir Mohamad decided on a remedy to strengthen English while staying within the constitutional framework: Mathematics and Sciences were to be taught in English from Year One in all schools. It was hoped that students would learn enough general English to transfer from these subjects into other areas of life. A number of serious shortcomings made success unlikely. The divide between rural and (large) urban schools led to the fact that schools in rural areas suffered considerably more than urban ones; they showed a shortage of teachers and of other amenities so that the gap with urban areas was growing. Exam results showed that rural students were unable to cope with the two subjects taught in English. There was an acute lack of competent subject teachers in English and re-training was not done with enough verve. So the hoped-for transfer from the teaching of Mathematics and Sciences in English into other domains is doubtful to have happened. Complaints about the lack of English did not disappear; quite the contrary. The policy was phased out in 2012 and English was replaced by Bahasa Melayu and vernacular languages in these subjects. Obviously, there was a public outcry among the more highly educated, affluent and urban middle classes, who considered English proficiency crucial and a critical skill for obtaining good jobs and for social mobility. They believed that the earlier children learn English, the more proficient they will become. While there was an ethnic element in these controversies, with the Chinese being stronger in the urban middle class, the protests cannot be reduced to ethnicity. To counter such broad criticisms by all communities, a promise was made to teach more English as a second language, which has happened with additional hours allocated for this. One will have to wait and see if that is a better remedy than the one before.

Following Kirkpatrick's opposition to the early introduction of English into subjects, language specialists have pointed out that English is not relevant to very young children and plays no role outside school where other languages are used (e.g., Coleman, 2006; Kirkpatrick, 2010). This remark certainly does not apply fully to urban and tourist areas such as Malacca or Langkawi, nor to Kuala Lumpur or Johor, which attracts massive foreign investments. But a debate is absent even in the *Blueprint* on whether other local languages (than Malay), should be given a bigger role. They would get sidelined if English is allocated more teaching hours. Such a debate is therefore more than necessary and solutions would go beyond the opposition between English and Malay.

English in ASEAN and beyond

These policy responses must be seen as addressing mainly national needs that aimed at creating a Malay-based and cross-ethnic identity. Within that intellectual framework one may indeed be sympathetic to the opposition against English. But the foundation of a large regional body, the Association of South-East Asian Nations (ASEAN) in 1967, has introduced a new dimension for policies and has added pressure to maintain and to strengthen English in the education system. Malaysia, Singapore, the Philippines, Thai-land and Indonesia had been the founding members and they assumed English to be, and be made, the only official and working language from the beginning in 1967 (Kirkpatrick, 2010). There was no debate and it came with some surprise to outsiders. The new ASEAN member states, namely Cambodia, Laos, Vietnam, and Burma (later Myanmar), which had no English colonial past and whose economic standing was such that they depended on outside help, did not, and could not, raise any objections when the status of English was officially sanctioned with the signing of the ASEAN Charter in 2009. Article 34 states that "the working language of ASEAN shall be English". The fact that English had by then become the global language of aid in all institutions such as the UN, the IMF, and the World Bank undoubtedly strengthened its position in the region. As the language of diplomacy among all the members of ASEAN, it would bring with it other advantages such as multinational and intraregional trade and mobility which would contribute to the nations' growth. This has led institutions of higher education to strategise including on which language should be medium of instruction and given greater focus. The academic environment has therefore had to deal with challenges to the university management, pedagogies used and also in the social interactions now taking place in their environment (Azirah & Leitner, 2014; Chew, 2014; Kirkpatrick, 2014; Lau & Chia-Yen, 2014).

Though at different stages of nation-building, all ASEAN member countries of today aspire to become integrated nations by 2015 and to be regional and global players with partners within ASEAN and beyond. While a tussle between English and other languages can be seen in all countries, English is promoted as a vehicle of empowerment and participation from an ASEAN and global angle. Within novel, multi-lingual and cultural spaces, it is being used for multiple functions as a second, foreign or even first language and is accepted as the lingua franca for regional and global purposes. It has acquired a dynamic role in regional communication and serves as a lingua franca in communication between neighbours. What Bolton (2008, p. 3) states for the whole of Asia, that "across Asia, the numbers of people having at least a functional command of the language have grown exponentially over the last four decades, and current changes in the sociolinguistic realities of the region are often so rapid that it is difficult for academic commentators to keep pace", is true also of South-East Asia, where English has gone hand in hand with economic growth.

As a result of its expansion and its embeddedness in a multilingual languages habitat, its texture has changed. New varieties have emerged that belong to what Kachru (1992) has called the Outer Circle countries in the former colonies or protectorates of Malaysia, Singapore, Brunei and the Philippines. These varieties get exported to the other ASEAN countries through networks of cooperation, knowledge transfer and training within the region and therefore it is not just British, American or Australian English that people are exposed to. It is different varieties in complex multilingual and functionally-differentiated settings (Azirah & Leitner, 2014; Leitner, 2014).

There is a regional lingua franca at the level of educated speakers whose properties are being investigated in a large-scale international project initiated and led by Andy Kirkpatrick (Azirah & Jagdish, 2011; Kirkpatrick, 2012). Even at more informal and less educated spoken levels one can notice family relationships between, say, Cambodian or Laotian uses of English and Malaysian English

(Leitner, 2014). The extent to which these varieties will ever develop norms of their own and become national forms of English like Malaysian and Singaporean English is doubtful. But there may emerge a cluster of varieties that cut across national boundaries. To what extent the established national varieties interact and create a new ASEAN *lingua franca* remains to be seen. It depends on the strength of national language policies that still adhere strongly to native norms even in former Anglophone colonies whether that can happen in the education domain.

At the same time, there is a great concern that the increased emphasis on English will threaten not only local languages but local cultures. As stated by Kirkpatrick (2010, p. 17), "the fact that English is now being introduced as a compulsory subject into the primary curriculum in all ASEAN countries with the exception of Indonesia adds to the threat for local languages, as English almost always replaces a local language in the primary curriculum". In ASEAN countries, the establishment of a national language or languages together with the need to continue using English to ensure a country does not lag behind due to lack of English does indeed lead to some neglect of local languages. Debates on how a balance can be struck between local languages and English are being carried out in countries in the region with differing outcomes. The proponents of English as a medium of instruction and the government support their demands with reference to the fact that:

(1) the best way to learn a language is to use it a as medium of instruction;
(2) to learn a second language you must start as early as possible; and

From an economic angle, English will become even more essential if ASEAN works toward a single market and production base. The agreement to form the ASEAN Free Trade Agreement (AFTA) and the ASEAN Economic Community (AEC) will see the streamlining of banking, finance, human capital mobility, for example. Eight Mutual Recognition Arrangements have been signed on the free flow of skilled labour in a number of fields. In the Tourism industry, ASEAN has laid out specific job titles that are open for free flow of labour within ASEAN countries. There are competency frameworks and employment expectations and the requirement that workers are able to communicate in English. Therefore, those lacking this competence will be unable to secure jobs at management level. Migration of skilled labour will result in brain drain. There will be a greater flow of workers from poorer countries with English competency to wealthier countries leading to greater discrepancies between the ASEAN nations.

The ASEAN dimension in education

This section will now turn to the effects of English as a lingua franca in South-East Asia and of ASEAN's language policies and suggest ways of mediating its repercussions. As ASEAN countries integrate economically, politically and socially, issues concerning equitable distribution, identity and opportunities will arise.

If ASEAN wishes to be a major player in the globalising world, then important consideration must be given to the effects of the language policy.

English is now taught from the lowest forms of primary schools in all countries in Southeast Asia. The general trend is that children are learning English at an even earlier age. As a result, the function of English in the curriculum will no longer be that of "foreign (or second) language", but that of a "near universal basic skill" (Graddol, 2006, p. 72). The education systems would need to see how to produce a skilled labour force for markets in the region and beyond. It would be important to produce well qualified workers and at the same time able to communicate effectively with other ASEAN workers. As English is the language of business, language teaching and learning is being increasingly done in English. There is also more and more interest in English as a Lingua Franca and a shift away from English as a Foreign Language. There is less stress on native English fluency and more on achieving communicative competence in multilingual environments. As Malaysians will be communicating in English mainly to other non-native speakers, the school curriculum must respond to these developments. At higher education level there will be a demand for English teaching that prepares graduates for a multilingual environment and for a globalized world. Students should be exposed to different English varieties and develop intercultural competences to cope with the diverse group of workers they will encounter.

As mentioned in the previous section, ASEAN considers a range of competencies to be important for the future success of the region. These competencies and mind-sets include critical, innovative and adaptive thinking; entrepreneurship; collaboration and cross-cultural working and digital literacy. This set reflects the thinking of the Assessment and Teaching of 21st Century Skills (ATC21S) (http://www.atc21s.org) headquartered at the University of Melbourne, a group of more than 250 researchers across 60 institutions worldwide. That organization has categorised the 21st century skills for an internationally mobile workforce and has developed four broad categories of essential skills for a knowledge-based economy:

- Ways of thinking – creativity, critical thinking, problem-solving, decision-making and learning
- Ways of working – communication and collaboration
- Tools for working – information and communications technology (ICT) and information literacy
- Skills for living in the world – citizenship, life and career, and personal and social responsibility.

This reflects the international outlook of the ASEAN community and the need that their graduates must be empowered to compete successfully in a regional and global marketplace. What seems particularly distinctive is the strong link with industry, a strong role in the knowledge economy, and the opportunity to develop new models of universities unconstrained by history or established systems. In terms of higher education harmonisation in ASEAN, there are efforts to improve mobility and cross-border education. Students spend time in other countries, graduates from one country are recruited by employers in other countries leading to multi-national workplaces throughout ASEAN. Many graduates lack the necessary skills needed for today's workplace which would affect economic and social development. English is a key to developing a global community; therefore, being able to communicate in English is important for realising the ASEAN Community.

Globalisation, internationalisation of education and the spread of English have clearly impacted educational systems in the region. In Malaysia, this can be seen clearly in the education policies adopted especially in the medium of instruction for mathematics and science. Tan and Santhiram (2014, p. 164) name two important causal factors: transnational corporations and the advent of ICT. For the first, the country needs to ensure that there is a workforce that is proficient enough in English as these corporations are necessary for the country's economic development. The second causal factor spurs the emergence of the knowledge-based economy and Malaysia, like other countries, is moving toward a knowledge-based economy. Like the Bologna Process, the move to English would facilitate staff and student mobility and ease credit transfer across universities in the region. Kirkpatrick (2014) also provides three main sources for the move to English as medium of instruction. The first is that a number of English-speaking countries have set up campuses in Asia, such as Monash University and Nottingham University in Malaysia, and Nottingham University in China. The second is that a number of programmes have been set up in partnership with universities in English-speaking countries. Curtin University has courses offered at its partner universities in Asia. The third is the set-up of regional universities which also use English as medium of instruction to cater to the diverse student market.

Malaysia's modern response in education

Education is the key to achieving a balance between Malay and English at the national level and the promotion of English for ASEAN and global markets. The Malaysia Education Blueprint 2013–2025 spells out the most recent policy shift to balance national and international needs. Prime Minister of Malaysia, Najib Razak, has said this in the foreword:

- "Education is a major contributor to our social and economic capital. It inspires creativity and fosters innovation; provides our youth with the necessary skills to be able to compete in the modern labour market; and is a key driver of growth in the economy . . . we must ensure that our education system continues to progress in tandem [with other policies]. By doing so, our country will continue to keep pace in an increasingly competitive global economy". (Foreword)
- To meet today's challenges ". . . will [2–4] . . . require students . . . to have strong universal values such as integrity, compassion, justice, and

altruism, to guide them in making ethical decisions. At the same time, it is important to balance the development of global citizenship with a strong national identity".

It is worth noting in passing that, while the policy is framed in an economic discourse, there is mention of another type of ethical value discourse. The former would promote English, the latter Malay but this need not be one-sided. Many experts see an increasing demand for high quality education and English as the language of modernisation, of access to knowledge, as against older policies that tended to create or preserve national identity and to strengthen national priorities. Globalisation now places pressure on governments to adopt policies and especially language policies that make citizens proficient enough in English so they are not to be left behind in this competitive era. Education reforms have aggressively taken place here and in other South-East Asian countries in the last few years in line with global reforms. Rankings such as Times Higher Education and QS World University Rankings have influenced the way universities conduct themselves as many international and local students use them as indicators and guidelines for choosing a university. With Malaysia wanting to become an education hub, foreign universities are setting up branch campuses. In light of competition at the world and the national level, universities are implementing more and more stringent key performance indicators to improve academic performance. Many universities market their programs and services around the world and actively network with other universities. Publication in high impact journals has become very much a priority.

While it is true that older policies tended to emphasise national needs, Malaysia had formulated a number of responses to the global challenges, with the Blueprint (2013) being the crystallization of past responses and the formulation of new ones (*see* Tham, 2013). The following are the historical stages of higher education development in Malaysia:

> Stage 1 (1990)- convergence of (a) the plan to reverse the 1980s higher education overseas exodus, and (b) new educational requirements of the *First Industrial Master Plan* (1990 policy to reverse *Higher Education Export Model*)
> Stage 2 (1996)- landmark reforms of the 1996 Higher Education Acts (including National Council of HE Act and Private HE Act) especially with regard to private institutions which now have access to the college sector.
> Stage 3 (2001)- Following 9/11 in 2001, Middle East students have become a strategic focus of the renewed internationalisation policy
> Stage 4 (2010)- In 2010 Higher Education was designated National Key Economic Area (NKEA) within the wider New Economic Model (NEM); EduCity and related policies

This growth of English as medium of instruction in Higher Education was and is linked to the increasing diversity of student populations, the demand from stakeholders about what kind of education is required in working life and in global competition and so forth. English is the language of academia and the sciences, and the language we have to use if we wish to prepare our students for an international career in a globalising world (Coleman, 2006, p. 7). Unsurprisingly, English is the most taught language in South-East Asia and in virtually all countries in the world. In many countries it is taught from primary level, hence consolidating its position. Graddol has described this trend and its sociocultural and economic consequences in these words:

> One of the most significant educational trends world-wide is the teaching of a growing number of courses in universities through the medium of English. The need to teach in English, rather than the national language, is well understood: in the sciences. Up-to-date text books, research articles and information are generally obtainable more easily in one of the world languages and most readily of all in English.
>
> (Graddol, 1997, p. 45)

Graduates who went through an English medium education, he believes, would usually extend the language to social use and use it with their children believing that that would give them a competitive edge or indicate social privilege: "English-medium higher education is thus one of the drivers of language shift, from L2 to L1 English speaking status" (1997, p. 45).

The primacy of research universities, the emphasis on research, and the need to publish in English has been widely accepted in Asia despite predictable problems. A case in point is the well-meant compromise between strengthening English as a second important language for economic reasons while maintaining the constitutional stipulation by Dr. Mahathir's government. Recent reversal of teaching Mathematics and Science in English by the government was motivated by failures in implementation (inadequate language skills of staff and students, lack of sufficient Anglophone subject specialists, lack of investment in training), an ideological policy discourse (perceived as threat to cultural identity and the status of the native language as a language of science), and an emotive stance against English (unwillingness of local staff to teach through English). The acceptance of English as a global necessity still jars with the demands of education at the primary level. The opposition to English might find support in social rights arguments that the expansion of English has brought about a need to go against capitalism and imperialism and protect human and community rights (Canagarajah, 1999; Kachru, 1992; Pennycook, 1994; Phillipson, 1992). But both the economic and the social rights discourse have a global dimension with the latter being mainly expressed through English.

Implications for language policy and planning in Malaysia and ASEAN

The role of English in the regional context has several implications that language policies have to address. The first is about the status of English and other

Malaysian languages, the second deals with the codification of English in the domain of education. The first has to address the balance of languages in language habitats vis-à-vis English (in its diverse societal functions). While this may be relatively easy in Singapore and, somewhat less so, in Malaysia, Brunei and the Philippines, this amounts to major change in the former Indochina. The status of English is often discussed in terms of an economic policy discourse (see Malaysia's *Blueprint*), but an economic discourse ignores the rights of all other languages in a national habitat. A social rights discourse would need to complement the economic discourse and lead to a (more) comprehensive national language policy in education (Azirah & Leitner, 2014).

The second implication permits three options: (i) the choice or maintenance of an exo-normative native-English (say, British) model; (ii) the choice of a local ("Englishes") model, following Kachru's Outer Circle; and (iii) the shift to a (South-East Asian) lingua franca model. That concept represents a new paradigm for the way English can be viewed and taught (Kirkpatrick, 2010, 2012; Seidlhofer, 2001, 2011). According to Kirkpatrick (2012), that concept would affect language learning goals, language teacher training, teaching practices, curriculum design and, one should add, teaching/learning materials design. Kirkpatrick believes English should be presented as an "Asian" lingua franca spoken by multilinguals who usually need English to talk to fellow ASEAN speakers rather than native speakers thereby making the acquisition of idealised native speaker norms hardly relevant. The main goal of these people would be to learn English to be able to communicate successfully with other multilinguals. As for language testing, Kirkpatrick (2007, 2012) recommends that learners be measured against the norms of successful Asian multilinguals rather than against native English norms. Aspirations of wanting to sound native-like no longer exist as strongly as they did in the past since speakers from each ASEAN country view their English as a quasi-native variety, native to their own nation. Pending more empirical research with tangible results, such an assumption is, we believe, still highly arguable. But other scholars have put forward similar views. McKay (2009, p. 238), for example, has proposed that "reliance on a native speaker model as the pedagogical target must be set aside". That demand has significant repercussions on the traditional second language acquisition paradigm. Testing criteria must be developed that place emphasis on how successfully people use the language in contexts relevant for them. This is especially difficult since in Asia bi- and multilinguals communicate and interact with other bi/multilingual Asians. They will use English in multilingual contexts in which they normally operate, and code-switching has to be taken into account as a normal phenomenon in oral communication.

Domains that would benefit particularly from such a new perspective are higher education institutions, science, research and technology, export trade, and so forth. Universities, for instance, are evaluated in a global marketplace where they are ranked in world league tables. Academics are expected to publish in top journals which almost always use English. Universities attempt to get bigger numbers of international staff and students so that more courses have to be taught in English. As curriculums become more international, more students can go on attachments abroad. These developments strengthen the need for proficiency in English and, more specifically, require the teaching of academic and *lingua franca* English. They require curriculums that promote awareness of diversity in terms of culture, religion, work experience and learning preferences. Different students from different cultural and educational backgrounds will come with different expectations and concerns and bring different perspectives with them. Key competencies would include those defined by Assessment and Teaching of 21st Century Skills (ATC21S) discussed earlier. Having these competencies is not enough as they must be expressed in English. Education systems will need to look into how to educate students to have globally relevant competencies, and this may differ from country to country, and job to job in terms of status and texture.

References

Asmah Haji Omar. (2012). Pragmatics of maintaining English in Malaysia's education system. In Ee-Ling Low & Azirah Hashim (Eds.), *English in Southeast Asia: Features, policy and language in use* (pp. 155–174). Amsterdam: John Benjamins.

Azirah Hashim. (2009). Not plain sailing: Malaysia's language choice in policy and education. *AILA Review, 22*, 36–51.

Azirah Hashim, & Leitner, G. (2014). English as a lingua franca in higher education in Malaysia. *Asian Journal of Applied Linguistics, 1*(1), 16–27.

Azirah Hashim, & Kaur, Jagdish. (2011). *ELF Data, ELF corpora: Structural characteristics of ACE*. Paper presented at the 16th World Congress of Applied Linguistics, 23–28 August 2011, Beijing Foreign Studies University, China.

Bolton, K. (2008). English in Asia, Asian Englishes, and the issue of proficiency. *English Today, 24*(2), 3–12.

Canagarajah, A. S. (1999). *Resisting linguistic imperialism in English teaching*. Oxford: Oxford University Press.

Chew, P. G-L. (2014). The role of English as a lingua franca in institutions of higher education in Singapore. *Asian Journal of Applied Linguistics, 1*(1), 28–35.

Coleman, J. A. (2006). English-medium teaching in European higher education. *Language Teaching, 39*(1), pp. 1–14.

Department of Statistics of Malaysia. (2010). Retrieved from www.statistics.gov.my

Graddol, D. (1997). *The future of English*. London: British Council.

Graddol, D. (2006). *English Next. Why global English may mean the end of 'English as a Foreign Language'*. London: British Council.

Kachru, B. (1992). *The other tongue: English across cultures* (2nd ed.). Chicago, IL: University of Illinois Press.

Kirkpatrick, A. (2007). *World Englishes: Implications for international communication and English language teaching*. Cambridge: Cambridge University Press.

Kirkpatrick, A. (2010). *English as a Lingua Franca in ASEAN: A multilingual model*. Hong Kong: Hong Kong University Press.

Kirkpatrick, A. (2012). English in ASEAN: Implications for regional multilingualism. *Journal of Multilingual and Multicultural Development, 33*(4), 331–344.

Kirkpatrick, A. (2014). The language(s) of HE: EMI and/or ELF and/or multilingualism? *Asian Journal of Applied Linguistics, 1*(1), 4–15.

Lau, K., & Chia-Yen, L. (2014). The role of English as a lingua franca in social integration: The case of the international students of a university in Taiwan. *Asian Journal of Applied Linguistics, 1*(1), 36–49.

Leitner, G. (2014). Transforming South-East Asia's languages habitats. *World Englishes, 33*(4), 512–525.

Lim, B. S., & Poedjosoedarmo, G. (2016). Bahasa Indonesia and Bahasa Melayu: convergence and divergence of the official languages in contemporary Southeast Asia. In Leitner, G., Azirah Hashim, & Wolf, H. G. (Eds). *Communicating with Asia*, Cambridge: Cambridge University Press. 170–187.

McKay, S. L., & Bokhorst-Heng, W. D. (2009). *International English in its sociolinguistic contexts: Towards a socially sensitive EIL pedagogy*. New York, NY: Routledge.

MoE. (2013). *Malaysia education blueprint 2013–2025*. Putrajaya: Ministry of Education Malaysia.

Pennycook, A. (1994). *The cultural politics of English as an international language*. London: Longman.

Phillipson, R. (1992). *Linguistic imperialism*. Oxford: Oxford University Press.

Seidlhofer, B. (2001). Closing a conceptual gap: The case for a description of English as a lingua franca. *International Journal of Applied Linguistics, 11*(2), 133–157.

Tan, S. I. (2013). *Malaysian English: Language contact and change*. Frankfurt: Peter Lang.

Tan, Y. S., & Santhiram, R. (2014). *Educational issues in multiethnic Malaysia*. Selangor, Malaysia: Strategeic Information and Research Development Centre.

Tham, S. Y. (Ed.). (2013). *Internationalizing higher education in Malaysia*. Singapore: Institute of Southeast Asian Studies.

6 Technical and vocational education and training in Malaysia

From policy to implementation***

Kee-Cheok Cheong, Hwok-Aun Lee, Kuppusamy Singaravelloo and Abdillah Noh

Background

Malaysia's aspirations to achieve developed country status have been fuelled by several decades of heady economic growth. This growth has seen the Malaysian economy transformed from a primary commodities producer to a major manufacturing hub, earning the country membership into a group of economies that the World Bank in its report *The East Asian Miracle* (World Bank, 1993) called High Performing Asian Economies. When the last decade of the 20th century began, it did not appear far-fetched to Malaysia's leadership that making the transition from middle- to high-income by transforming to a "knowledge (K)" economy was a feasible endeavour. Vision 2020, announced by then Prime Minister Mahathir Mohamad in 1991, was to give substance to this plan.[1] Technical and vocational education and training (TVET) would have to be an integral part of human capital deepening.

But Malaysia's TVET program is more than a matter of ambition. It is also one of necessity – for several reasons. First, rapid economic growth had elevated the demand for labour that could not be matched by the increase in labour supply from population growth. At the same time, labour supply itself was depleted by the rapid expansion of enrolment in both secondary and post-secondary education. Malaysia had thus little choice but to import labour. Thus was born the low-cost imported labour model. In this model, Malaysian workers would move

---

*** This chapter is based on research by the authors in a World Bank project on Workforce Development under the title "Systems Approach for Better Education Results" (SABER). This research is fully reported in a country report for Malaysia issued by the World Bank (World Bank, 2013). Malaysia is one of a number of countries participating in this project. We are very grateful to members of the World Bank's SABER team covering Malaysia, particularly Jee-Peng Tan, Kiong-Hock Lee, Ryan Flynn and Joy Nam, for their comments on the substance of our research. Comments from Ximena del Carpio and Mauro Testaverde are also much appreciated.

up the skills ladder with unskilled work performed by imported labor. How would these skills be acquired? TVET was an obvious answer.

Second, not long after the launch of Vision 2020, the development model Malaysia employed, manufacturing using low-cost labour, began to fray. Despite redistributive policies based on extensive affirmative action, income inequality has increased; not all segments of the population have benefited, and development has come with increasing environmental cost. The Asian Financial Crisis (AFC) that befell Malaysia in 1997 also put an end to the high growth phase. From year 2000 until 2008, Malaysia's GDP grew at just 5.5 percent, still respectable, but nowhere near the average 9.1 percent from 1990 to 1997 (NEAC, 2010). With other countries in the region experiencing equal or more rapid growth, the country's position as regional leader was also eroding. Private fixed investment failed to recover even as net foreign direct investment (FDI) leveled off with the rise of alternative FDI destinations such as Indonesia and Vietnam. External factors such as the bursting of the tech bubble in the US during the turn of the century did not help (Lee & Tham, 2009, pp. 920–921). The deceleration in growth has raised concerns among the country's leadership that Malaysia may be in danger of falling into the "middle-income trap". The heart of this challenge is the country's inadequate labour supply in both quantitative and qualitative terms. TVET again takes centre stage if this challenge is to be met.

Third, the growth in numbers notwithstanding, quality issues in the Malaysian education system especially relating to the physical sciences are on display in the data provided by the Trends in Mathematics and Science Study (TIMSS), conducted every four years[2] and in the OECD study Programme for International Student Assessment (PISA) in 2009.[3] Malaysia's TIMSS scores for the three most recent studies show that in both mathematics and science Malaysia falls far behind the leaders, made up of the Newly Industrialized Economies (NIEs).[4] More worrying, the absolute scores have declined over time, with mathematics and science scores lower in 2011 compared to 1999. This is despite improved student results reported for national examinations every year. Malaysia's universities are also nowhere near the top Asian universities in terms of ranking.[5] A sound TVET system could, even if partially, make up for inadequacies in academic education.

These developments have elevated TVET to a central role in Malaysia's human capital development. The overarching objective of this chapter is to assess if Malaysia's TVET system is up to this task. The specific objectives are to (1) examine the system's performance in three areas: policy-making, system oversight and program delivery, (2) review the progress made in each of these areas over the decade 2000–2010, (3) draw lessons from the above analyses, and (4) provide recommendations in light of these lessons. The focus is on the public sector, partly because information on non-state provision of TVET is far from complete, but also because the public sector dominates the TVET landscape both in terms of policy and delivery.[6]

The rest of this chapter is structured as follows. Section 2 provides an overview of Malaysia's TVET system. An evaluation of the three dimensions of performance over the first decade of this century follows in Section 3. Section 4 draws together lessons of experience from the above reviews. Section 5 concludes with policy recommendations based on lessons drawn.

Malaysia's TVET system

Malaysia's education system can be broadly categorised as consisting of three streams (Table 6.1). The second and third streams make up the TVET system.

These streams are not watertight, and pathways exist for students to transfer from pursuing studies in one stream to doing so in another. As Figure 1 shows, transfer from the academic to the vocational stream could occur upon the completion of primary education.[7] Students opting for the vocational stream then complete 3 years of junior vocational education, in parallel with those enrolled for 3 years in lower secondary education in the academic stream. The next opportunity for transfer to vocational education occurs when students are enrolled in upper secondary education. Transferring students then enroll in vocational institutes. A final avenue for transfer exists at the tertiary education level, where students are free to transfer between universities and university colleges and vocational institutes of higher education.

The relative simplicity of Figure 6.1 belies the large number of agencies in charge of an even wider array of institutions delivering training at different skill levels. The details of these are shown in Figure 6.2. No fewer than 13 federal

Table 6.1 Main Streams of Malaysia's Education (and Training) System

Stream	Institutions	Workplace Preparation
Academic education	Universities and other tertiary education institutions, both public and private	Managerial, professional occupations, including those requiring technology
Technical and vocational education	Polytechnics, technical institutes/colleges and community colleges	Supervisory occupations, including technical assistants and supervisors
Vocational skills training	Skills training institutions, both public and private	Skilled and semi-skilled occupations

Source: Pang (2010), Table 2.2.

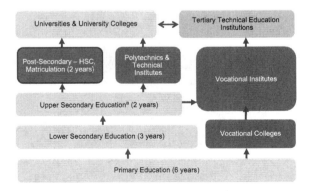

Figure 6.1 Pathways in Malaysia's education system.
Source: Adapted from Abdul Rahman Ayub (2012).

[a] Includes secondary technical and vocational education.

Ministry or Agency[a]	No. of Institutions	Total Enrollment	Under the Malaysian Skills Certification (SKM) System					Bachelor of Eng Tech
			Certificates			Diplomas		
			1	2	3	4	5	
MOE	88	25,000	Technical and Vocational schools[b]					
MOHE	99	17,000	Community colleges					
		88,000	Polytechnics					
	3	24,000						UTEM, UNIMAP, UTHO[c]
MOHR	27	10,800	Industrial Training Institutes (ITIs)					
		3,200				Japan-Malaysia Institute of Technology (JMTI)		
						Advanced Technical Training Centre (ADTEC)		
	1	538[d]				Centre for Instructor and Advanced Skills Training (CIAST)		
MRRD	234	2,000				German-Malaysia Institute		
		10,000	MARA Vocational Institute (IKM)[e]					
		2,700	MARA Higher Skills College (KKTM)[e]					
		19,000	Local Youth Awareness Movement (GiatMara)[f]					
		20,500				Universiti Kuala Lumpur[g]		Universiti Kuala Lumpur[g]
MYS	17	8,200	National Youth Skills Training Institute (IKBN)[e]					
						National Youth Higher Skills Training Insitute (IKTBN)[e]		
MOA	7	700	Ministry of Agriculture Institutes[h]					
MOD	5	805	Institutes of the Armed Forces Ex-Servicemen Affairs Corporation (Perhebat)					
MOW	6	37,000	Construction Industry Development Board (CIDB)					
States	13	20,000	State Institutes					
Private	n.a.	60,000	Accredited Centers					

Figure 6.2 Federal, State and Private Institutions Providing TVET by Skill Level, 2012

Source: CIDB (2011), Department of Skills Development (2013a), GiatMARA (2008), Mohd Gazali Abas (2012), Pang (2011).

a Full names of the ministries or agencies are shown in the list of abbreviations at the end of the report
b Some programmes lead to the Sijil Pelajaran Malaysia Vokasional (SPMV, Malaysian Certificate of Vocational Education).
c The acronyms refer, respectively, to Universiti Teknikal Malaysia Melaka (UTEM), Universiti Malaysia Perlis (UNIMAP), and Universiti Tun Hussein Onn (UTHO).
d Enrolment only in courses leading to Vocational Training Officer Certificate (VTO), SKM level 3 and VTO, Vocational Instructor Advanced Diploma (DLPV).
e Acronyms stand for the Bahasa Malaysia equivalent of the terms in English; see list of abbreviations for the full explanation.
f GiatMARA (Gerakan Insaf Anak Tempatan), established in 1986 as a non-profit, grassroots training institution under MARA, provides skills training and lifelong learning to school dropouts, retrenched workers and poor students from the *Bumiputera* ethnic community.
g Includes the British Malaysian Institute (BMI), Malaysia France Institute (MFI), Malaysian Spanish Institute (MSI), Malaysian Institute of Aviation Technology (MIAT).
h Examples include Institut Akuakultur Marin, Institut Perikanan Malaysia, Institut Veterinar Malaysia, and various institutes.

ministries oversee their own institutions, with the largest number of institutions (234 as of 2012) under the Ministry of Rural and Regional Development. Added to this phalanx of federal level institutions are training institutes under each of the 13 states. An unknown number of private sector institutions running government-accredited training programs catered to an estimated 60,000 students in 2012. Even if institutions running non-accredited programs, for which no information is available, are excluded, this complexity renders programme coordination and standards harmonisation a real challenge.

Assessing TVET performance

Assessing TVET performance requires attention to three areas. The first relates to policies supporting the system's development. The second refers to supervision of the system while the third consists of implementation of TVET programs on the ground. These three dimensions are clearly interconnected. Without coherent and supportive policies, effective implementation cannot occur. And without effective supervision, the link between policy and implementation would be lost.

Policy and strategic direction

At the policy level, what matters is policy clarity in setting a strategic direction for the country and involvement of key stakeholders to ensure their needs are met. The strategic direction for Malaysia, with implications for human resource development, was set in 1991, when then Prime Minister Mahathir tabled the Sixth Malaysia Plan in Parliament and launched Vision 2020 (*Wawasan 2020*), which would see Malaysia becoming a developed nation by the year 2020, 30 years from its launch. To him, development meant much more than a high level of income; it incorporated all the characteristics of a developed society.[8] This grand vision has been given substance and embellished in successive development plans (Government of Malaysia, 2000, 2001, 2006, 2010) and in occasional rhetoric from the leadership. For instance, during the launch of the 2000 Budget, the plan for Malaysia to become a knowledge economy was made explicit.

TVET was given greater attention under Vision 2020. This strengthened focus was reflected in successive development plans. In the Seventh Malaysia Plan (1996–2000), the focus on vocational education had been at the secondary level, with the conversion of vocational secondary schools into secondary technical schools (Government of Malaysia, 1996). The Ninth Malaysia Plan (2006–2010) pledged to increase focus on initial vocational education training (IVET) (Malaysia, 2006), but it was under the Tenth Malaysia Plan that much greater emphasis has been placed on TVET, including IVET (Government of Malaysia, 2010).

Policy rhetoric and planning have not been matched by action on the ground, however, and the several associated initiatives, especially the k-economy, had failed to take off for a number of reasons, one being the country's inadequate human resource base (Cheong, Selvaranam, & Goh, 2012; Lee & Nagaraj, 2012; World Bank, 2007; Yap & Rasiah, 2013). Additionally, policies put in place were reactive rather than proactive. Thus, the passage in 1996 of the Private Higher Education Act and the launch of the *Lembaga Akreditasi Nasional* (LAN – National Accreditation Board) to regulate private sector education was the government's response to the surge in enrolment in private higher education institutions (PHEIs) (See Hill et al., 2014).

With little to show even as Malaysia's growth rate and FDI fell after the Asian Financial Crisis, a degree of urgency was injected with the prospect of Malaysia falling into a "middle-income" trap (see Gill & Kharas, 2007). The decade 2000–2010 saw several developments in TVET. First, the regulatory framework for TVET was strengthened with the passage of the Skills Development Act 2006. Second, budgetary allocations were increased between the Eighth and Ninth Plans (Government of Malaysia, 2000, 2006). Third, an organisational framework was built around the Cabinet Committee on Human Capital Development (JKPMI) formed in 2009. The Malaysian Qualifications Framework was approved in 2005 and the Malaysian Qualifications Agency (MQA) to oversee this Framework was established in 2007. The latter was preceded by the establishment of the Department of Skills Development in the Ministry of Human Resources (MOHR) in 2006.

The installation of Najib Razak as Prime Minister in 2009 saw Malaysia taking a more proactive approach in achieving Vision 2020. Obviously eager to stamp his signature on a position to which he was appointed rather than elected, Najib introduced a raft of new policy initiatives. In rapid succession, a group of international experts was called upon to produce a "New Economic Model" for Malaysia, and Economic (ETP) and Government (GTP) Transformation Programmes were launched, with the ETP overseen by a newly established Performance Management and Delivery Unit (PEMANDU) in the Prime Minister's Department. The year 2010 also saw the launch of the Tenth Malaysia Plan to support the transformative programmes under the above initiatives. Despite periodic positive pronouncements by PEMANDU, the outcomes of these initiatives remain to be seen.

But policy effectiveness requires more than the sustained articulation of a consistent strategy. It also requires incorporating other stakeholders into the decision-making process to ensure that policies are also demand-driven. This means engaging employers in shaping the country's TVET agenda, collaborating with private sector training providers to maximise training outreach and impact, and consultating trainees to understand their aspirations and needs. Although estimates of manpower needs have been made in development planning, industry involvement in this exercise has been limited until formal consultations were organised as part of the ETP, the output from which was presumably incorporated into the Tenth Malaysia Plan. Indeed, projections of manpower needs had been made mostly by foreign consultants (BCG, 2009; Blumenstein et al., 1999; Pang, 2010; World Bank, 2005, 2009) although tracer studies done by the Ministry of Education in 2002 and 2006 and a telephone survey by the Malaysian Employers Federation in 2006 were also used.

Further, despite the private sector's growing role in providing tertiary education in general and TVET in particular, the government sees the sector as the object of regulation rather than collaboration, at least until the launch of the ETP. This was clear from the establishment of LAN, which was tasked with the supervision of only the PHEIs. As major stakeholders, private sector training providers had no role in policy making. And the beneficiaries of TVET, be they students in the vocational stream of the education system or workers in firms, have no say at all.

Malaysia's policy articulation with respect to TVET can thus be summarised as being strong on policy rhetoric and planning, but less so in translating these into initiatives on the ground, and even less so in achieving results. It is primarily a top-down process with limited involvement from other stakeholders.

System oversight

Ensuring policies are effectively implemented requires a robust framework for supervision and coordination. This framework would have oversight of the funding allocation and of the public sector's relations with the private sector, both as beneficiaries of TVET and as training providers. These relations include regulation, but also coordination of activities.

At the aggregate level, Malaysia's TVET suffers no shortage of funding on paper, whether fiscally from the federal government or through levies on companies based on their revenues. Funding for IVET and CVET[9] comes both from fiscal sources, through taxation and the taking on of debt for public sector training provision, and also from a dedicated training fund contributed by companies, the Human Resource Development Fund (HRDF) for training of private sector employees.[10] Given the dominant federal government role in national governance, it is no surprise that the bulk of public sector TVET funding comes from this source. The actual funding mechanism for development expenditure is allocated under Malaysia's five-year development plans, and disbursed through the annual federal government budget. In practice, however, the emphasis given to tertiary academic education may mean that funds allocated to TVET have been less plentiful. Scholarships awarded by the government and government-linked companies have been mainly for tertiary academic education.

While recurrent funding for TVET has increased over the decade of 2000–2010, such funding has been based primarily on past expenditure and enrolments with scant attention to funding efficiency and equity (see EPU, 2004; Nor Azlina, 2013; Siddiquee, 2013). On the private sector side, it has also been reported that little of HRDF funds had gone to SMEs in 2000 (HRDF, 2010). There are, however, encouraging signs. Especially since 2009, greater focus on specific needs has been reflected in such programs as the Graduate Employability Program introduced in 2009 and available to all public higher learning institutions, and in the HRDF's efforts to target SMEs, with the result that the utilisation rate among SMEs rose from 34% in 1999 to 76% in 2010 (Government of Malaysia, 2003, pp. 113–114).

Effective system oversight also requires proper institutional coordination and harmonisation of training standards. The framework governing both is shown in the following Figure 6.3, which also shows the legislation governing both institutions and standards.

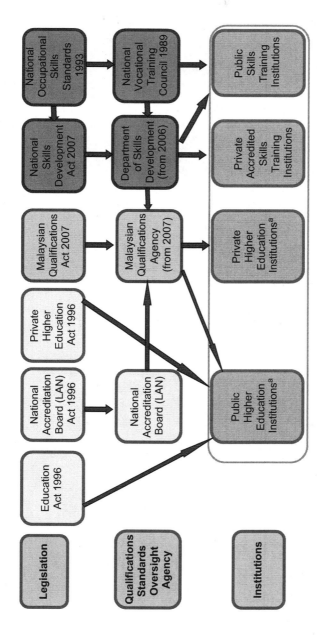

Figure 6.3 Oversight Structure of Malaysian TVET, 1989–2010

Source: Authors' construction

[a] Includes tertiary TVET institutions.

Malaysia has done well with respect to establishing competency standards and a qualification framework on a national scale. In 2000, Malaysia did not have a national qualifications framework, and whatever standards that existed were fragmented. At the tertiary level, LAN only covered private sector institutions. The National Occupational Skills Standards (NOSS), introduced in 1993, likewise covered only 467 occupations in 2000 (Government of Malaysia, 2000, p. 109; Pang, Jailani & Spottl, 2009) (Figure 6.4). The ensuing years however saw further improvement in qualification standards. By 2010, the National Skills Development Act 2006 and Malaysian Qualifications Agency Act 2007 had put in place a national qualifications framework – the Malaysian Qualifications Framework. NOSS has since been subsumed under this Framework, while the MQA had been

NOSS Definition	A specification of the competencies expected of a skilled worker/professional gainfully employed in Malaysia for an occupation area and level as required by industries		
Job Function	*Type of Malaysia Skill Certificate under NOSS*	*SKM[a] Level or Equivalent*	*Definition of Competency*
Management	Advanced Diploma (Diploma Lanjutan Kemahiran Malaysia [DLKM])	5	• Competency in applying a significant range of fundamental principles and complex techniques across a wide and often unpredictable variety of contexts • Very substantial personal autonomy and often significant responsibility for the work of others and allocation of substantial resources • Personal accountabilities for analysis and diagnosis, design, planning, execution and evaluation
Supervision	Diploma (Diploma Kemahiran Malaysia [DKM])	4	• Competency in performing a broad range of complex technical or professional work activities, performed in a wide variety of contexts with a substantial degree of personal responsibility and autonomy • Some responsibility for the work of others and the allocation of resources
	Advanced Certificate	3	• Competency in performing a broad range of activities, performed in a variety of contexts, most of which are complex and non-routine • Considerable responsibility and autonomy with guidance from others
Operations and Production	Certificate	2	• Competency in performing a significant range of activities (both routine and non-routine), performed in a variety of contexts • Some individual responsibility and autonomy
	Certificate	1	• Competency in performing a range of varied activities, most of which are routine and predictable

Figure 6.4 The National Occupational Skill Standard (NOSS) System.

Source: Department of Skills Development (2013a)

[a] SKM refers to Sijil Kemahiran Malaysia (Malaysian Skills Certification)

given much more resources and authority compared to the LAN, the agency it replaced. Also, the Department of Skills Development (DSD) under MOHR had taken responsibility for NOSS accreditation.

The above was accompanied by the broadening of coverage of occupations and range of occupational skills. Thus the coverage of NOSS had expanded to reach 1,585 by 2010, compared to just a few occupations in 2000 while the range of skill levels had also been enlarged. All NOSS-based training was required to be accredited by the National Vocational Training Council (NVTC) and LAN in 2000 and by the Department of Skills Development (DSD) and the MQA in 2010. Enforcement of these standards has been helped by the requirement that all publicly funded programs had to be accredited.

Institutional coordination is a different story. The structure of Malaysia's TVET system renders coordination a challenge. First, as shown in Figure 6.2, 13 federal ministries have responsibility over TVET, each with its own institutes running a wide variety of programs at different levels. Second, private sector provision of TVET programs has increased with the rapid growth of private higher education. Yet, as the paucity of data on this segment makes clear, the precise magnitude and nature of its role is not fully known.

This dispersal of jurisdiction over public training provision has resulted in substantial overlap in mandates and responsibilities. For instance, the Ministry of Higher Education (MOHE) is responsible for community colleges and polytechnics, while the Ministry of Youth and Sports (MYS) and the Ministry of Rural and Regional Development (MRRD) also oversees post-secondary public training institutions. It is also unclear if coordination exists in projections made by ministries for their respective institutions.[11] To the extent that different ministries tend to provide programs that accord with their priorities and suit their level of expertise, the degree of overlap in the training substance delivered may be reduced somewhat. This lack of attention to coordination may reflect Malaysia's top-down, supply-driven system.

Efforts at coordination of TVET were made in 2007 when the National Advisory Council on Education and Training (NACET) was established under the Ninth Malaysia Plan but little of anything concrete has been achieved during its tenure.[12] In 2009, the Cabinet Committee on Human Capital Development (JKPMI) was established, and appears to have superseded NACET in its coordination role. The difference between JKPMI and NACET is that JKPMI has no private sector representation, so that coordination of TVET has thus taken a step backward.

System oversight of Malaysia's TVET can thus be summarised as requiring improvement both in giving attention to efficiency and equity of funding and in strengthening institutional coordination of a highly fragmented system. The system might have fared worse had it not been for the successful establishment and harmonisation of skills standards within a national quality framework and the strong mandate and enforcement provided to the MQA under the National Skills Development Act 2006 and Malaysian Qualifications Agency Act 2007.

Program delivery

What are the factors determining the quality of TVET programmes? Are TVET programmes relevant to industry needs? How extensive is TVET programme monitoring? Who are the main stakeholders and players in TVET provision? Is there a role for private sector providers? What is the extent of industry's involvement in TVET? These questions produce varying answers when we look at Malaysia's TVET program delivery over the years.

Malaysia's TVET system consists of a mix of state and non-state training providers. This is more an unintended policy consequence than deliberate policy. The rise of private education was the result of the demand for tertiary education exceeding what public universities could absorb. Private post-secondary education provision burgeoned to cater to this unmet demand. Though the Private Higher Educational Institutions Act in 1996 (Government of Malaysia, 2000) resulted in a more than two-fold increase in the number of private higher education institutions from 280 to 611 in the four years from 1995 to 1999,[13] regulations prohibited private institutions from becoming universities. Furthermore, even though there is now an eclectic range of public and private sector education providers, there is yet little synergy in TVET provision between the public and private sectors, thus putting on hold Malaysia's ambition to become an education hub for the region.[14]

The government provides almost no direct incentives for non-state provision, the main indirect incentive since 2000 being the benefits of adopting NOSS, in terms of accredited content and standards, a marketing bonus for these training providers. Another indirect financial incentive consists of eligibility to undertake training using reimbursements from levies paid to HRDF. For private sector providers, profits from training are definitely a major form of incentive. While it is obvious that the raison d'etre of private sector TVET providers is profit and that the courses offered are demand-driven, the challenge for the government and for Malaysia is to ensure that in the pursuit of profits, private sector providers do not compromise on standards.

TVET provides a different challenge to the public sector. The profit motive is clearly absent among public institutions. Instead, for each ministry engaged in TVET, government targets for enrolment, graduation and job placement rates had to be met; these targets become particularly important with the emergence of skill shortages. Despite all these requirements, it is not known if a reward system existed for training institutions under the above ministries should they achieve their targets.

Nor is there a link between autonomy and accountability among these institutions, reflecting the historically top-down, supply driven approach that emphasised inputs rather than outputs as benchmarks of performance. That being said, the degree of autonomy exercised by these institutions was rather limited. Thus, the Ministry of Education's (MOE's) training institutions for secondary education had little autonomy, with major decisions coming from the central government. Similarly, MARA's individual Vocational Institutes (IKMs) and MYS'

(IKBN) centres also enjoy little or no autonomy in their operations. Decisions are typically made at central ministerial level, with training institutions simply following instructions. Nor is there autonomy in curriculum development and implementation. Political considerations also sometimes weigh in on decisions over the location of training institutes, resulting in some being distant and delinked from industrial zones.

Have efforts been made to engage industry in programme delivery? Increased engagement over the last decade has taken the form of giving industry a major role in curriculum design. Industry experts play important roles in curriculum design in MOHE's training institutions, and since 2006, MARA has designed its curricula based on inputs from industry experts and academicians. Industry experts also had opportunities to provide curriculum feedback through the MARA Council in which they were represented.

Links between training providers and research institutions, vital to ensure curricula and training methods are up-to-date, have increased, albeit from a very low base. In 2000, it was reported that MOE instructors were trained in institutions that lacked a research orientation or were full universities. This changed somewhat by 2010, with one university (the Faculty of Technical Education, Universiti Tun Hussein Onn) playing the lead role in training vocational school teachers for a new NOSS-based curriculum. In 2012, community colleges were reported to have begun to undertake research, but it was in collaboration with research institutions. Industry involvement was evident at training institution level but this was only in respect of facility improvement and/or utilisation of equipment they provided to these institutions. Input to curriculum development occurs at the ministry level, however.

In terms of faculty enrichment, in-service training in industry appears to be the most feasible avenue, given that public sector training institutions appointments are made within a civil service system which is hierarchical and positions are filled by internal promotion. However, it is unclear to what extent such training has enhanced their and their respective institutions' capabilities, especially in meeting industry needs.

Monitoring performance is essential for accountability in training delivery. This is less of an issue for private sector training institutions, which are tested in the market through the choices of fee-paying trainees. For public sector institutions, however, the monitoring function requires the generation and use of relevant data. This is particularly important for Malaysia with its many training institutions under various oversight bodies. A lack of information serves to entrench misconceptions of the status and role of TVET in relation to academic education.

In this respect, Malaysia has made progress both in terms of the amount of data collected and of making these data publicly available but this progress was uneven across public training institutions. For instance, secondary and tertiary education institutions under the MOE collected data on enrolment and administration, graduation rates and job placement, which were compiled in annual reports initially for internal use only but now also for public dissemination. Non-state post-secondary institutions were also required to report data, and most did, but it required visits from MOE officials to obtain them. Reporting requirements for MOHE which took over post-secondary level institutions were initially similar to those of MOE, but were progressively enhanced. MOHE also monitored data collection by non-state institutions, although only partial compliance was achieved. Other public training providers – MARA, those under MOHR – also generate and disseminate substantial administrative data but also data on client feedback and tracer studies.[15] The MYS' institutions, however, generated much less administrative data. Even as of 2010, there was no systematic requirement for them to submit reports.

Effective performance monitoring is only possible when data generated, no matter how voluminous, is put to good use. It is unclear if this has been done. An area of concern is that much of the data collected are for administrative purposes, and not much emphasis has been placed on data collection specifically to measure impact, beyond indicators of student feedback, graduate absorption, and tracer studies mentioned earlier. Thus, the MOE and other ministries conducted surveys on specific issues, including impact evaluation of specific activities only on an ad hoc basis. There remains room for improvement in effective data use.

Malaysia's performance in TVET program delivery may thus be summarised as having shown improvement over the past decade. This improvement took the form of an expanding corpus of training providers from both the public and private sectors and of greater input into training content by industry. Areas for further improvement remain, mainly in fostering a more collaborative public-private sector relationship and in making better use of data for monitoring performance.

Drawing lessons from the Malaysian experience

Several lessons can be drawn from the survey of Malaysia's TVET performance. Like every TVET system, there are both strengths and challenges. And like every TVET system, contextual factors as well as structural ones; those relating to the structure of the system, have played important roles.

The system's main strength lies in its application of a nationwide harmonised system of standards, the NOSS which has wide coverage of occupations and types of skills. Harmonisation of standards has been achieved through the expanded coverage of the NOSS and the MQA, with accreditation made mandatory for government recognition ensuring its adoption. More rational recurrent funding of TVET, especially CVET, has elevated public sector TVET programmes from being a minor player in education and training with limited coverage to a major player with nationwide reach. Accessibility has also been enhanced through a widening set of learning pathways and articulation criteria for training, including prior learning. Public provision has been augmented by rapid expansion of private provision. In terms of program content, incorporation of industry in curriculum development and training (internships and in-service training) reflects greater attention to industry needs. The approach to program evaluation by public sector training providers has also progressed from being input-driven – how much was spent – to being output-driven – how many were trained. These positive developments, representing significant improvement over the decade 2000–2010, are taking place within a framework of strong policy commitment by the leadership, driven both by ambition as well as the recognition that the country will lose its competitive edge if human resources are not deepened.

At the same time, challenges with public provision remain. Foremost among these is that policy formulation and announcements have not been supported by commensurate attention to implementation and programme monitoring. One manifestation is that despite the change in emphasis in programme evaluation from input to output, impact assessments of training beneficiaries beyond employment are still largely absent. Nor was there much evidence that funding and other inputs were linked to targets to be achieved and/or to considerations of efficiency in public sector training.

The public-sector focus of TVET programmes affords limited roles for non-government stakeholders. While a role has been found for industry as mentioned before, other important stakeholders – non-state training providers and workers – have found practically no voice in this process.[16] This state of affairs raised two important issues. First, while industry needs should be incorporated, whether these needs accord with the government strategy of building a technologically capable workforce needs to be given serious consideration. Second, the lack of synergy with non-state providers represents a lost opportunity to make full use of existing resources for TVET.

Organisationally, Malaysia has multiple public agencies engaged in TVET with limited interagency coordination. While the harmonisation of standards referred to earlier has ensured coordination of programme content and competencies required, this lack of institutional coordination has left inefficiencies in the geographical distribution of programmes that may result in programme duplication and poor resource allocation, especially financial and human. It also leads to confusion among potential beneficiaries of the system, already affected by a public perception that TVET is only for those who cannot make it in the academic stream.

Major changes in organisational structure and education policies (such as the establishment of the Ministry of Higher Education (MOHE) to take over some functions of the Ministry of Education (MOE) and then merging these again in 2013 (with a similar fate befalling the teaching of mathematics and science in English) have not been helpful to institutional building and to maintaining an institutional memory. Both are essential to building a strong TVET programme. Also not helpful, despite the greater willingness to disseminate TVET data, is the culture of information confidentiality that pervades government as a whole in developing strong public-private sector collaboration and in building the public confidence needed to change the current negative perceptions of TVET.

Conclusion: Implications for policy

Several policy recommendations emerge from these lessons. First is the need to give much greater emphasis to implementation and its oversight. In particular, given improvements needed to ensure efficiency and equity in the use of funds, monitoring and evaluation based on impact rather than output need to be strengthened. Doing so does not require more personnel; Malaysia has already more public sector staff per capita than most countries in the world but greater institutional capability. This means more careful consideration given to institutions, their role and structure so that frequent changes can be avoided. It must be recognised, however, that this capability depends on the quality of the country's education system output as a whole, a clear reminder that TVET cannot be strengthened without strengthening the entire education framework.

Intensifying the focus on quality also requires a new approach to training provision that embraces the contribution of private providers. In Malaysia, the private providers of education and training emerged to fill the gap that public sector provision cannot fulfill. This suggests a complementary, not competing, role, and to the extent they are competitive with public sector providers, this helps promote service delivery efficiency. The increasingly competitive environment together with Malaysia's skill deficit suggests there is considerable room for both providers to coexist. But for this to happen, the current attitude that private institutions are not a match for public ones and should be more tightly controlled should give way to incorporating them fully into the TVET process. While regulating and monitoring are needed so that private for-profit providers do not engage in practices that drive profit at the expense of trainees' interests, these should be undertaken on a level playing field for public and private providers. By this criterion, if incentives are available to public providers, they should be available to private providers as well.

That TVET is more receptive to what the industry wants does not mean the industry should get whatever it wants. Industry should get what it wants provided that it is also beneficial to the national interest in the long term. While avoiding capture of the state by vested interests is a tall order for all countries, it is particularly acute for Malaysia with the dominant role played by government-linked companies that are among the largest companies in the country. Yet, unless there is the political will to align TVET to strategic priorities that have been stressed repeatedly at the highest circles, realising Vision 2020 will remain an elusive target.

Institutional coordination remains a high priority. This is particularly important given the large number of public agencies involved in public provision, and likely an equally large number of non-state providers. There is also an overall need for efficiency in public spending with the already large and rising public debt burden. Malaysia's record has not been exemplary. Despite allocating among the highest proportion of public funding for education as a share of GDP in Asia, the performance of Malaysia's education system continues to go south in international benchmarking assessments. Beyond efficiency is also the equity dimension of catering to those in greatest need. For the sake of TVET and of the country as a whole, spending efficiency and equity as part of fiscal responsibility needs to be taken much more seriously.

There is however one area where decentralisation would improve training flexibility and relevance. That is curriculum development. However, this remains highly centralised. Recent moves toward greater specialisation of functions and offerings by specific institutions represent a degree of compensation for this lack of institutional coordination. Greater autonomy for individual training institutions would have strengthened their respective institutional capabilities.

Finally, although much improvement has occurred over the past decade, greater transparency in what public sector agencies have been doing and the assessment and/or impact of their activities from studies they conduct or commission will help the public learn about their achievements and empathise with the challenges they face. Indeed, transparency, rather than any public relations exercise, will likely be more effective in reversing negative public perceptions of TVET. Greater access by local researchers to data collected will help to promote independent assessment of training provision and providers' performance. And easier access to government official data and documents would also foster public confidence in the government's commitment to accountability.

Notes

1 Vision 2020 (*Wawasan 2020*) was announced by then Prime Minister Mahathir Mohammad during the tabling of the Sixth Malaysia Plan (Government of Malaysia, 1991).
2 TIMSS is an international assessment of mathematics and science achievement of students in the fourth and eighth grades (or their equivalents) in participating countries. It was developed by the International Association for the Evaluation of Educational Achievement. (www.oecd.org/pisa)
3 The OECD's Programme for International Student Assessment (PISA), "is an international study that was launched by the OECD in 1997. It aims to evaluate education systems worldwide every three years by assessing 15-year-olds' competencies in the key subjects: reading, mathematics and science" (OECD, 2016).
4 These are Hong Kong, Korea, Singapore and Taiwan.
5 Mukherji and Wong (2012) provide an interesting comparison between the University of Malaya and the National University of Singapore, which shared common roots, to show how these institutions diverged in performance.
6 Apart from sources cited in the text, information on ministries and training institutions had been gathered through interviews with officials of ministries and departments with oversight over TVET in the World Bank project referred to earlier.
7 This is a recent development. Earlier, the transition to vocational education occurred upon the completion of lower secondary education.
8 This vision was also laid out in a working paper Mahathir used at the Malaysian Business Council in 1991 (Mahathir, 1991).
9 At the beginning of the decade, funding for retraining had been minimal, even for workers retrenched in the aftermath of the 1997–98 Asian Financial Crisis. Worker retraining did not receive public fund allocations, and the number of workers benefiting from HRDF was a mere 572 in 1998 and 426 in 1999 (Jomo & Lee, 2000).
10 The HRDF consists of a mandatory levy on companies employing 50 workers or over. However, under the provisions of the Human Resources Development Act 2001, the Minister of Human Resources is empowered to exempt fully or partially any employer from payment of the mandatory levy (*Pembangunan Sumber Manusia Berhad Act 2001*, incorporating all amendments up to 1 January 2006, Act 612, Laws of Malaysia, Part III, Section 19).

11 This can occur even within the same ministry. For instance, the MOHE decided that the target of 120,000 trained graduates would complete the National Modular Certificate at these colleges by 2015 (MOHE, 2012, pp. 124–127). In addition, these colleges were to contribute around 33 percent of skilled manpower in Malaysia. Polytechnics are also expected to produce 490,000 trained graduates by 2020 (MOHE, 2012).
12 The BCG Report (2009, pp. 46–47), while stating that NACET was to meet three times a year, noted that it had met only twice since it was formed.
13 Under this Act, non-government institutions such as tuition centers, training institutes, language centers (like the British Council), and professional organisations (e.g., the Malaysian Institute of Management) were all classified and had to register as higher education institutions. But not all private institutions were for-profit. NGOs such as the Monfort Boys Town also offered vocational courses. And state and semi-state owned institutions like the Sekolah Agama Darul Ehsan Islam (a religious polytechnic funded by the Selangor State Government) and Yayasan Pelajaran MARA (MARA Education Trust) were also required to register as private education institutions (Tan, 2002, p. 124).
14 The National Higher Education Strategic Plan, formulated in 2006 with the launch of the Ninth Malaysia Plan, has as one of its seven main thrusts the "intensification of internationalization" of Malaysian higher education (Ministry of Education, 2006).
15 The MOHR conducted tracer studies of graduates from 2004, while student evaluations were conducted bi-annually to evaluate courses, equipment, and instructors (in compliance with ISO 9001 requirements).
16 Perhaps this lack of voice could be explained by the government's ability to maintain economic paternalism toward labour (Turner, 2006, p. 343).

References

Abdul, Rahman Ayub. (2012). *Implementing skills training in the higher education syllabus (Vocational College Model)*. Paper presented at the Higher Education Conference 2012: Trends and Growth Strategies, Kuala Lumpur, July 3–4.

Blumenstein, G., Borgel, H., Greinert, W., Grunwald, E., Jarck, K., & Kaloo, U. (1999). *Basic study on the design of a dual vocational training scheme in Malaysia*. Eschborn, Germany: Deutsche Gesellschaft fur Technische Zysammernarbeit.

Boston Consulting Group (BCG). (2009). *Strategy package for higher growth and structural change: Human capital for a higher income economy, Malaysia*. Final report submitted to the Economic Planning Unit, Prime Minister's Department, Putrajaya.

Cheong, Kee Cheok, Selvaratnam, Visvanathan, & Goh, Kim Leng. (2012). Education and human capital formation. In Rajah, Rasiah (Ed.), *Malaysian economy: Unfolding growth and social change*. Shah Alam: Oxford University Press.

Construction Industry Development Board (CIDB). (2011). *Laporan Tahunan (Annual Report) 2010*. Kuala Lumpur: Construction Industry Development Board.

Department of Skills Development. (2013a). *Laporan Tahunan (Annual Report) 2012*. Putrajaya: Ministry of Human Resources.

Department of Skills Development. (2013b). SKM/PC statistics 1994–2011. Ministry of human resources. Retrieved from http://www.dsd.gov.my/index.php/en/component/phocadownload/category/19?download=228

Economic Planning Unit (EPU). (2004). *Development planning in Malaysia*. Putrajaya: Author.

GiatMARA. (2008). *Local to global*. Paper submitted to the 2008 Commonwealth Association for Public Administration and Management (COPAM) International Innovations Awards, Ottawa. Retrieved from http://www.capam.org/assets/mal004.pdf

Gill, Inermit, & Homi, Kharas. (2007). *An East Asian renaissance: Ideas for economic growth*. Washington, DC: World Bank.

Government of Malaysia. (1991). *Sixth Malaysia plan, 1991–1995*. Kuala Lumpur: National Printing Department.

Government of Malaysia (1996). *Seventh Malaysia Plan 1996–2000*. Kuala Lumpur: Percetakan Nasional Malaysia.

Government of Malaysia. (2000). *The Eighth Malaysia plan, 2001–2005*. Kuala Lumpur: Government Printers.

Government of Malaysia. (2001). *The third outline perspective plan, 2001–2010*. Kuala Lumpur: Economic Planning Unit, Prime Minister's Department.

Government of Malaysia. (2003). *Mid-term review of the eighth Malaysia plan, 2001–2005*. Kuala Lumpur: Percetakan Nasional Malaysia.

Government of Malaysia. (2006). *The ninth Malaysia plan, 2006–2010*. Putrajaya: Economic Planning Unit, Prime Minister's Department.

Government of Malaysia. (2010). *The tenth Malaysia plan, 2011–2015*. Putrajaya: Economic Planning Unit, Prime Minister's Department.

Hill, C., K.C. Cheong, Y.C. Leong, & Fernandez-Chung, R. (2014). TNE – transnational education or tensions between national and external? A case study of Malaysia. *Studies in Higher Education, 39*(6): 952–966.

HRDF (2010). *Annual Report 2010*. Kuala Lumpur: Human Resources Development Fund.

Jomo, K. S., & Lee, Hwok Aun. (2000). Some social consequences of the 1997–98 economic crisis in Malaysia. In *Social impacts of the Asian economic crisis in Thailand, Indonesia, Malaysia and the Philippines* (pp. 167–228). Bangkok: Thailand Development Research Institute.

Lee, Kiong Hock, & Shyamala, Nagaraj. (2012). The crisis of education. In Hal Hil, Tham Siew Yean & Ragayah Haji Mat Zin (Eds.), *Malaysia's development challenges: Graduating from the middle* (pp. 213–232). London: Routledge.

Lee, Poh Ping, & Tham, Siew Yean. (2009). Malaysia ten years after the Asian crisis. *Asian Survey, 47*(6), 915–929.

Mahathir, Mohamad. (1991). *Malaysia: The way forward*. Working paper presented at the Inaugural Meeting of the Malaysia Business Council, February 28th, in Kuala Lumpur. Retrieved from http://unpan1.un.org/intradoc/groups/public/documents/apcity/unpan003223.pdf

Ministry of Education. (2006). *National Higher Education Strategic Plan 2006–2010*. Kuala Lumpur.

MOHE. (2012). *The National Higher Education Action Plan: Phase 2 (2011–2015)*. Kuala Lumpur: Percetakan Nasional Malaysia.

Mohd, Gazali Abas. (2012). *Skills development in the 21st century: Concept and Malaysia experience*. Putrajaya: Economic Planning Unit, Prime Minister's Department.

Mukherji, H. and P.K. Wong (2012). The National University of Singapore and the University of Malaya: Common roots and different paths. In P.G. Altbach & J. Salmi (Eds.), *The Road to Academic Excellence: The Making of World-Class Research Universities* (pp. 129–166). Washington DC: World Bank.

National Economic Advisory Council (NEAC). (2010). *A new economic model for malaysia: Part 1: Strategic policy directions.* Kuala Lumpur: National Printers.

Nor Azlina Ariffin. (2013). Financial administration I: Government budgeting. In Noor Alam Siddiquee (Ed.), *Public management and governance in Malaysia: Trends and transformations* (pp. 102–120). Abingdon, UK: Routledge.

OECD (2016). "Programme for International Student Assessment (PISA)". At http://www.oecd.org/pisa/home/.

Pang, Chau Leong. (2010). *The integration of the national occupational skills standard-based training system and the national dual training system in Malaysia.* Batu Pahat: Penerbit Universiti Tun Hussein Onn.

Pang, Chau Leong. (2011). *Key reforms in revitalizing Technical and Vocational Education and Training (TVET) in Malaysia.* Presentation at the Regional Conference on HRD through TVET as a Development Strategy in Asia, Colombo, Sri Lanka, August 2–3.

Pang, Chau Leong, Jailani, Md Yunos, & Spottl, G. (2009). Comparative review of the National Occupational Skills Standard (NOSS)-based training system and the National Dual Training System (NDTS) in Malaysia: Issues and themes. *Malaysia Labour Review, 3*(1), 110–138.

Siddiquee, Noor Aslam. (2013). Managing ethics: Drives for fighting corruption and enhancing integrity. In Noor Aslam Siddiquee (Ed.), *Public management and governance in Malaysia: Trends and transformations* (pp. 179–198). Abingdon, UK: Routledge.

Tan, Ah Mei. (2002). *Malaysian private higher education: Globalization, privatization, transformation and marketplaces.* London: Asean Academic Press.

Turner, Donna. (2006). *The Malaysian State and the regulation of labor: From colonial economy to K-economy.* Unpublished Ph.D. thesis, Asian Research Centre, Murdoch University, Perth.

World Bank. (1993). *The East Asian miracle: Economic growth and public policy.* Washington, DC: Oxford University Press.

World Bank. (2005). Malaysia: Firm competitiveness, investment climate, and growth. Poverty Reduction, Economic Management, and Financial Sector Unit (PREM) Report No. 26841-MA, Washington DC.

World Bank. (2007). Malaysia and the knowledge economy: Building a world-class higher education system. Human Development Sector Report No. 40397-MY, East Asia and the Pacific Region. Washington, DC: World Bank. Retrieved from https://openknowledge.worldbank.org/bitstream/handle/10986/7861/403970MY0Kn owl1white0cover01PUBLIC1.txt?sequence=2

World Bank. (2009). Malaysia economic monitor: Repositioning for growth 2009. Bangkok: World Bank. Retrieved from https://openknowledge.worldbank.org/bitstream/handle/10986/3132/516240ESW0WHIT1sitioning0For0Growth.pdf?sequence=1

World Bank. (2013). Malaysia workforce development. SABER Country Report. Washington DC: World Bank. Retrieved from http://wbgfiles.worldbank.org/documents/hdn/ed/saber/supporting_doc/CountryReports/WFD/SABER_WfD_Malaysia_CR_Final_2013.pdf

Yap, Xiao Shan, & Rasiah, R. (2013). *The lost tiger: Technological learning trajectory of Malaysian semiconductor firms.* Paper presented at the 10th Asialics Conference, Tokyo, September 20–21.

7 Education policy and human capital transformation strategy in Malaysia

Hussein Haji Ahmad

Currently, Malaysia is facing tremendous challenges from within and without due to the unanticipated effects of globalisation, liberalisation and development of the information technologies and communication systems. One of the critical challenges is how to steer and develop its future economy so as to base it upon the strategy of the knowledge industry, or in short, the K-Economy.

The document of the 10th Malaysia Plan reports that investment in human capital would be given greater emphasis during the Plan period (2011–2015). This policy thrust was designed to sustain economic resilience and growth, drive the knowledge-based economy as well as foster a community with an exemplary value system. This will be achieved through greater synergy and collaboration between the Government, the private sector and the community. In this regard, the human capital policy thrusts are:

1 Undertaking comprehensive improvement of the education and training delivery systems
2 Strengthening national schools to become the schools of choice for all Malaysians to enhance national unity
3 Implementing measures to bridge the performance gap between urban and rural schools
4 Creating universities of international standing and ensuring that tertiary institutions meet employer needs
5 Providing more opportunities and access to quality education, training and lifelong learning at all levels
6 Nurturing an innovative society with strong Science and Technology capabilities and the ability to achieve and apply knowledge
7 Strengthening national unity and developing a Malaysian society with a progressive outlook, exemplary value system and high performance culture as well as with an appreciation for tradition and heritage; and
8 Enhancing the forum of engagement and consultation between the government, private sector, parents and community in human capital development

In retrospect, for more than five decades, the education sector was able to demonstrate its rapid growth and development, principally in providing basic infrastructure and facilities and also in addressing the equally pertinent issues of accessibility, equity and quality education.

New economic model, 10th Malaysia plan and education

In the past several decades, Malaysia's national socioeconomic development programmes have been underpinned by the application of principles of the New Economic Policy (NEP) which was targeted at restructuring society and eliminating poverty. While the policy has had its impact in transforming Malaysia's population for about thirty years, certain other issues have not been well addressed particularly in terms of per capita income, stagnating productivity level, low labour productivity growth as well as declining annual GDP growth. Coupled with these issues are also factors that have been found to have contributed to the sluggish economic growth of the country.

The National Economic Action Council (NEAC) which was instituted by the government in mid-2010 in preparation for the 10th Malaysia Plan (2011–2015) had analysed and identified the most critical factors. They include, among others: decline of private investment in the economic sector, bureaucratic difficulties in relation to doing business in the country, existence of low value-added industries, persistence of low skill jobs and low wages for workers, insufficient knowledge and lack of initiatives in productive areas, and a general lack of appropriate skilled human capital.

Given such a scenario, the government has adopted a new socioeconomic development formula for the whole nation. It is labeled as the New Economic Model (NEM) that will address three principal targeted objectives: high income target of US$15000–20000 per capita by 2020; inclusiveness wherein all communities regardless of ethnicity, religious background and social status must fully benefit from the wealth of the country; and, sustainability in terms of meeting present needs without compromising future generations. The overall goal of the NEM has been synthesised as the total improvement of quality of life of all Malaysians. The targets have been conceptualised by the NEAC as in the following Figure 7.1.

Adoption of the strategy is important in order to ensure that the country would not only be economically competitive in the global arena but also would progress along a sustainable development trajectory in all sectors of the economy through the year 2020. This challenge demands that the country develops its human capital potentials to the maximum, specifically to enhance its competitive edge in the global economy toward achieving the goal of becoming a developed nation in 2020.

Education has been acknowledged as the principal vehicle to develop the qualities of resilience and resourcefulness of the human capital potentials. In this regard, the Ministry of Education is expected to focus on developing and expanding the respective systems toward achieving higher level of quality student outputs. The strategy is to develop and provide quality educational programs that will produce knowledgeable, skillful and ICT literate citizens with good moral

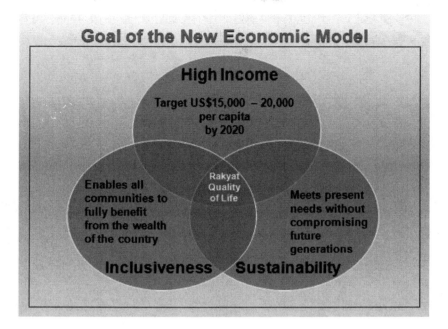

Figure 7.1 The New Economic Model.
Source: PEMANDU-Secretariat of the NEAC, Economic Planning Unit, Prime Minister's Department 2010.

values and attitudes based on the National Philosophy of Education, while at the same time able to fulfill the aspirations of the individual self, family, society and the nation in general.

Strategic policy approaches

The formulation of the educational development policy and strategy of the 10th Malaysia Plan (10th MP) takes into consideration the generalised policy and planning strategies of the Vision 2020 concept, the principal thrusts of the Long-Term Third Perspective Plan (RRJP3), and the planning policies of the Ministry of Education in the development plans between 2001–2010.

National educational development in the 10th Malaysia Plan (2011–2015) also takes due consideration of the national vision strategy. It is aimed at creating a resilient citizenry, and a society based on a set of characteristics: social equality and justice, sustainable economic growth, perseverance in the face of international competition, knowledge-based economic development, enhancement of human capital development, and the continuation of sustainable environmental development policy.

In order to achieve the national development goals, the Third Long-Term Perspective Plan (RRJP3) of 2001–2010 has defined the strategies, programs and projects that placed strong emphasis on qualitative development toward achieving the aspirations of a developed nation. In this regard, quality educational programmes will be continued as a long term strategy, particularly toward achieving the over-riding goals of restructuring society, reduction of absolute poverty, and provision of quality human capital and workforce for the nation.

Given the broad spectrum of the challenges mentioned, the human resources planning issues must always be studied in relation to the labour market trends where the emphasis seems to focus on the following points:

1 The need for multi-skilled generalists, or specifically skilled graduates who will become effective and efficient members of the workforce
2 The process and impact of contract labour saving technology on human resource planning
3 Portfolio career paths for new entrants into the graduate workforce
4 The increased importance of lifelong learning for professional and personal development of fresh graduates

Indeed, just as there is a clear pattern of an ever changing technology in the ICT world, there is also an ever changing expectation for a graduate profile. In this regard, several suggestions have been offered in the recent literature regarding the relevant profile of a typical graduate in the new society of the current millennium.

In essence, it has been anticipated that the graduate of the 21st Century is expected to have acquired the following attributes:

1 Up-to-date knowledge of the field, both general and specialised in character
2 The ability to apply theoretical knowledge to practical situations and problem-solving
3 A range of social and communication skills, often labeled as "soft skills" which will allow them to function effectively in an increasingly globalised world. These include capacities in terms of:
    a Relationship building and professional rapport with others
    b Self-managerial and organisational skills in related fields of industry
    c Leadership and management abilities, competences and capabilities
    d Fundamental knowledge of industry and business acumen
    e Foreign language competency, especially English, French, German, Chinese, Japanese, Arabic, Russian
    f Mastery in applying ICT or "computer savvy"
    g High commitment to professionalism and work orientations
    h Strong resilience and perseverance in the working culture
    i Readiness to become "glocal"— (an effective integrationist behaviour, capitalising on both local and global elements of the new economy)

Indeed, the checklist is endless. However, what is far from evident is whether these capacities can be guaranteed by the education and training offered in each and every higher education institution in the country.

Some of these institutions, especially the private sector universities, have serious and critical constraints. The majority of them lack the financial, infrastructural and human resources necessary to meet the rising expectations and demands of students and the general clientele.

The Malaysian case

In the Malaysian context, two approaches have been adopted by the government. Firstly is the formulation of the Education Act 1996 for the public sector which includes public education at all levels. Secondly is the formulation of the Private Higher Educational Institution Act 1996 for the private sector education system. Both these Acts have been geared toward achieving human capital development of the country through the year 2020 and beyond.

Education and the blueprint strategy

In order to relate its role and function with the strategy of the national socio-economic development strategy, the Ministry of Education has organised dialogues and discussions for the purpose of coming up with a 'Blueprint' for Educational Development' for the years covering 2001 through 2010. The Blueprint apparently covers the educational policy and strategy in terms of the national as well as its development goals within the context of the National Philosophy of Education.

The 'Blueprint' is aimed at ensuring all citizens of the country benefit from the policy of access to quality education. The aim is also to develop their individual potentials as a whole in a well-integrated and balanced way in line with the National Education Philosophy aspirations, and to generate the elements of creativity and innovation within the context of the culture of knowledge creation, science and technology, and lifelong learning. The final objective of the Blueprint is to provide an efficient system of world class education, and to transform Malaysia into a centre of educational excellence through upgrading the quality of the national education system to the international level benchmark. The planning and implementation of the educational development strategy at the current stage was, thus, based on a set of principal development thrusts, which have been continuously used since the early Five-Year Plans through the current 10th Malaysia Plan. There are six principal policy thrusts adopted in the Blueprint. There are:

1 Building of a Malaysian Nation towards enhancing national unity, creating a national identity and patriotism, and developing human resource in alignment with national needs
2 Developing human capital that have the knowledge, skills and noble human values
3 Strengthening of the national schools by ensuring that all national primary and secondary schools become the first choice of Malaysian parents

4   Closing the education gap between locations, socio-economic status and students' level of ability
5   Improving the teaching profession through enhancing teacher quality, career and welfare
6   Enhancing the educational institutions in the country toward excellence

In essence, the Blueprint (2006–2010) strategy developed in the 9th Malaysia Plan was designed to address the following strategic development parameters:

1   Accessibility of quality education to all children
2   Equity issues in education
3   Quality of educational programmes
4   Efficiency in the management and organisation of the education system

Implementation strategy

To ensure a successful implementation of the Plan, since 2010 several new strategies and action plans have been identified for all levels of the structure of the education system, so that all Malaysian citizens of school-going age have the opportunity to attend schooling up to eleven years on the basis of the principles of access, equity and quality.

The strategy to improve accessibility is focused on the efforts of ensuring an increased percentage of the young citizens benefit from education from preschool through the secondary level of education. This strategy involves the sub-strategies of increasing and improving the infrastructure and educational facilities, increasing the participation rates and reducing student dropout rates, as well as improving and expanding the varied educational programs to cater to the diversity of student populations especially in terms of aptitudes, abilities, inclinations and interests. The structure of integrated framework of human capital development is summarised in Figure 7.2.

To improve equity in education, a strong focus is given to the sub-strategy of narrowing the "education gaps" between urban and rural schools, the variations between sexes and ethnic groups. Strong emphasis is also focused on the sub-strategy of ensuring schools and educational institutions have all of the infrastructure and physical facilities, headmasters, principals and management staff, teaching staff, adequate teaching and learning materials, sufficient educational curricular and co-curricular programs and assistance, so that students have equitable access to a well organised learning environment.

In addressing the issue of quality education, emphasis is directed to the sub-strategy of ensuring quality for all inputs of the whole system of education through programmes, projects and activities and thereby quality student outputs as the products of the system. The strategy to ensure efficiency and effectiveness in educational management encompasses a wide range of sub-strategies. Effective and efficient delivery systems in all aspects of management of institutions, data management and information systems, programmes and project monitoring,

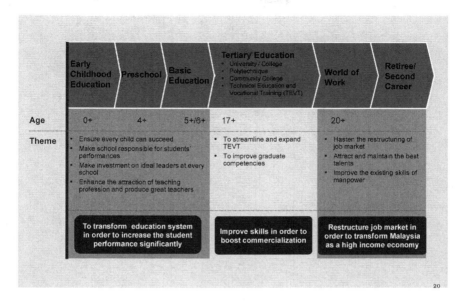

Figure 7.2 An integrated framework of human capital development.
Source: Economic Planning Unit, Prime Minister's Department, Malaysia

Table 7.1 Statistics of Schools, Teachers, Students and Support Staff as at 2011

	Primary School	Secondary School	Total
Schools	7,715	2,285	10,000
Teachers	225,459	178,557	414,016
Students	3,037,112	2,302,452	5,339,564
Support Staffs	41,575	32,000	73,578

Source: EPRD (EMIS Ministry of Education), 2011

evaluations, research and development have been the major emphases addressed by the Ninth Malaysia Plan in the sub-action plans.

At the beginning of 10th Malaysia Plan (2011–2015), the statistics of schools, teachers, students and staff at both primary and secondary levels are shown in Table 7.1.

Fundamental bases of planning and implementation

The planning and implementation principle of programmes and projects for the 10th Malaysia Plan takes into consideration two principal factors. Firstly, programmes and projects of the 8th and 9th Malaysia Plans, and their continuation through the 10th Malaysia Plan, including committed projects that have been deferred and projects implemented through deferred payments; secondly, programmes and projects of the 8th and 9th Malaysia Plans that have not been started have been revised in terms of their needs and priorities in the 10th Malaysia Plan.

Against the background of the accomplishment of the 8th and 9th Malaysia Plans, for education, the priority programmes and projects under the 10th Malaysia Plan are specifically focused on addressing the critical six policy-related issues of the educational development blueprint. These are: building up strong citizenship culture through education; enhancement of quality of national schools; strengthening of curriculum and co-curriculum contents; balancing of urban and rural educational development disparities; raising the quality and status of the teaching profession; and expanding ICT application in teaching and learning and effective educational management systems.

Policy approach: NKRA in education

Under the new strategy of the Government Transformation Programme (GTP) introduced in 2010, four "National Key Results Areas (NKRA)" for the education sector have been identified. The strategy was designed in conjunction with the preparation of the 10th Malaysia Plan in order to expedite achievement of the qualitative goals of Vision 2020. However, it should be noted that the issue is not only should equal opportunity of access to every level of education be efficiently provided to all Malaysian citizens, but it must also be in tandem with the philosophy of quality at every level of schooling – preschool, primary, secondary, and tertiary.

In short, the quantitative expansion and development of the education system has to be underpinned by the qualitative factor since these two factors are inseparable in any educational transformation process. The strategy of applying the NKRA also suggests that rates of student enrolment or participation (an indicator of input) and achievement (an indicator of output) need to be maximised while the rates of failure and dropouts be minimised. All aspects of the measurable indicators, principally rates of student participation, literacy level, achievement scores and dropout rates have to be consistently monitored. All of these issues have to be evaluated against the backdrop of management and leadership behavior of school principals and headmasters.

It cannot be denied that the NKRA for education is an important catalyst for transformation of the education system. If well implemented, it should benefit all students generally. In this regard, the NKRA have identified four sub-indicators that need to be given serious attention, namely: 1) pre-school, 2) educational literacy and numeracy (3R's and linguistic communication), 3) high performance schools (curriculum and co-curriculum activities), 4) new deal for principals and headmasters. Elements of the transformational initiatives are conceptualized in Figure 7.3.

The transformation of the educational system at school level in order to improve students' performance significantly (1/2)

	Transform education system		
How?	Ensure every child can succeed	Make school responsible for students' performances	Make investment on developing ideal leadership at every school
Main Initiative	? Prepare stronger education foundations to more children ? Increase enrolment and preschool quality to 87% at 2012, and 92% at 2015 (NKRA) ? Lower starting age for schooling ? Ensure the mastery of literacy and numeracy (LINUS) ? Give prominence to Bahasa Melayu and strengthen the command of the English Language	? Introduce the School Performance Development Programme in order to close the performance gap of low achieving school. ? Create 100 High Performance School by 2012 in order to improve the school standard to international level (NKRA)	? New Offer (Bai'ah) for principal and headmaster to improve their performance through the new achievement management approach. ? Strengthen training, support and guidance at school for principal

Figure 7.3 Educational transformation goals.

Source: Economic Planning Unit, Prime Minister's Department, Malaysia

One of the Sub-Indictors of the NKRA in Education is in the preschool area. Within the preschool Transformation Concept, several indicators of standard have been identified. They are:

National preschool curriculum standard

a) Introduction to literacy and numeracy
b) Introduction to basic thinking and problem-solving skills
c) Inculcation of confidence and positive attitudes
d) Practice of safe living and healthy life
e) Practice of self-reliance, cooperation and give-and-take attitude
f) Promotion of creative ideas and appreciation for arts and music
g) Exhibit characteristics of inquisitiveness and responsibility
h) Readiness to progress to the primary school

Under the NKRA strategy, the move toward standardising the assistance to all government preschool centres to ensure quality education has assumed a policy priority. Hence, it is envisaged that all government preschool centres will continue to receive per capita fund assistance and equipment support. The amount of financial allocation, though, will vary between centres, according to regional needs, being higher for Sabah and Sarawak preschools than that of the peninsular.

The NKRA strategy also involves new initiatives to ensure quality education. The initiative will formalise the approach of Key Performance Indicators (KPI).

This is to ensure quality delivery process of preschool education and the criteria of standards achieved would include concepts of 'excellent performance', 'good', 'satisfactory' and 'not satisfactory'. In addition, to complement programmes to ascertain standards of teacher quality, continuous training sessions would be intensively conducted for all preschool teachers. As a policy direction for the future, all preschool teachers to be recruited will be university level graduates, particularly from the Malaysian Teacher Education Institutes.

It should be noted that, at present, it is estimated that more than three hundred and twenty five thousand children, aged five and six, are not enrolled in preschool centres. With the opening of new government-sponsored preschool centres, it is anticipated that an additional two hundred thousand new pupils would be registered. This would result in an increase to about eighty seven percent (87%) of children who would be enrolled in preschool by 2012. Specific strategies to manage and expand the private sector preschool education centres are also in the pipeline including the regulating of student fees.

Literacy and numeracy (LINUS) at the primary level

The Government Transformation Plan (GTP) is determined that every child should master the basic skills of literacy and numeracy after three years of preschool education by 2012. The LINUS concept which is the short form for 'Literacy and Numeracy Domain' area is a remediation programme designed to ensure that students master the basic skills of literacy and numeracy in Malay Language (Bahasa Malaysia) at grade three of their primary schooling. While the programme is targeted at students with learning problems and difficulties in respect of the Three R's, there are six sub-strategies of the LINUS programme which would target at ninety percent of the relevant cohorts and they are as follows:

1   Student Domain (Year 1, Year 2, Year 3)
2   Development of educational learning materials
3   Teacher pedagogical skills enhancement
4   School and community awareness programme
5   Evaluation, supervision and monitoring
6   Development of FaciLINUS (LINUS Facilitator)

The LINUS programme would focus on early interventions (Year 1 through Year 3) for literacy and numeracy skills. Previously the intervention programme has primarily focused on literacy skills or is conducted at Year 4; remediation teacher-student ratio would be improved to 1:15 from one remediation teacher for each school. The Quality Assurance monitoring and management role would be undertaken by the District Education Office and the School Inspectorate. Previously such function was sole centrally conducted. Under the new policy approach, best and excellent teachers would be assigned to such classes; whereas, previously, such teachers were assigned to teach the Year 6 examination class.

Education policy and human capital 115

Several other strategies and new initiatives have also been identified and considered for successful LINUS programme implementation. These include creating the FaciLINUS team at the District Education Office; deploying the best and experienced teachers under the direct purview of the 154 Offices, to be supported by a Team of 2–10 LINUS teachers per district, with a ratio of 1 FaciLINUS for 30 schools within a given district. The professionally trained LINUS teachers' role is to assist the State Education Office in delegating and streamlining the LINUS programme with respective headmasters besides providing training, mentoring and capacity building activities for remediation teachers with the concurrence of the school management. They are also expected to assist the related primary schools with designing plans for corrective actions.

High performance schools approach

Under the High Performance Schools Approach, the plan is to enhance and promote schools which have attained excellent performance record. The approach would be undertaken under the strategic quality enhancement programme, especially through providing greater autonomy and accountability and by allowing schools to generate innovations in managing the centralised curriculum and education service personnel. The principal aim in the long run is to produce excellent student output of international standards in respective fields of competence. The main initiative on the human capital development as reflected in 10th Malaysia Plan has been conceptualised by the Economic Planning Unit of the Prime Minister's Department as reflected in the following Figure 7.4.

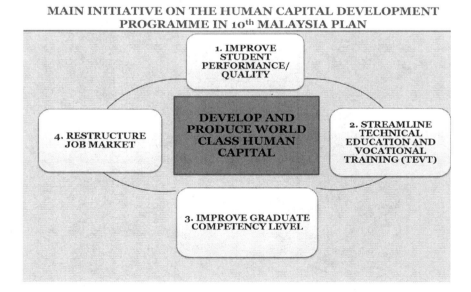

Figure 7.4 Human capital development under the 10th Malaysia Plan.
Source: Economic Planning Unit, Prime Minister's Department Malaysia

While the overall goal is to narrow the gaps between schools in terms of performance standards, the underlying strategic assumption is to provide inspiration to those schools which so far have been unable to address the issue of underperformance nationally and internationally. The criteria of selecting this school-type is comprised of two principal indicators; firstly academic excellence and secondly Verification Score through the Malaysian System of Education Quality (MSEQ). Related to these two indicators is a set of sub-criteria, which include, namely Ideal Personality Achievement of Individuals and Influential leaders; achievement and recipient of national awards and accolades; linkages and partnerships for credit transfers and student exchange with world class institutions of similar levels internationally; institutions are used as benchmarks for national achievement standards.

In relation to the above mentioned indicators, the assignment of school leaders would be based on absolute achievement scores as well as improvement scores. Incentives to principals and headmasters who could surpass the targeted achievement level would be in the form of cash or equivalent to be shared with the staff or attachment programmes with world class institutions for schools which have consistently demonstrated high performance record, or quicker promotions to higher scales and the award of appreciation certificates.

Labeled as the 'New Deal' in terms of reward and incentives to excellent principals and teachers, this approach has generated a lot interest as well as controversies among educators in the country. For example, the main issue very often debated by the general public is on financial rewards to individual principals and teachers who have successfully achieved the goals determined by the composite scores of the Malaysian System of Education Quality (MSEQ). In order to achieve the rewards, the composite scores are based on the following two dimensional indicators; public schools examination results and schools self-assessment inventory as shown in Figure 7.5.

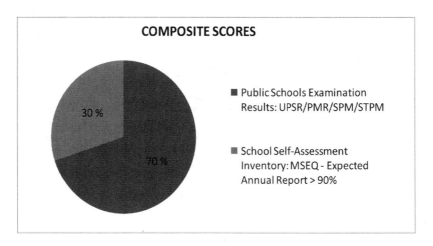

Figure 7.5 Composite scores for Malaysian schools.
Source: Ministry of Education

A specific strategy has been adopted to enhance education quality in schools in order not only to achieve the targeted national key performance indicators but also to address clear performance differences between schools. This strategy relates to the creation of special schools that have been accorded special status in terms of clear-cut definition as well as specific goals and objectives. While small in number within each classified status, they would become the model for other schools of their category. The special status is a motivational factor for other schools of their characteristics to emulate.

The classification of these schools include: the 'High Performance School' (HPS). These are schools which have ethos, character and a unique identity quality which enable them to excel in all aspects of education. The specific goals and objectives are to promote innovation and creativity in school management and to improve student productivity. Wholly owned by the Ministry of Education, in 2010 the number of schools in this category is 20 at the inception stage.

The second category is the 'Cluster School' which is aimed at being the centre of educational excellence (within each school grouping) focusing on niche areas such as music, sports, ICT, science, language and other disciplines. The principal objective is to accelerate the creation of excellent primary and secondary educational institutions in the country and to develop them as exemplary schools within or outside the cluster. Also wholly owned by the Ministry of Education, the number that had been identified was 120 beginning in 2007. This number is expected to increase in future.

The third category of the special status school is the 'SMART School'. The definition of "Smart School" is one that uses a technology platform as a medium on which distance learning and specific teaching expertise are made. The Malaysian Smart School is one of the nine flagships premised on the strong belief that ICT is a key enabler to imparting knowledge. As a learning institution, the approach of pedagogy has systematically been reinvented especially in teaching and learning methods as well as improvement of leadership and the school management process. It was designed with 88 schools in the beginning of 1997 by the Ministry of Education with the aim of preparing students to make a successful transition to a modern and global environment.

The fourth category is the 'Vision School' whereby all the major primary school types namely National Schools (SK), National-type Chinese School (SJK (C)) and National-type Tamil School (SJK (T)) that share the same compound and facilities but maintain a separate school administration, management and leadership. The concept was introduced in order to encourage greater teacher-student interaction and to foster the spirit of national unity and integration at the younger age. At its inception in 2004, there were 8 schools identified by the Ministry of Education.

The fifth category of the special status school is the 'Premier' educational institutions which have strong tradition, history and culture associated with their establishment since the colonial era. Most schools belonging to this category are over 100 years old and they have been selected as premier schools based on their records of academic and co-curricular achievements. The objective of classifying this school as Premier institutions is to recognise not only their academic and co-curricular excellence but also to ensure they continuously produce future national leaders, scholars, scientists, corporate figures, professionals and sportsmen. Highly recognised by the Ministry of Education and the Malaysian community at large, the number of these special schools in 2006 is only 4.

The sixth category is the type of school labeled as "Pintar". It is an acronym to indicate the status of the school that has the potential to become excellent and high-performing. It is organised along the principle of collaborative social responsibility initiative by Government-Linked Companies (GLCs) and Malaysian private corporations. The strategy is designed in order to foster higher academic excellence, especially among the underprivileged, disadvantaged and underserved schools nationwide. Its principal objective is to enhance education levels in the schools through greater participation of concerned companies. The number of schools belonging to this category at its inception in 2006 was 212, out of which 33 were under the purview of business corporate organisations.

The seventh category in the special status school is "Trust School" which was established in 2011. The principal thrust of this category is that it is jointly managed by the private and public sectors in order to especially improve performance and student outcomes. Spanning across socio-economic and demographic dimensions, the objective of this status school is to create step-change improvement in all aspects of education through interventions of public and private sector expertise. Organised under the AMIR Foundation in collaboration with the Ministry of Education, the number of schools beginning 2011 was 10.

The basic policy thrust of the school categories mentioned above is underpinned by clear development philosophy of an enhanced school improvement programme. The programme covers sub-strategies under the School Improvement Toolkit (SIT). It also includes School Examination Analysis System (SAPS) in terms of coordinating student test and examination scores, School Improvement Partner (SIPartner) and School Improvement Specialist Coaches (SISC). The total school transformation programme is geared toward the school performance development programme to be coordinated by the District Education Office, State Education Department and intensively monitored by the Ministry of Education.

Human capital development: Public higher education

The human capital development model in higher education of any country is normally directed at two strategic initiatives, namely the public higher education sector and private higher education sector. In the past, manpower planning especially for the public sector has regulated the accessibility factor to various areas of education and training, so as to meet national development requirement in terms of the world of work and manpower resources. However, today, when a diploma or a degree in a particular field can be commonplace, and often over-subscribed, a number of emerging new policy related questions must be considered and addressed by governments of developing countries, especially Malaysia. One of the critical questions is:

How should higher education system in developing countries diversify?

In this context, the government has adopted two approaches. First is the formulation of the Education Act 1996 for the public sector which includes public education at all levels. Second is the formulation of the Private Higher Educational Institutional Acts 1996 for the private sector education system. Both these Acts have been geared toward achieving human capital development of the country through the year 2020.

Strategic policies for human capital development through the public higher education system take a different form. New initiatives have been undertaken, though not fully accomplished. Nonetheless, the initial initiatives under the planning and commitment of the government's concern have shown some encouraging progress under the Phase 2 Action Plan and Strategic National Higher Education Plan. These include the launching of the innovative human capital action plan at tertiary, Metro Polytechnics and AkEPT Young Leaders Programme as well as the disbursement of Research Grant under the 10th Malaysia Plan. These initiatives are designed by government to enhance the role and capability of the higher education sector as one of the critical contributors in the National Transformation Plan. This is apparently evident in the Budget of 2012 whereby about RM12.9 billion has been allocated to the higher education sector compared to RM37.2 billion that goes to Ministry of Education as a whole. All these initiatives are targeted at upgrading the quality of higher education academic staff, enhancing the quality of research and development (R&D) capability, improving the programmes of student personality development particularly on soft skills and internationalisation of the higher education system; eventually good staff development will produce quality graduates to realize the national human capital development needs.

The following five (5) critical strategies have been adopted through the Budget 2012:

1 Enhancement of quality academic staff through an increase of advanced degree programme allocations especially in the pure sciences disciplines
2 Enhancement of research and development (R&D) capabilities through bigger Research Grants for high impact research activities focusing on Innovative Human Capital Incubator Programmes, with the purpose of generating patented design industrial and business products and the creation of Centers of Excellence (CoE) in the higher education system

3 Development of ideal student personality and competencies through several sub-strategies including:

   a   Professional Recognition Programmes
   b   Graduate Marketability Programmes
   c   Graduate Business Development Programmes
   d   Excellence Sports Programmes

4 Internationalisation Programmes to be promoted to the immediate developing countries in the region particularly Cambodia, Laos, Myanmar and Vietnam (CLMV) and regional branding of Malaysia through confidence building programmes (Soft Power)
5 Streamline technical and vocational training by establishing polytechnics in order to empower the population to become highly skilled human capital and improve the performance of polytechnics making them comparable to that of universities to ensure the polytechnics serve as alternative institutions for students wishing to pursue their higher education in the advanced technical and technological domains

The number of government tertiary education institutions with respect to entrants, enrolments and graduates at Degree, Diploma and Certificate level for year 2009 is indicated in the following Table 7.2.

Table 7.2 Number of Government Institutions, Entrants, Enrolments and Graduates in 2009

No. of Universities	*Entrants*	*Enrolments*	*Graduates*
20	153,470	437,420	104,870
No. of Polytechnics	*Entrants*	*Enrolments*	*Graduates*
27 (Diploma Level)	26,526	60,480	19,316
(Certificate Level)	11,936	25,950	12,110
No. of Com. Colleges	*Entrants*	*Enrolments*	*Graduates*
63 (Diploma Level)	431	846	443
(Certificate Level)	8,714	16,415	7,242
Level	*No. of Graduates*		*%*
Degree Holders	104,870 (Universities)		72.8
Diploma Holders	19,759 (Poly & Com. Colleges)		13.7
Certificate Holders	19,352 (Poly & Com. Colleges)		13.5
Total	143,981		100

Source: EPRD, MOE and MOHE – Malaysian Educational Statistics 2010 (adapted)

Human capital development: Private higher education

As suggested by Thalha (2003), there has been a popular demand in private sector education in the country in the past two decades. However, many of the courses offered in the past are related to four basic areas: business and accountancy, ICT especially software-related studies, technological engineering courses including electronic, power, mechanical and petroleum, as well as industrial arts and graphic design especially at the Diploma and basic Degree levels.

The population data of 2010 indicates that currently the average age of Malaysians is around 25.6 years old. This implies a fairly young national population that could lead in the formation of new households, thereby leading to an increase in income, urbanisation and greater demand for education beyond the secondary level. While it is apparent that in 1990, the labour force in Malaysia was around 7 million, in 2010 it has increased to 12.9 million. Of late, there is thus a greater demand for higher education and training for the fast growing labour force.

Liberalisation of the Education Act in terms of development of private sector education especially for the establishment of private universities, has led to a phenomenal increase of not only local students studying in private sector institutions but also foreign students. This has also led to an increase in the number of private university level institutions whether owned by Malaysians or foreign-based institutions. One hidden factor that has contributed to national income of the country is in the earning of foreign exchange through private sector education. However with changing scenarios in private sector institutions, strategic approaches need to be addressed especially in terms of laws, regulations, governance, quality and standards of the private sector education in the country.

The number of private tertiary institutions with respect to entrants, enrolments and graduates by field of education at Certificate, Diploma, Advanced Diploma and Degree level for 2009 is indicated in the following Table 7.3.

Table 7.3 Private Institutions, Entrants, Enrolments and Graduates by Field of Education at Certificate, Diploma, Advanced Diploma and Degree in 2009

FIELD OF EDUCATION	ENTRANTS	ENROLMENTS	GRADUATES
ARTS & SOCIAL SCIENCES	92,644	265,706	58,993
SCIENCES	49,183	137,325	24,446
TECHNICAL	20,542	650,154	12,246
TOTAL	162,369	468,044	95,685

Source: EPRD, MOE and MOHE – Malaysian Educational Statistics 2010 (adapted)

Implications of the paradigm shift

There is, in fact, an active debate among policy makers in Malaysia as to what exactly the new paradigm should be to ensure particular institutions of higher education in the country can effectively operate and contribute to the new "1 Malaysian" society of the 21st Century. In general, several concerned educationists have suggested that the higher educational process must move from:

- Instructor/lecturer-centred-learning of instruction styles to resource-oriented and problem-solving learning culture
- Provider-driven curriculum to user-centred curricular modules and packages
- Closed to open systems without rigid disciplinary parameters
- Classroom to work and performance-based learning context
- Isolated to networked environments
- One-way to highly interactive instructional teaching methodologies
- Local to national to global perspectives and vice-versa
- Change resistant to open and anticipatory educational management style.

The paradigm shift is a most challenging task for institutions of higher learning to handle. Even more challenging in the paradigm shift is that the change process should and must be driven by the higher education sector itself. Otherwise, it could result in the output profile of graduates being heavily shaped and manipulated by market forces which focus on short-term return and profits to the few individuals, rather than for long-term benefits of the wider net of individuals in society in general. Indeed, all institutions of higher learning in Malaysia have constantly been urged to provide a pro-active role in engendering all the necessary attributes of modern 21st Century institutions that emphasise a broad and super dynamic model of higher education.

Transformation through innovation, creativity and change

In essence, innovations are necessary especially for old but established institutions of higher learning (example: the University of Malaya), which must possess the pro-active attributes necessary to face the challenging but daunting task of transformation and change, head on. This is because innovative and pro-active institutions of higher learning in the country are expected to face up to the challenges or perish in the waves of the globalisation era.

Hence, the higher education policy directions and missions of Malaysia must be governed by concrete strategies and actions in:

- Offering quality higher education programmes, training and research
- Ensuring entry, based on intellectual merit without sacrificing equity and equality
- Pursuing high intellectual scholarship, development and professionalism
- Exhibiting total institutional commitment to community social development

- Offering lifelong learning opportunities for all regardless of creed and background
- Establishing links to the world of work for graduates nationally and internationally
- Engendering social debates and healthy criticism from within and without
- Providing impartial advice and expertise for decision makers and implementers
- Upholding academic freedom, justice, integrity, morality and high ethical standards
- Serving local, national, regional and international development needs.

These social expectations, underpinned by the five broad policy perspectives of quality, pertinence, relevance, effective management of human resource and finance, are critical for the higher education transformation process in Malaysia.

Thus, for Malaysia to achieve an effective transformation process, a whole range of issues and challenges will require close scrutiny and deliberation. In general, these include: well-organised institutional profiling of the student body, participatory leadership and management training of staff and student leaders, constant innovation in teaching, training and research activities, provision of excellent essential services such as career counseling, graduate placement and tracer studies, recognition of cultural diversity, and total commitment for the inclusion of the marginalised social groups.

Strategic agenda for policy-related research programme

The new social expectations of the role of higher education in many developing economies, for example Malaysia, seem to reflect a tall order as underlined in the preceding discussion. In terms of university-level leadership and governance, the social expectations are underpinned by five broad policy perspectives. They are: relevance, pertinence, quality, management and finance. These perspectives are critical in the public and private higher education institutional transformation process.

In terms of "relevance", higher education must essentially be considered in relation to its fundamental social role in society, and to its mission of providing education, training and research.

Also, equally important is its pertinence such as linkage with the world of work and in the context of its relationship with the human capital development policy of the country.

As a third perspective, quality is inseparable from social relevance. The quality of higher education depends on the quality of the academic staff and their level of intellectual productivity, programmes and curricular content, diversity of student compositions, up-to-date research infrastructure and facilities, and evaluation systems and mechanisms. These factors are fundamentally critical to be continually addressed by the relevant institutions.

With respect to management, policy related examination of higher education is posited on the conviction that it is a set of sub-systems which include philosophy, visions, missions, structures, resources, admission procedures and the intellectual climate that should interact with one another at the national and the supra national levels. The management of higher education institutions cannot be reduced to the level of book-keeping operation and activities solely on the basis of economic considerations, but must be evaluated also on the criteria of social relevance, quality of instruction, training and research, and productive consultancy services.

In terms of finance, the funding of higher education faces the huge challenge of mass number of intakes and admissions into the public universities and the related costs and services as required of the procedures and requirements. Policy-related research in higher education financing is an indispensable activity that must be undertaken by the system.

Indeed, to achieve the intended transformation of higher education, a whole range of policy issues and teething problems must be continually addressed. The issues and problems require close scrutiny in terms of policy-directed research, reviews and re-evaluation by the concerned parties. In general, the activities related to the perspectives outlined above will invariably include regular re-examination of: institutional profiling of student body, advanced leadership and management training of university leaders and administrators, periodic reviews of programs and curricular content toward improvement and relevance, updating of instructional methodologies based on innovations in effective teaching, training and research activities, as well as regular reviews of essential student services through studies and career counseling.

Conclusion

National educational transformation is undoubtedly linked to national development policies, strategies and priorities. The challenges of Vision 2020 demand that Malaysians be able to rise to meet the global challenges of the 21st Century. The development of a quality workforce and resource of highly qualified, innovative and creative human capital is based on the model of the "glocalised" (combination of global and local characteristics) human capital development programmes. Not only has the strategy become a top priority, but the task of creating such a workforce has to depend on overcoming several critical factors and challenges. The overall strategy is to ensure that there is a greater commitment and a more effective private sector involvement in order to complement as well as augment the government's initiatives in the transformation process.

References

Malaysia, Ministry of Education. (2003). *Education Development Plan 2001–2010*. Putrajaya: EPRD, MOE.

Malaysia, Ministry of Education. (2004). *Malaysia educational statistics*. Putrajaya: EPRD.

Thalha, M. (2003). Trends in private higher education: Is there a gap between aspirations & achievement? A thematic discourse Paper presented at the Faculty of Education, University of Malaya, Kuala Lumpur, Malaysia.

8 Graduate employability in government discourse
A critical perspective

Zuraidah Mohd Don

In Malaysia, graduate employability has become a dominant issue, and graduates face major problems in obtaining employment commensurate with their academic qualifications. Drawing on the insights from Critical Discourse Analysis, this chapter offers a critical appraisal of the way graduate employability is identified as a problem to be addressed through policy solutions, and the way graduates, higher education and employers are positioned in discourse. In the context of a fast growing economy primarily driven by foreign investment and export growth, and a more competitive and knowledge-intensive labour market, graduates are required to have the kind of knowledge, skills, creative potential and dispositions to maintain and enhance their attractiveness in the jobs market. Universities are assigned the responsibility for producing employable graduates, while employers positioned as clients want quality "products", and graduates themselves have to face increasing competition and continuously develop the essential skills and attributes required by employers. In this chapter it is argued that these graduates are disadvantaged and face potentially damaging consequences as a result of the discourse of employability, which puts the emphasis on individual responsibility, and takes insufficient account of social inequalities.

Introduction

In the increasingly knowledge-driven context of changing global economies, in which theories of human capital represent the backdrop against which policies and government official documents on higher education (henceforth "HE") are drafted, the Malaysian government has identified improvements in the quality and skills of graduates as a means of increasing national prosperity and economic growth. Great emphasis is placed on the economic value of HE both to individual graduates, and through them to the nation's economy. By implication, this emphasis puts universities in the role of the leading future trainer and supplier of the workforce, a fact turned to advantage by the Malaysian government as it gives a reason to encourage universities to reorganise their approach to the HE system to meet the demands of the knowledge economy. The lack of employability skills among Malaysian graduates is being used to justify increasing government involvement in HE in the context of policy making in order to bring about reform in the HE sector for national economic development.

Neoliberal influences have touched many aspects of HE in Malaysia including the importance given to entrepreneurial activity and the increasing importance of university-industry partnerships. In their critique of the new model of education which mirrors what is happening in HE where it is packaged to meet economic needs and the demands of graduates, Lambert, Parker and Neary (2007) contend:

> This is an 'instrumental' education, [. . .] it is about the development of human resources and economic prosperity much more than notions of personal achievement, growth and fulfilment and the promotion of education for the social good.
>
> (p. 52)

For the government, graduate employability (henceforth "GE") is concerned with producing trained human resource to meet manpower needs and with the enhancement of graduates' level of job market potential and access to jobs commensurate with their academic qualifications. The fact that government and other stakeholders are now addressing the problems faced by graduates in obtaining employment marks a dynamic shift in the relationship between universities, the jobs market and future economic growth (Stiwne & Alves, 2010). An appreciation of the connection between economic success and HE has made GE a new political priority. The growing pressure on universities to increase graduate employability foregrounds the long-standing relationship between HE and the economy (Yorke & Knight, 2007) and the political concern that HE should make an appropriate contribution to developing trained human capital.

This chapter takes as its object of research "a social problem that has a semiotic aspect" (Fairclough, 2001, p. 236), namely GE, and uses insights and analytical tools from Critical Discourse Analysis (henceforth "CDA") to examine the way it is identified as a problem to be addressed through policy solutions, and analyse the way relevant social actors including Institutes of Higher Learning (henceforth "IHLs") and graduates are positioned in the selected texts. The perspective taken here is influenced by Bacchi's " 'What's the Problem Represented to be?' ('WPR') approach, [. . .]regarded as an innovative tool for examining social issues and responses to them (Bletsas & Beasley, 2012, p. 1). Bacchi (2007, p. 1; cited in Mackinnon, 2012, p. 14) argues that "governments . . . give a particular shape to social 'problems' in the ways in which we speak about them and in the proposals we advance to 'address' them. Governments in this understanding are active in the creation of particular ways of understanding issues".

A critical perspective on higher education and graduate employability

The emergence of the knowledge economy, primarily driven by the production, distribution and application of knowledge and new communication technologies, has transformed HE to the extent that the dominant rationale for education is economic, and designed to create human capital capable of innovation and economic performance (World Bank, 1994). Powell and Snellman (2004, p. 5) assert that there "is greater reliance on intellectual capabilities", which forces universities to rethink their role in the new knowledge era. HE is now seen as a driver of economic growth "for producing an educated workforce, [...], and generating innovations in science and technology that resonate throughout society" (Kinser & Hill, 2011, p. vi). Making a link between "employability" and the contributions made by universities to knowledge and skills development implies a reframing of the university role, marking a shift of responsibility of the definition of what constitutes employability away from universities to the state (Boden & Nedeva, 2010, p. 38). The emphasis is on the economic role of graduates and the capacity of universities to equip them with "employability skills" for the job market.

Yorke (2006, p. 3) contends that "the employability of graduates has become an aim that governments around the world have [...] imposed on national higher education systems". Annamalai (2013) sees the primary role of education as "Producing knowledge workers for companies" (p. 199), and this applies equally to HE. Gumport (2000) talks about a shift in priorities within HE, which is seen more as an industry than a social institution, and where corporate interests play an increasingly influential role in determining its purpose.

The contemporary discourse of GE brings with it a new way of describing graduates as part of the nation's workforce. The focus is now not on the universities alone but also on the graduates themselves, who are described as employable or unemployable rather than employed or unemployed (Garsten & Jacobsson, 2004). Graduates are positioned as lacking and in need of employability skills, and employability is "used as an explanation, and [...] a legitimation, of employment" (Strath, 2000 cited in Fejes, 2010, p. 90). In short, employability is here presented not only as the key for success in the job market, but the very condition for employment, and as a result "less emphasis is placed on structural inequalities and problems in the labour market" (Fejes, 2010, p. 90).

This new discursive framing makes employability more open to different interpretations. From the perspective of a critical policy analysis, Fejes (2010, p. 90) sees employability as "planet speak" discourse, which is "a way of reasoning that seems to have no structural roots, no social locations and no origin". Hillage and Pollard (1998) relate employability to the abilities to gain initial employment, maintain employment and obtain new employment if required. For employers, employability is often associated with immediate work-readiness with graduates possessing the knowledge and "employable skills" for the effective functioning of their organisation (Harvey et al., 1997). For graduates, employability is concerned with their propensity to get employment defined in terms of the knowledge, skills and attributes they have, and the way they use them and present them to employers and the context in which they seek employment (Hillage & Pollard, 1998, p. 2). Yorke (2006) asserts that employability "implies something about the capacity of the graduate to function in a job" (p. 7) and "should not be confused with the actual acquisition of a 'graduate job' ... which is subject to influences in the environment" (p. 2).

Data and analytical perspective

The main document from which the extracts are drawn is The National Graduate Employability Blueprint (2012), which expounds an ambitious government reform agenda on GE published in November 2012 after extensive consultations with key participants from public and private sectors. The practice of soliciting stakeholders' views is a way of "testing reactions to government initiatives as part of a wider strategy for managing consent" (Fairclough, 2010, p. 179). The *Blueprint* establishes the government's own position, and forms part of the MoE's initiative to improve the labour market relevance of university programmes. The increased use of employability in policy discourses illustrates the influence of globalisation in HE. Selected texts concerned with graduate employability are analysed to bring out how the dominant issues are problematised and to illustrate the positioning of stakeholders, in particular the government, students, and IHLs and employers, with respect to graduate employability.

Relevant extracts from the *Malaysia and the Knowledge Economy: Building a World-Class Higher Education System* (2007, henceforth "MKE") will be introduced to enrich the analysis and interpretation of the texts drawn from the *GE Blueprint*. MKE is a report prepared to help "develop a strategic vision for the evolution of the country's universities towards becoming world class" (MKE, 2006, p. vii). The two documents together illustrate that the "employability" of graduates is high on the government's agenda, and puts pressure on IHLs to produce an employable workforce not only matching employers' needs but also capable of contributing to economic competitiveness (*GE Blueprint*, 2012).

Taking a CDA approach and using appropriate analytical tools for critical analysis, this chapter analyses selected texts to examine how GE and relevant stakeholders, especially IHLs and graduates, are positioned from the government's perspective. Fairclough (2001) argues that CDA focuses on linguistic aspects of "social issues and problems" (p. 227) with the aim of showing "how the [. . .] properties of a text connect with what is going on socially" (p. 140), which is relevant to the focus of this study. According to Rogers (2011, p. 10), CDA has three main features: it deals with discourse, it has to be critical and it is analysis. Being "critical" means raising awareness of the link between language and other elements in social life to produce critical knowledge (Wodak & Meyer, 2009, p. 7). Discourse is defined by Jorgensen and Phillips (2002) as "a particular way of talking about and understanding the world or any aspect of the world" (p. 1). For this chapter, the discourse analysed takes the form of extracts drawn from the *relevant* documents on graduate employability. The role of discourse in social practice has to be established through analysis, and there is an increase in the use of discourse analysis to analyse policy discourses (Moreau & Leathwood, 2007), within the context of HE.

Analysis

Like other Malaysian government documents, the *GE Blueprint* has two distinctive sections. The first is the intertextual element in the front matter which consists of a Foreword (p. i), a Message (p. iii), a Preface (p. v) and an extract from the Prime Minister's (henceforth "PM") 2013 Budget Speech (p. viii). The second, the body of the document, is divided into three main sections: Introduction, Current Graduate Employability Background and Graduate Employability Framework. *MKE* draws attention to the problem of graduate unemployment. This explains why *MKE* brings into discussion the interplay of several factors which contribute to unemployment, including the supply of and demand for graduates, the job search process and skills mismatch (p. 67).

The *GE Blueprint* is structured in the form of "problem"(graduate employability) and the proposed solution (*GE Blueprint*) which reflects a top-down pyramid where governmental and national interests are deeply involved and legitimised by the necessity to ensure that the education system is "responsive to the growing demand for more employable graduates" (*GE Blueprint*, p. ii). This tendency is reflected in the front matter and topics of the *GE Blueprint* which define the global coherence and the most important information in the text. Four major recurring topics are woven together into a coherent discursive formation which essentially consists of (1) the need for trained human capital to face the challenge of a more competitive global labour market (2) the lack of employability attributes among the graduates (3) the IHL as the provider of a trained labour force for industry and contributor to the development of the nation's knowledge economy (4) the *GE Blueprint* designed to help the IHLs to adapt their HE system to the needs of the knowledge economy and produce employable graduates.

Graduate employability

Extract A from the front matter presents the government's GE agenda, expressed intertextually through the voices of institutional authority: the then Minister of HE, the Ministry of Higher Education (henceforth "MoHE") Secretary General and the chairman of the Critical Agenda Projects. These voices give the document its legitimate power, and ensure that universities will embrace the government's agenda and include it in their missions.

Clearly, the discourse of employability that dominates the texts is economically driven. The focus on producing employable graduates in the dynamic and competitive labour market is presented as justifiable because of the role that HE plays in developing human capital, which is regarded as "a key enabling factor in our pursuit for prosperity and a sustainable national economy" (NHE, 2007, p. 5). This explains why GE has become an issue of political concern, and the Ministry of Education (henceforth "MoE") has put it at the centre of their national HE strategies.

The selected texts in Extract A exemplify how the HE system is subject to governmental intervention, which takes the form of putting in place several measures to increase GE, including those proposed in the *GE Blueprint*. The implication is that "change" is necessary because the HE system is increasingly ineffective in addressing the problem of graduate employability.

130 *Zuraidah Mohd Don*

Extract A

Foreword

(1) [. . .] graduate employability [. . .] has become an issue of concern. (2) The publication of this Graduate Employability Blueprint, the result of many months of deliberation and discussion by key representatives from academia, the public sector and industry players, therefore is timely. (3) Prospective employers complain of fresh . . . graduates lacking the pre-requisite attributes; more than 50% . . . are deemed to be unsatisfactory in English communication skills, and yet, many of these young inexperienced job-seekers expect unrealistically high-starting salaries.

(p. i)

Message

(1) As a fast growing and open economy, Malaysia is faced with the challenge of a more competitive employability landscape and the increased need for 21st century skills especially for the graduates of Institutes of Higher learning. (2) In essence, the IHL system has to be responsive to the growing demand for more employable graduates to continue to help propel the various industries with creativity and innovations. (3) In this regard, the Ministry of Higher Education, [. . .] has developed a blueprint for Graduate Employability that leverages the strength of IHL to address the challenges [. . .].

(p. iii)

Preface

(1) As higher education becomes a cornerstone in Malaysia's development, it has become imperative that IHL graduates become more employable within the growing economy. (2) This National Graduate Employability (GE) Blueprint is stipulated to serve as a guide to what IHL graduates need to know and should be able to do with respect to their employability attributes.

(p. iii)

In the *Foreword*, GE is problematised (1), and "IHL graduates" are described as lacking "the pre-requisite attributes" and "English communication skills", and "young and inexperienced job seekers", who nevertheless expect "unrealistically high-starting salaries" (3). This justifies the publication of the *GE Blueprint* produced after consultation with the stakeholders and considered "timely" given the problem of employability (2). The discourse of employers focuses on the mismatch between their requirements and expectations and the skills and capabilities graduates possess, which implies that the HE system "has some significant limitations to overcome" (MKE, p. xiv). The complaints about the lack of employability attributes are made legitimate by the personal authority of the "prospective employers" in whom authority is vested because of their roles as employers in the labour market. Here, the government's view on graduates reflects the views of the prospective employers.

Meanwhile, in the *Message* Malaysia is presented "as a fast growing and open economy" which justifies the need to prepare graduates for "the challenge of a more competitive employability landscape and the increased need for 21st century skills" (1). This perspective continues in (2) which puts the obligation on the HE system "to be responsive to the growing demand for more employable graduates" justifying the development of "a blueprint for Graduate Employability" (3). The MoHE, which is activated as the developer of the *GE Blueprint*, is positively represented as leveraging "the strength of IHLs to address the challenges" (3).

Framed as crucial in Malaysia's development in the *Preface*, HE has to produce "more employable graduates within the growing economy". "More" in the Preface and also in the Message (2) implies some kind of deficiency with graduates falling short of the employers' expectations, hence contributing to making them less employable. To address the problem the government initiated the development of the *GE Blueprint* "stipulated to serve as a guide to what IHL graduates need to know and should be able to do with respect to their employability attributes" (p. v).

The inclusion of the PM's Budget Speech in the *Blueprint* (Extract B) placed strategically before the content page (p. ix) reflects how seriously the government is tackling the problem of graduate employability which has been elevated to the status of national concern. Extract B represents a political initiative aimed at making graduates employable:

Extract B

> [. . .]. The government will launch the Government Employability (GE) Blueprint to assist the unemployed graduates by the end of 2012. The GE Blueprint focuses on strengthening the employability of graduates. The Government will establish a Graduate Employability Taskforce with an allocation of RM200 million.
>
> (p. viii)

This extract represents the government's view that the investment in human capital is central. A taskforce with an allocation of RM 200 million was set up to ensure that 75% of Malaysian graduates are employed within six months of graduation. This initiative illustrates how the government has responded to the growing number of unemployable graduates and how important it sees the relationship between investment in education and training and its productive economic value within the labour market.

With respect to modality in the clause there is a shift from modal auxiliary 'will' which indicates the future launching of the "Government Employability Blueprint", to factuality when describing the focus of the *Blueprint* which is "on strengthening the employability of graduates" and back to "will" when referring to the future establishment of the Task force "with an allocation of RM200 million", a promise of financial support from the government. The PM's speech suggests that there is a serious problem with the employability of graduates, and as the PM he has the authoritative resources and legitimation to speak on behalf of the government and formalise government intervention, namely through the launching of the GE Blueprint, and by setting up a task force with financial support.

Immediately after the extract from the Budget Speech is a description of the *GE Blueprint*:

Extract C

> [. . .] a comprehensive guide for policy administrators, IHL leaders, and programme managers to obtain a quick understanding of the [. . .] (GE) charter and to embark on a roadmap of necessary measures in order to enhance the graduate employability programmes and activities within their institutions.
>
> (p. 1)

The main social actors, namely "policy administrators, IHL leaders, and programme managers" are "authoritative people" from IHLs grouped together and functionalised to assimilate the meaning of the Blueprint quickly, and embark on the roadmap. The *Blueprint* is evaluated positively as "comprehensive". Students and prospective employers are not mentioned. There are three purpose relations indicated by 'to' and 'in order to' which foreground legitimation: "*to* obtain a quick understanding of the graduate employability (GE) charter and *to* embark on a road map of necessary measures *in order to* enhance the graduate employability programmes and activities".

Producing "employable graduates" for the country is legitimising discourse, which "embodies new notions of what university education is [. . .], and new forms of relationships between universities and the states that largely fund and regulate them" (Boden & Nedeva, 2010, p. 37), marking "a transition of authority over the definition of what constitutes employability away from HE to the state" (p. 38). Paragraphs 1 and 2 (Extract D) are structured as an argument to legitimise the need for government interventions which are presented as necessary responses to the perceived lack of employability skills among graduates. Together they are built around a 'problem-solution' relation. Fairclough (2003, p. 91) argues that this kind of "higher level semantic relation" is pervasive in policy texts.

Extract D

Paragraph (1)

(1) The Malaysian economy is an open economy driven primarily by foreign direct investment and export growth. (2) Thus, the education system must recognise the changing demand conditions in terms of the needs of multinational and large corporations. (3) This is important to ensure the country is able to produce adequately and appropriately trained human resource and does not face a skills-shortage problem.

Paragraph (2)

(1) The Critical Agenda Project (CAP) was created to accomplish the mission of the National Higher Education Strategic Plan which is to convert higher education in line with the objective of establishing Malaysia as a worldwide centre of excellence for higher education. (2) [. . .], CSP has embarked on developing a Graduate Employability (Blueprint). (3) It is hoped that the Blueprint will ensure a higher education environment that encourages the growth of premier knowledge centres and graduates who are competent and knowledgeable, and innovative with high moral values in order to meet national and international needs.

(*GE Blueprint*, p. 1)

Paragraph 1 puts the onus on the HE system to ensure that the country produces "adequately and appropriately trained human resource". Sentences 1, 2 and 3 suggest that HE will have to face "new realities" (Harvey, 2000): the Malaysian economy, ". . . driven primarily by foreign direct investment", needs an education system that recognises "the changing demand conditions in terms of the needs of multinational and large corporations" which explains the need to ensure that "the country is able to produce adequately and appropriately trained human resource". Sentence 1 is a kind of report which makes a link between "is" and "must" – what "The Malaysian economy is" and what "the education system must" do. "Must" reinforces the unequal relationships between the ministry and the IHLs. In (3) graduates are referred to as "human resource", and as a supplier of human resource it is implied that the IHLs have to ensure that the country "does not face a skills-shortage problem".

Paragraph 2 explains why the government "has embarked on developing" a *GE Blueprint* (2), which is to ensure that the HE environment is conducive for the "growth of premier knowledge centres" and produces "graduates [. . .] competent [. . .]to meet national and international needs" (3). It foregrounds legitimation, namely explaining the need for the *Blueprint*.

The graduates

Both *GE Employability* and *MKE* emphasise the employers' perspective on employability and the perspectives of graduates are excluded, their voices silent. This is evident from intertextual elements in the two documents which make explicit what employers want from the graduates and the IHLs. Graduates are classified as a group assigned specific characteristics which define what they are and not what they do. They are impersonally categorized as 'workforce', 'talent pool', 'job seekers', 'human resource', and 'manpower' which draws attention to their functionality as a group, and they are appraised in terms of their state of employability, as "employable" or "unemployable".

The shift from academic qualification now regarded as a 'threshold requirement' to employability attributes has been criticised as reflecting a narrow view of educational aims (cf. Boden & Nedeva, 2010). The state of employability is constructed as primarily a matter of an individual's skills and personal attributes. Several main problems associated with the graduates themselves have been identified as contributing to unemployment as illustrated in Extract E:

Extract E

> [. . .] the most common problems identified by employers are poor command of English (55.8%), poor character, attitude and personality (37.4%) [. . .] no demonstrated ability to solve problems (25.9%), and skill knowledge not in depth enough (23.8%). As the main demand of industry is to employ graduates with GSA (Generic Student attribute) centred, . . . it is obvious that these skills are lacking among graduates.
>
> (p. 9)

Through the voice of the employers, graduates are positioned as lacking the required employability attributes which explains why they are not meeting "the main demand of industry", namely "to employ graduates with GSA [. . .] centred". Employability is framed as a "supply-side" problem associated with deficiencies in employability attributes. The percentages given in brackets add to the objectivity of this characterisation of graduates. The heavy emphasis on the employment incapacity of graduates position them as "unfinished products" the outcome of prior educational experiences and processes which have failed to help them make the transition from HE to the workplace. By implication, there is a general pressure on both graduates and IHLs to improve their performance with regard to employability.

The emphasis on the supply side of employability places employers in the position of power. The survey in Extract F draws attention to the dilemma of firms facing the shortage of employability skills among graduates:

Extract F

(1) According to a survey conducted by Manpower Inc. (2008), the five most sought after attributes by Malaysian firms [. . .] identified comprised strong communication skills and the ability to relay information to others [. . .]. (2) Consequently, the five most difficult attributes to find in the talent pool [. . .] were loyalty and a willingness to make a career commitment to the firm, critical thinking, reasoning and problem-solving skills, [. . .]

(p. 10)

The lack of employability attributes among graduates is presented as a mismatch between demand, namely "what Malaysian firms want" (1) and supply, namely "what is lacking" (2). It foregrounds the gaps between the worlds of HE and of work which could provide leverage for change.

Higher education

In the *GE Blueprint*, employability is presented as "a performative function of universities, shaped and directed by the state" (Boden & Nedeva, 2010, p. 37) whose goal is to ensure that there is an adequate and appropriate supply of employable graduates matching employers' needs. Following increasing numbers of unemployed graduates since 2000, concerns have been expressed about the quality of HE and its relevance to the workplace (MKE, 2007, p. xx). Extract G raises doubts about the relevance of HE from the perspective of employers, and identifies the weaknesses in the system:

Extract G

(1) Concerns about the workplace relevance of tertiary education remain. (2) Tracer studies, commissioned research, and employers point to the need for tertiary education institutions, public universities in particular, to better build into their curricula soft skills [. . .], link faculty to industry, provide students with workplace experience through job attachments in the private sector, and provide counselling. (3) These steps should help to reduce problems in the initial transition of new graduates from university to the labour market.

(MKE, p. xx)

The key task for HE is to supply a trained workforce to "multinational and large corporations", who have the "authority" to determine the type of workers they want. The call for a change in the HE system (3) is attributed to tracer studies, commissioned research and employers (2) which represent the demand side as opposed to the supplier-side signalled by 'their'. Here is a categorical assertion concerning the shortcomings of HE which need to be addressed. The "steps" recommended "to reduce the problem in the initial transition" (2) suggest a mismatch between what students learn at university and the skills required in the job market. Fairclough (2010) criticises this view of education which assumes that key skills, for example, communication skills, are easily transferred from one sphere of life to another.

The government is in a position to ensure that public universities respond to employers' demands, as it provides a large portion of the funding. This authority is expressed by the MoHE as follows: "Being owned and funded by the Government, public higher education institutions must ensure that their strategic objectives are in line with those of the Ministry's." (National Higher Education Action Plan, 2007, p. 18). The mission of the IHLs (p. 1) is presented to foreground the message:

Extract H

> To produce competent graduates in order to fulfill national and international manpower needs with 75% of the graduates employed in their relevant fields within the six months of their graduation.
>
> (*GE Blueprint*, p. 4)

Here again IHLs are functionalised as suppliers of competent human resources for the job market. Their core purpose is foregrounded explicitly by 'to', namely "To produce competent graduates" with the assumption of "75% of the graduates employed in their relevant fields within the six months of their graduation". This reflects an attempt on the part of the government to develop links between HE and the country's manpower needs which unfortunately may narrow "the purpose of education towards serving the needs of the economy" (Fairclough, 2010, p. 557).

Extract I (*GE Blueprint*, p. 4) exemplifies a common contemporary genre which emphasises the need to act in certain ways made inevitable by the way the world is now:

Extract I

> *Paragraph 1*
>
> While the IHL have always been regarded as the cornerstone of a country's supply of quality and talented human resources, the changed and changing industry landscape, both at home and abroad, has given rise to GE implications that need to be understood and challenges that need to be faced.

Paragraph 2

(1) In the continuing debate on the priorities of IHL and whether they should be knowledge-driven or industry-driven, pragmatism suggests a middle path. (2) It is there in that context that IHL should work to address the many urgent issues and challenges of GE. (3) IHL should take upon themselves to be proactive in improving GE rather than fault industry for being overselective or for their reluctance to contribute to training.

In Paragraph 1, the change in the industrial landscape suggests that the IHLs are required to act in certain ways, namely to understand the GE implications and face the challenges, despite being recognised as the supplier of "quality and talented human resources". However, in Paragraph 2 they are explicitly told what they should do, foregrounding their obligations for the employability of their graduates: "should work to address the many urgent issues and challenges of GE" and "should take upon themselves to be proactive in improving GE". Sentence (3) puts the obligation for GE on the IHLs to the exclusion of other contributory factors. The second half of sentence 3 implies that the IHLs have attributed the fault to industry rather than being proactive themselves.

Extract J (*GE Blueprint*, p. 3) exemplifies the burden faced by IHLs in making their graduates employable: having to satisfy the employers' demand for quality "employees" when the students they have to "train" constitute "poor intake":

Extract J

(1) As shown by the graph on page 9, there are significant shortcomings that IHL need to address [. . .]. (2) Industry players are the employers [. . .], they are the "buyers" who seek value for their money. (3) It is therefore the responsibility of IHL, who produce the "products" to meet the expectations and demands of "customers".

(4) Although IHL may take the effort to develop and revise the current curriculum to equip graduates with the required exit attributes as specified by employers, it is important to realise that because of poor intake attributes these efforts may not fully produced the desired outcomes.

[. . .] Such awareness of the poor quality of intake attributes and specific efforts made to address this shortcoming will provide the IHL with the opportunity to positively impact GE.

The IHLs are told that they are required to produce graduates that "meet the expectations and demands" of employers who are placed in a powerful position as "buyers" and "customers" that have the right to demand. Reference is made to a graph to support the assertion that HE has "significant shortcomings" which they are required to address to meet the demands of employers positioned in the powerful position as "buyers". Although the students are deemed to be of poor quality on entrance, the IHLs are nevertheless expected to turn out graduates meeting the high standards of employers. The dehumanisation of graduates as "products" presents them as a homogeneous output of an industrial process rather than as people from varying social backgrounds.

The employers are however not totally absolved of responsibility. They are assigned the role of providing "further training" which implies the existence of basic training, the responsibility of the IHLs:

Extract K

> (1) Companies [. . .] are prepared to invest reasonable time and money to train fresh graduates provided they can be convinced that those they hire have the required attributes. (2) The onus therefore is on IHL to teach their graduates to acquire these attributes. (3) While IHL have taken the steps to introduce certain tailor-made courses to suit industry requirements, these fundamentals must be complemented by the right attributes which should be instilled and nurtured before these graduates join the workforce. (4) It is the industry's responsibility to provide further training and develop graduates' potential so as to make them experts in their profession. [. . .] (5) Briefly, IHL provide the diamond industry polish that rough diamond to become the precious gem it can be. Such joint responsibility of IHL and industry will provide a win-win situation.
>
> (GE, p. 14)

The responsibility of companies towards GE is interestingly not represented as an obligation or duty but as a willingness on their part indicated by "prepared" (1). They are represented positively as being prepared to invest "reasonable time and money", but with a condition attached, namely that they need to be convinced the graduates have "the required attributes". The demands of the companies take precedence (2), so that the IHLs are positioned as being responsible for producing graduates with employable attributes before they even join the workforce (3). As gatekeepers, the companies are given the privileged position of being able to dictate what the IHLs should teach their students, namely preparing a trained workforce to meet the company's needs.

Discussion and conclusion

The impact of global economic forces increasingly causes HE to be viewed as an investment in human capital, requiring it to shift the focus from being concerned solely with knowledge advancement to creating a trained workforce for a competitive global labour market. The positioning of GE as a problem in the *GE*

Blueprint (2012) provides an important site of analysis, allowing the examination of how the government sees the need for some form of intervention and how this fits with the requirements of concerned stakeholders. Although the *GE Blueprint* was apparently produced after consultation with industry and IHLs, only one set of solutions is offered, namely the Government's. There seems to be a one-way communication with the government instructing IHLs what action to take, which leads us to infer that there is little space for dialogue.

The government discourse on employability is economically driven, a reform globally legitimised by the requirements of the Knowledge Economy including the need to produce graduates with particular employability skills who can compete in a changing global environment. As evident from the analyses of selected texts, the change in the orientation of the labour market policy from "job security" to "employability security" has affected the IHLs in fundamental ways, including requiring them to produce "work ready" graduates that will make them more appealing to employers.

An issue arising from the analyses is what subject is produced and positioned as responsible for graduate employability. The government is represented as an "enabler" providing the financial support as well as prescribing and putting in place measures to help universities increase their graduate employability to meet the knowledge economy needs. In the context of globalisation, the demands of national and multinational corporations take precedence, so that universities are positioned as responsible for producing employable graduates accommodating the future demands of employers. Findings from the analysis of selected texts show that universities should provide their students with the necessary employability skills and competences required for the world of work through planning, improved curricula and by providing appropriate work-related training. What is interesting is a relative lack of emphasis on employer responsibility to train their newly recruited employees to fill the gaps in employability skills.

The focus on the productive capabilities of fresh graduates reflects a heavy emphasis on the supply side of the problem, with relatively less emphasis on wider issues including socio-economic factors that result in inequalities as in the case of graduates from non-English-speaking backgrounds, and who cannot get employment because of their inability to communicate in English. The reality for many students, particularly those from humble backgrounds, is that getting a degree at all is a remarkable achievement in itself. Nothing is gained by ignoring what they have achieved, and concentrating only on what they have failed to achieve. If they need further training, then it should be provided; but that does not mean that they have been given the wrong training in their undergraduate courses.

A fundamental belief underlying the discussion of these deficiencies is that they can and must be remedied, and this legitimises the positioning of universities in relation to such a responsibility. The term *lacking* is used for a condition which can in principle be remedied. The discussion of problems however serious is thus tempered by hope and confidence in the availability of solutions in the form of recommendations in the *GE Blueprint*, with the problem solver the government itself.

References

Annamalai, E. (2013). India' economic restructuring with English: Benefits versus costs. In W. Tollefson (Ed.), *Language policies in education: Critical issues* (pp. 191–207). New York, NY: Routledge.

Bacchi, C. (2007). What's the problem represented to be: An introduction. Retrieved from http://www.flinders.edu.au/medicine/fms/sites/southgate/documents/theory%20club/2007-oct/IntroducingWP_Bacchi.pdf

Bletsas, A., & Beasley, C. (2012). *Engaging with Carol Bacchi: Strategic interventions and exchanges.* Adelaide, Australia: The University of Adelaide Press.

Boden, R., & Nedeva, M. (2010). Employing discourse: Universities and graduate 'employability'. *Journal of Education Policy, 25*(1), 37.

Fairclough, N. (2001). The discourse of new labour: Critical discourse analysis. In M. Wetherall, S. Taylor, & S. Yates (Eds.), *Discourse as data: A guide for analysis* (pp. 229–266). London: Sage/Open University.

Fairclough, N. (2003). *Analysing discourse: Textual analysis for social research.* London: Routledge.

Fairclough, N. (2010). *Critical disourse analysis: The critical study of language.* Kuala Lumpur: Pearson Education.

Fejes, A. (2010). Discourses on employability: constituting the responsible citizen. *Studies in Continuing Education, 32*(2), 89–102.

Garsten, C., & Jacobsson, K. (2004). Learning to be employable: An introduction. In C. Garsten & K. Jacobsson (Eds.), *Learning to be employable: New agendas on work, responsibility and learning in a globalized world* (pp. 1–22). New York, NY: Palgrave Macmillan.

Gumport, P. (2000). Academic restructuring: Organizational change and institutional imperatives. *Higher Education, 39*, 67–69.

Harvey, L. (2000). New Realities: The Relationship between Higher Education and Employment. Opening presentation at the Fifth Quality in Higher Education Seminar, Warwick University, in Coventry, UK, 28 October. Retrieved from http://www.qualityresearchinterantional.com/ese/relatedpubs/Employability5thQHE.doc

Harvey, L., Moon, S., Geall, V., & Bower, R. (1997). Graduates' Work: Organisation change and students' attributes. Birmingham: Centre for Research into Quality (CRQ) and Association of Graduate Recruiters (AGR).

Hillage, J., & Pollard, E. (1998). *Employability: Developing a framework for policy analysis.* London: Department for Education and Employment.

Jorgensen, M., & Phillips, L. (2002). *Discourse analysis as theory and method.* London: Sage.

Kinser, K., & Hill, B. A. (2011). *Higher education in tumultuous times: A transatlantic dialogue on facing market forces and promoting the common good.* Washington, DC: American Council of Education.

Lambert, C., Parker, A., & Neary, M. (2007). Entrepreneurialism and critical pedagogy: Reinventing the higher education curriculum. *Teaching in Higher Education, 12*(4), 525–537.

Mackinnon, A. (2012). From women's history to women's policy: Pathways and partnerships. In A. Bletsas & C. Beasley (Eds.), *Engaging with Carol Bacchi: Strategic interventions and exchanges* (pp. 9–20). Adelaide: University of Adelaide Press.

Malaysia and the Knowledge Economy: Building a World Class Higher Education System (2007). Washington, DC: The World Bank.

Manpower Inc. (2008). *The Agenda for the New Service Workforce*. Kuala Lumpur: Manpower Staffing Services.

Ministry of Higher Education, Malaysia. (2007). *National higher education action plan*. Putrajaya: Ministry of Higher Education.

Ministry of Higher Education, Malaysia. (2012). *The national graduate employability blueprint 2012–2017*. Putrajaya: Author.

Moreau, Marie-Pierre, & Leathwood, Carole. (2007). Graduates' employment and the discourse of employability: A critical analysis. *Journal of Education and Work, 19*(4), 305–324.

Powell, W., & Snellman, K. (2004). The knowledge economy. *Annual Review of Sociology, 30*(1), 199–220.

Rogers, R. (2011). *An introduction to critical discourse analysis in education*. New York, NY: Routledge.

Stiwne, E. E., & Alves, M. G. (2010). Higher education and employability of graduates: Will Bologna make a difference? *European Educational Research Journal, 9*(1), 32–44.

Strath, B. (2000). After full employment and the breakdown of conventions of social responsibility. In B. Strath (Ed.), *After full employment: European discourses on work and flexibility* (pp. 11–31). Brussels: Peter Lang.

The National Graduate Employability Blueprint. (2012). Serdang, Selangor Darul Ehsan: Universiti Putra Malaysia Press.

Wodak, R., & Meyer, M. (2009). Critical discourse analysis: History, agenda, theory and methodology. In R. Wodak & M. Meyer (Eds.), *Methods for critical discourse analysis* (pp. 1–33). London: Sage.

World Bank. (1994). *Higher education: The lessons of experience*. Washington, DC: Author.

World Bank. (2007). Malaysia and the knowledge economy: Building a world-class higher education system. Report commissioned by the Ministry of Higher Education, Malaysia. Washington, DC: Author. Retrieved from http://sitere sources.worldbank.org/INTMALAYSIA/Resources/Malaysia-Knowledge-Economy2007.pdf

Yorke, M. (2006). *Employability and higher education: What it is – and what it is not*. York, UK: Higher Education Academy.

Yorke, M., & Knight, P. (2007). Evidence-informed pedagogy and the enhancement of student employability. *Teaching in Higher Education, 12*(2), 157–170.

9 Going forward

The need to rethink education policies

Suseela Malakolunthu and Nagappan Rengasamy

This book on policy discourses of Malaysian education aimed at substantiating the inquest of how education has played a closely intertwined role with politics in shaping the country as a nation. Presumably, the two are inseparable entities be it in a developing or developed country. You cannot talk about one without having to delve into the other. The chapters included in this edition cover several aspects of education policies and how they have unfolded over the years affecting the many facets of national development. Nevertheless, they encompass materials that would tell more or less the interplay between education and nation building in alliance with politics, economics, and sociocultural development. The editors of the book should have expected more contributions providing greater in-depth and critical analysis in the individual cases of certain chapters, additional discourses on similar topics, and others of different aspects and perspectives of education such as religion, science and technology, sports, creative arts, talent creation, intellectual development, brain drain, citizenry, race relations and conflicts, political affiliations, extremism, civic and moral education, inter or multiculturalism, and a score of others. Even the philosophy of education for the nation could have been explored. Also, a couple of chapters on the distant confederates of Sabah and Sarawak would have proffered a greater intellectual experience with the book. The hope was to add on to the extant literature in the various areas that would bring about a greater understanding on the role of education in nation building, at the same time to put to scrutiny, diagnosis, contemplation, and reflection the peculiar case of the country in this regard. In doing so, it would be crucial to take into consideration its confederation, demography and historical backgrounds. Much may be learned from the foils and failures as well as successes to guide and affect the future for the better. Alas, because of time and space constraints we could not add these topics to this volume; we can only take them as missed opportunities for now, and move on. We hope that another companion volume with chapters on other aspects of education in Malaysia will be authored soon. Nation building and the role of education in it will always be a work in progress.

As far as the integrative role of education and nation building is concerned the Malaysian experience does stand out quite interestingly as an effective episode of national history; however, not without a share of tense periods of change and turbulence. We, the authors of this chapter, may draw some relevant insights for the stance we make based on our individual experiences. We are full-fledged citizens of this country as we were born here within the span of a decade before and on the year of independence. At least one of us was privileged to the first sound of hailing of "Merdeka" (Freedom), for Malaya, by the first Prime Minister, Tunku Abdul Rahman, at the tick of a historical clock that heralded the day of independence and the birth of a new nation; later, at school going age, we were exposed to the tell-tale stories of the formation of Malaysia. We passed our childhood and headed into adulthood when the country was still in the grip of poverty and hardship, and was trying to escape underdevelopment and a commodity-based economy. We witnessed, in fact, without being affected personally until much later, the onset of change and its rapid advancement into a nationwide growth and quality of life. We graduated, entered the labour market, and became urban dwellers. Thereon, we have held, both as operatives and in consultative capacities, a close connection with the nation as it made its mark on the world map industrially and economically, and even culturally. In reminiscence, we recognise that we were essentially the products of the Malaysian Education, at least of our time. Thus, we may lay claim, rightfully, of course, that we are contemporaries, subjects and living witnesses of the period of the country's historical moments and movements of nation building through sovereignty and of becoming a nation that is globally renowned with unique accolades.

What Malaysia has become may not be the ideal model of a nation, at least not yet, if there can be an illustrative definition for it or the existence of another country to refer to as one. Malaysia's neighbour and one time partner, Singapore, is often viewed in comparison as a better achiever, but our historical, demographic, geographical, and political dynamics do not hold common grounds. Perhaps, it is the reason Singapore opted out of the alliance. Malaysia has to be viewed fairly and objectively on its own context which was more complex and complicated than that of its neighbour. Nevertheless, Malaysia has grown as a nation, and is aiming to become part of a larger entity in the years ahead. It would never be a smooth journey but it would have to be embarked. Based on the past, there is much scope for learning, experimenting, and realigning to make the journey a success. The symptomatic assurances of a greater future, light at the end of the tunnel, are fairly perceivable. However, the opportunism and optimism may not be emboldened overly so as not to be blinkered about a potential slippery slope.

It is not in our interest to wrap up this book by arriving at some convergent or collective decisions or assumptions of the role of education in nation building based on the policy discourses of the chapters; neither do we want to call out any predictions for the country. Also, we do not wish to recapitulate the chapters with a summary or individual commentary which would be mostly repetitive and redundant. We thought we would construe a complementary perspective of what may underlie as mental models and catalysts of influence in the various chapters and how they may translate into the future.

The knowledge and proclamations wielded by the authors in the book would certainly encourage the reader to readily acknowledge that Malaysia as a fast developing country has also projected itself as stable and viable despite its industrialisation and urbanisation having taken place in a relatively short period. The quality of human resource for the whole nation has also stepped up manifold. It is for the strength of its human capital that the government, for the most part of the last decade, has been making strategic advances to turn the economy into a knowledge-based one. It has also been gearing up transformations in the government, economy, and education to elevate itself to the world's elitist club of high income nations by the forthcoming decade.

In retrospect, we wanted to utilise this concluding chapter to scoreboard Malaysia on the basis of eventualities that appear to be trendy and entrenched in the administration of the people and the nation. We want to be able to pick out those distinctively perceivable mental models and belief patterns that corroborate and/or compete in the shaping of the national mind-sets which, in turn, substantiate the on-going discourses and accentuate the events that unfold on the people's daily life. We also want to be able put forth our take on what may have to be altered within educational policies to further the nation building process.

Five phases of development

For a foreigner, or another who may lack knowledge of the historical and cultural background of Malaysia, it would certainly help to approach a study of Malaysian education and how it may have coupled with politics in the instrumentation of nation building in terms of five phases of development, namely: colonisation, nationalisation, socioeconomic restructuring, internationalisation, and globalisation. These five phases may be aptly optimised both for academic purposes and for the sake of historical interpretation; however, they may not be regarded as completely linear and distinctly separable from one another either in time or substance. In fact, they overlap to the extent that activities and initiatives of any two phases may be observed as occurring alongside the other even in later phases. Sometimes, the evidence is laid quite bare that some tensions especially of the earlier phases are dragged into the most recent ones without being resolved. Certainly, scholars would find these phenomena in nation building interesting to study as they may reveal the dynamics involved when one phase finally pulls or fails to pull itself out of an earlier one.

Colonisation

The colonisation phase actually set the groundwork for the nation building challenge. The colonisers, that is the British, harboured an indifferent attitude to the education of the population prior to and at the time of independence. It is also common knowledge that under colonisation the population was already mixed ethnically and culturally; however, it was segmented along racial lines to maintain their own identity and cultural normality. The British exploited the situation and found it propitious to allow an education system that would serve their economic convenience and at the same time satisfy ethnic group interests. Nation building was never in their list of options, only capitalisation. Apart from providing for race and ethnicity-based and preferred education practices and schools, the British introduced and promoted the English language schools which were also extended into secondary education, on the one hand, as a political exigency to curry favour from the Malay rulers and elite agents; on the other hand, to create a more dedicated labour force to handle their administrative chores. The English medium schools were operated largely by the missionary and local enterprise groups. Thus, the colonisation phase originated the basic order social norms and the structure of the Malaysian education system which was identifiably vernacular in form.

Nationalisation

In the nationalisation phase, the grandeur vision of the government of the day was to create a single unified education system preferably with the medium of instruction in Malay, the language of the indigenous people of Malaya, which was subsequently declared as the National language of the whole nation. The government tried to do this by enticing the people with a promise of unity and integration of the various ethnic groups as one nation; moreover, the modernisation of the new National language was set in motion. However, history reveals that the unified education system as envisioned by the government was able to succeed only partially. The desegregation of the multilingual primary school system created during the colonial period could not proceed because of the strong opposition from the non-Malay ethnic groups for fear of losing their traditional culture and language. At best, the government could only impose, besides a common delivery and evaluation system, a uniform school curriculum reflecting the local history, culture and interest in subjects of study for all the primary and secondary schools regardless of the medium of instruction, which made the study of Malay language a mandatory requirement in the non-Malay schools. Nevertheless, the government stood steadfast with the goal of a unified education with the medium of instruction in Malay, and implemented it in stages spanning across a couple of decades in all secondary schools and public universities. In due course, the goal was also extended to the new confederates of Sabah and Sarawak. However, it was not completely without revulsion from the non-Malays, especially the Chinese, who were insistent and, despite government pressure, continued to operate and fund their own secondary schools.

The elevation of the Malay language as the National Language and as the medium of instruction of education at all levels except the primary schools, where people's own language was used instead, reduced the value and significance of English language in Malaysia. It was reduced to being another subject of study. It ought to be noted that the government did hold a policy to do away with the English language as a medium of instruction altogether from the National Education system within ten years of independence.

Socioeconomic restructuring

The socioeconomic restructuring movement may be set alongside others as a phase because of its duration over two decades from 1970–1990, and the impact it made on the society as a whole as well as the politics of the country. In fact, scholars would deem it as a crucial turning point of the country's modern history. It took off a year after a racial riot attributed to the government's failure to improve the socioeconomic position of the Malays. Essentially, the policy named the New Economic Policy (NEP), aimed at eradicating national poverty and removing the identification of race with economic function by reconstructing a socioeconomic balance among the races. To begin with, the major concern for the government was the Malay education mobility and employment. It set up residential schools and higher education institutions for the indigenous people, created opportunities to study science, technical courses, engineering, and medicine, sponsored with scholarships and funding, and opened up the civil service, police and military for their employment. The government worked rather aggressively to achieve the NEP goals. It was also during the socioeconomic restructuring phase that the government pushed through many of the objectives of the Malaysian Unified Education system, for example the transcendence of the National language as the medium of instruction for all subjects in national and private schools and all public universities, and the language of communication in government offices.

But, the NEP, along with the Malay Affirmative Action initiatives created huge controversy between the Malay and non-Malay population. The government stance was that the Malays needed extraordinary help and push. On the contrary, the argument of the non-Malays was that there was too much preferential treatment affecting their morale and sense of citizenry rights. The latter was engulfed with much discontent and disillusion, and harboured them to this day. As far as objectives were concerned, the government was able to narrow the developmental gaps and wealth distribution between the different races.

Internationalisation

Naturally, the next phase of growth for Malaysia as a nation was internationalisation, a limited and restricted entry into a world that was already becoming global even when the Confederation was on the verge of formation. Of course, there are basic differences between internationalisation and globalisation. The former would refer essentially to diplomatic relations between and among nations covering socio-political cooperation and collaboration, cultural exchange, trade, treaties and agreements of mutual conduct, and investments, while the latter is a more open and borderless arrangement among nations that are reasonably developed and demonstrate a stable political and economic environment; the latter actually allowed for expansion of an individual economy into a communion of market facility constituted from a number of countries for the purpose of promoting global economy through free trade, free capital mobility, and politically sanctioned migrations.

In the case of Malaysia, internationalisation was adopted as a potential move to fast-track not only industry and technology-based economic activities but also to stimulate the thinking of the people culturally and intellectually to befit a modern world. Incidentally, the national manoeuvres of the internationalisation phase foreshadowed the events of the New Economic policy. The country drew a large number of foreign direct investments from other advanced countries on a whole range of industries and provided the necessary skilled labour and relevant manpower support for operational, management and engineering requirements. Educationally, there was noticeable realignment both in terms of policies and practices to raise the quality of human resource development to attract foreign investors for increased competitiveness and, thus, appease the local economic demands and aims. Greater emphasis on science and technology education was given compared to the traditional arts and social science subjects.

Going beyond the years of the New Economic policy, Malaysia also opened up to become a regional education hub, perhaps, in line with the policy of becoming a knowledge economy, to capitalise on underdeveloped and newly developing countries who were in dire need of higher education at a lower cost and reasonable quality. To these countries Malaysia became a haven to grow their own cultural and intellectual capital against countries such as the United Kingdom, USA, Australia, New Zealand, Canada, Singapore, and China. This further enhanced international cooperation and collaboration in corporatising higher education in the form of twinning programs, foreign university branches and brands, and off-shore campuses. Because of an increasing number of foreign students and professionals in the main cities of the country, international schools are also sprouting to cater to education for the young ones.

Globalisation

When internationalisation is firmly rooted it also serves as preparation to launch the country into globalisation. However, the country would have to gear up for the open economy via free trade, free capital flow and easy migratory practices. Globalisation would mean extreme competition and require high grade human resource capability, productivity and production. Malaysia may seem relatively competent as a developing country, but whether it will be able to step up to become a global player especially as it is seeking to become a developed nation in the near future will be awaited. Scholars, economic professionals and politicians hold differing views about it. The crucial ones are that Malaysia is trapped in the "middle income economy" model very much depending on foreign capital and cheap labour. Perhaps, the ASEAN Economic Bloc involving the ASEAN Free Trade Agreement (AFTA) and the ASEAN Economic Community (AEC) would give rise to new dimensions to test and explicate the real worth and readiness of the economy, human resource and socio-political conditions in the country. But, the real challenge will arise when the competition is set against the more established players especially the western powers, China, Japan and Korea.

Another aspect of the globalisation phase that Malaysia will have to deal with will be the need to harmonise rules and regulations in the administration as well as the economy and industries, even in the human rights issues, on par with international standards. Good governance and transparency will be in great demand.

Both politics and education will have to move beyond communalism, and be able to generate the necessary intellectual capital. Questions do arise in the public discourse if, indeed, Malaysia possesses the marks of these characteristics given the lingering concerns and controversies of the various institutionalisations and disparities of the New Economic Policy which, more or less, have evoked the new national make up. However, on the positive side, the government of the day has, indeed, launched several transformation programs to address culturally and racially sensitive vulnerabilities in governance, administration, education and economy. The public universities are being granted greater, if not full, autonomy. Research is emphasised, in some cases making it mandatory, in all higher learning institutions, and bigger budgets are allocated for the purpose. Teachers and university lecturers are encouraged and motivated toward securing graduate and postgraduate degrees respectively.

Tensions and challenges

From the standpoint of the five phases of development, the reader may be able to perceive the inter-coupling of education policies and the politics behind them in the making of a country. As far as Malaysia is concerned, on the one hand, education has played a crucial role, both in line with government objectives and via counter-productive reactions from the minority groups, to create a nation that it has come to be. Malaysia has certainly grown to be a reasonably renowned developing country, and is edging to become a developed one. However, the leapfrog development over the past fifty years or so is not without critics. Some claim that the material and economically focused advancement has denied the vision and wisdom of the founder members who had characterised how development should be approached. On the other hand, education, whether procured locally or in foreign countries, has produced a more liberal and literate society which takes keen interest and does not stop expressing opinions about national affairs and politics. Many have also turned themselves into activists and commentators of politics, or members of political parties. Voices in the public discourse may not be wholly amiss of the possibility of the Malaysian leaders at the helm having forsaken the opportunity to realise an alternate Malaysia as prescribed by the principles of the founding fathers. Taking into perspective the various counter-productive government measures and rising racial tension, somewhat sluggish economy, generally mediocre human resource capability, and declining quality of education in the recent decades one gets to wonder if, indeed, Malaysia has mishandled development; or, has its potential and accumulated wisdom been overstretched, making it difficult to cope with the next stage of growth. If it were not for these setbacks, could Malaysia have already become a developed nation or be in firmer footing to become one? Sieving through the various chapters in this book, it would not be too difficult to conceive the idea that Malaysia has, wittingly or otherwise, brought upon itself a "baggage" of conflicts and controversies that would not simply go away and, instead, create obstacles to advancement.

Political dynamics

Having a multiracial population that was fundamentally disintegrated because of the British colonial "divide and rule" policy, the best option the founding fathers had at the time of independence was to bring about a contractual agreement for a common front thus paving way for the ethnically different groups of people to survive together as a nation. This idea of consociational politics for the right of governance that weighed in the disparate needs of the majority Malays and minority Chinese and Indians was built on the basis of accommodation. The founding fathers had cautiously guarded themselves against acts of assimilation. Just as the indigenous people were to be privileged with certain special rights and prerogatives which were not to be disputed, the minority groups were to be left unchallenged and unbridled with regard to their ethnic identity and native language and culture provided their loyalty could be commissioned completely to the new homeland. And, to back up the accommodation principles, the founding fathers advocated pluralism, a multicultural approach, as a way forward to establish a degree of commonality among the different groups to promote the characteristics of a larger national society. The dynamics of consociational politics was also to be extended to the states of Sabah and Sarawak when they came into the fold as Malaysia. But, according to one view, along the way the so-called Social Contract was apparently sidelined and obviated as the Malay nationalistic sentiment that had been ignited as a pre-independent communal strife resurfaced and vied for greater political dominance, which in due course began to pervade all aspects of national institutional life. The minorities on their part stuck to their side of the bargain stipulated as the terms and conditions for being citizens of this country. Thus, the consociational arrangement turned into race-based politics which over the years manifested in intensity to become deviant, divisive, controversial, and some say, belligerent.

Backlashes in education

The conflicts in education may also have to do with the Malay dominance ideology which intensified during the socioeconomic restructuring phase via the New Economic Policy and Malay Affirmative Action initiatives. No doubt, Malaysia founded and operated a comprehensive education system that allowed it to achieve the United Nation's Millennium Development Goals in less than the targeted fifteen year period, and provided the much needed manpower support to construct and constitute all the services, industries and institutions that made the country immensely successful in the world. But, it was also cast with pitfalls along the way that have kept the different races unable to unite as one people. For example, the vernacular schools and the English language policy remained as unresolved issues to-date. As always, there are people on either side of the divide to engage in a war of words on these matters, and the government has not been able to diffuse them.

The vernacular schools in a multicultural environment may be an anticipated and welcome phenomenon. Moreover, they do fall in a framework of a single unified education system that the government appeared determined to establish as they were governed by the same common curriculum and regulatory measures. A similar paradoxical rationale may also be applied to the English language education in the country. This language issue has to be viewed in the context of globalisation. When the country was aiming to become a global player and a developed nation, and the world was being swept along by the forces of globalisation, it seemed incomprehensible for not being able to assimilate English language education in a systemic and structured way. Notwithstanding these bickering issues from the past, there is increasing uncertainty these days about the quality of education at all levels which observers claim has been deteriorating in recent decades. Evidence is shown by the results of performance in global assessment and evaluation surveys such as PISA for schools, and QS world ranking for the Universities, which in the latest couple of reports had fallen behind some neighbouring countries. A worse scenario may also be apprehended in the private sector with regard to vocational education and training. The entire industry may be erratic, weakly institutionalised and disintegrated and, if anything at all, poorly regulated. It appears to have barely any impact or consequence on the employers and employees. The government has yet to endorse a workable bridging mechanism between academic and vocational education and training as already available in a number of developing countries; steps are being taken to redress this situation, however, and this augurs well for the future.

Going forward

Much of what is going on in Malaysia, educationally and in nation building, that hinder continuous growth and progress par excellence at a time when they are most needed appears to be seeded due to the uncompromised tension between the accommodative or pluralist and assimilationist ideologies. The accommodative or pluralist ideology argues for co-existence of the various ethnic groups amicably and on equitable terms on the basis of multicultural advocacy, while the assimilationist ideology pledges for the unequivocal rights of the dominant group in governance, and cultural and religious practices. In the case of the latter, it is highly likely that the minorities in due course would be depleted of their ethnic and cultural fervour and practice. Apparently, the majority that is Malays in the country, at least at the level of policy makers and opinion drivers, are not in concurrence with the accommodative model as they do not see it good for their agenda, while the minority Chinese and Indians, now aligned in this category are the natives of Sabah and Sarawak who are tuning in their voice for their own statehood, are steadfast in defiance that they would not succumb to any assimilationist tactics. It seems that these socio-political developments underscore a framework within which Malaysia would have to work out its policies and strategies and, nevertheless, earn the people's support to carve its destiny; or, it would have to rework the framework itself in order to rediscover its future.

However, certain signs of change are evident: namely the rise of a moderate group representing either side of the divide that is encouraging a new discourse, one that is promulgating a multiracial and multicultural Malaysia. This is also reflected in the nation's political landscape. For the past couple of decades, more and more political parties appear to be breaking down their racial barriers and allowing membership of multiple ethnic background. In fact, the country is beginning to experience the rise of a two party system in which the opposition constitutes a coalition or alliance of three different parties which have been traditionally identified with a particular race but now have become openly mixed. Also, on the part of the ruling party the policies are becoming more accommodative and inclusive in tune with the multiracial and multicultural population as may be evidenced by the stand the government has taken in the recent Malaysia Education Blueprint 2013–2025. Besides, the latest Education Blueprint is acclaimed as having been developed taking into careful consideration the current state of affairs of the nation set against the aspirations of a developed nation as projected in Vision 2020.

The Malaysia Education Blueprint 2013–2025 as well as the recently launched Malaysia Education Blueprint (Higher Education) 2015–2025, and the increased budget allocation in the past few years are evidence that the government does cherish education as a priority sector. However, the government will have to introspect and possibly do some soul-searching as to how it will be positioning itself to tackle the politics and mercantile imperatives of globalisation. Additionally, education itself will have to be approached with a more liberal mind-set and balanced between the study of science, technology, and economy and that of social and societal development, which alone will create the intellectual aura and psychological appeasement to see Malaysia through the next stage of nation building.

Index

access 45, 46, 47, 48, 49, 55, 61, 62, 63, 65, 66, 71, 72, 73, 74
accessibility 106, 110, 119
access to education 24
accountability 96, 97, 101
affirmative action 46, 47, 56, 57, 59
alliance 31, 38
AMIR Foundation 118
articulation 98
ASEAN 11, 71, 72, 76, 77, 78, 79, 80, 82, 83, 84, 85
ASEAN Economic Community (AEC) 147
ASEAN Free Trade Agreement (AFTA) 147
Asian Financial Crisis 87, 91, 101
assimilationists 29
autonomy 94, 96, 97, 101

Bahasa Malaysia 20
beyond communalism 28
beyond politics 27
Borneo states, the: Sabah and Sarawak 45
British 29, 31, 37, 38, 41; decolonization 31; divide and rule 31, 37, 41; English-Malay bilingual school system 31; multilingual primary school system 31
Bumiputera 45, 46, 47, 56, 57, 58, 59, 60, 64, 65, 68, 70, 72, 73
bumiputra 19

Cabinet Committee on Human Capital Development (JKPMI) 91, 95
Cabinet Committee Report 8
census report 47
Chinese 29, 30, 31, 34, 37–8, 39, 40, 41, 45, 46, 55, 56, 57, 58, 59, 60, 61, 64, 72

Chinese educationists 30, 32, 33, 34, 35, 36, 37, 41
Chinese language 33
Chinese mother tongue education 34, 37
Chinese primary schools 35
Chinese secondary schools 30, 31, 35–7, 41; Education Act 1961 36
Cluster School 117
coexistence 10
colonisation 144, 145
communal politics 26
community colleges 48, 59
competitiveness 25
consociational democracy 38
consociational politics 15, 149
coordination 90, 92, 95, 99, 100
critical discourse analysis (CDA) 125, 126, 128, 140
cross-border 79
cultural issues 28
cultural pluralism 32
Cumulative Grade Point Average 58
curriculum design 97
curriculum development 97, 98, 100

democratisation 20
Department of Skills Development 95
desegregation measures 30, 32–4; integrated school project 32; national school as the school of choice 33–4; vision school project 32–3
divide and rule 5, 17
Dong Jiao Zong 23

education: private 96; tertiary 88, 91, 96, 97; upper secondary 88; vocational 88, 90
Education Act 1996 9
educational mobility 31, 37, 38, 41

Index 153

Education Blueprint (2006–2010) 33
employers 136
English (language) 71, 72, 73, 74, 75, 76, 77, 78, 79, 80, 81, 82, 83, 84, 85
English language policy 149
enrolment: age 18–14, 45, 49, 51, 55, 57, 58, 59, 61, 62, 70, 71, 72, 74; primary 48; secondary 68; tertiary 48–53
equity 45, 46, 47, 48, 55, 58, 61, 66, 73, 106, 110, 122
ethnic 45, 46, 47, 55, 56, 58, 59, 61, 64, 70, 72, 73, 74
ethnicity 58, 60
ethnic minorities 10, 29, 30, 31, 40
ethnic polarisation 31–2
ethnic quota 56, 58
Ethnic Relations Module 23
evaluation 87, 98, 99, 100

Federal Constitution 6, 46, 53
fees 66, 67, 71, 72, 73
financing 66, 68, 71, 73, 74
foreign branch campuses 48
funding 92, 98, 99, 100

gender 47, 61, 62, 64
globalisation 15–26, 105, 122, 139, 147, 150, 151
government discourse 125, 139
government linked companies (GLC) 73
Government Transformation Programme (GTP) 112, 114
graduate employability (GE) 125, 126, 127, 128, 129, 130, 132, 133, 134, 137, 138, 139
Graduate Employability Blueprint 12, 13
graduates 125, 126, 127, 129, 134, 136
Gross National Product 4

higher education (HE) 125, 126, 127, 128, 130, 131, 132, 133, 134, 135, 136, 137, 140
Higher Education Institution Act 9
Higher Education Planning Committee 56, 75
high performance schools 112, 115
human capital 86, 87, 91, 95, 105, 106, 107, 108, 109, 110, 115, 118, 119, 120, 123, 124, 125, 126, 127, 129, 131, 138
human capital transformation 12
human resource 133, 134
human resource development 2, 9, 12

Human Resources Development Fund (HRDF) 92, 96

Ibans 45, 56
identity crisis 28
ideological barriers 27
implementation 86, 90, 97, 99
inclusiveness 106
Independent Chinese Secondary Schools (ICSSs) 36–7; revival movement 36–7; Unified Examination (Tongkao) 37
Indian educationists 32
Indians 29–30, 31, 33, 34, 42, 45, 55, 57, 58, 59, 75
industry involvement 91, 97
industry needs 96, 97, 99
in-service training 9
Institutes of Higher Learning (IHL) 126, 130, 131, 132, 133, 134, 136, 137, 138, 139
institutional coordination 95, 98, 100
Integration Plan for Unity among Students 34–5
internationalization 146, 147

job market 126, 136

Kadazans 45
key performance indicators 113, 117
knowledge-based economy 105
knowledge economy 125, 128, 129, 139

Labour Force Survey 45, 65
labour market 125, 127, 128, 129, 132, 138
Ladang Teluk Sengat Tamil Primary School 32
language 19
language planning 82
language policy 29, 30, 41, 71, 73, 75, 79
lifelong learning 105, 108, 109, 123
literacy and numeracy (LINUS) 114
literacy rate 24
Lower Certificate of Education (LCE) 35

Mahathir Report 8
Majlis Amanah Rakyat (MARA) 38–9
Malay (language) 71, 72, 74, 76
Malay affirmative action 146, 149
Malayan/Malaysian Chinese Association (MCA) 31, 38
Malayan/Malaysian Indian Congress (MIC) 31, 38

Malays 29, 30, 31, 32, 37–9, 40, 41, 42, 45, 46, 55, 56, 57, 58, 70
Malaysia 29, 30, 31, 36, 40, 41, 42, 128, 131, 133, 140; affirmative action 87; demographic structure 29–30; Economic Transformation Programme (ETP) 91, 92; foreign direct investment 87, 91; Government Transformation Programme (GTP) 91; human capital 86, 87; human resources 90, 98; k-economy 90; low cost imported labour model 86; multiethnic society 29; New Economic Model 91; Ninth Malaysia Plan 90, 95; Seventh Malaysia Plan 90; Sixth Malaysia Plan 90; skill deficit 100; Tenth Malaysia Plan 90, 91; Vision 2020 86, 87, 90, 100
Malaysia Agreement 6
Malaysian education 143, 144, 145
Malaysia Education Blueprint (Higher Education) 151
Malaysian government 125, 128
Malaysian Higher School Certificate *see* STPM
Malaysian Qualifications Agency 91, 94
Malaysian Qualifications Agency Act 2007 95
Malaysian Qualifications Framework (MQA) 94, 98
Malaysian Students Studying Abroad 49
Malaysian System of Education Quality (MSEQ) 116
Mandarin 74, 75
MARA 96, 97, 98
matriculation 45, 56
May 13 race riots 38
medium of instruction 74, 75, 78, 80, 81
medium of teaching 71, 73, 82, 84
merit-based system 39
meritocracy 56, 58
Millennium Development Goals 149
Ministry of Education (MOE) 11, 47, 56, 96, 97, 98, 99, 106, 107, 109, 117, 118, 119, 129; Higher Education (MOHE) 95, 98, 99; human resources 91, 95, 98; Rural and Regional Development (MRRD) 90, 95; Youth and Sports 95
Ministry of Higher Education 11, 47, 56, 61, 62, 70, 72
minority groups 10
monitoring 97, 98, 99, 10
mother tongue education 30, 34

multicultural advocacy 150
multiculturalism 26
multilingual primary school system 30, 31–2, 35, 41

Nan Ya Chinese Primary School 32
National Accreditation Board 91, 94, 95
National Advisory Council on Education and Training (NACET) 95
National Economic Action Council (NAEC) 12
national educational policy 16
National Education Philosophy 109
National Front 31
National Higher Education Fund Corporation PTPTN 56, 68, 71, 72, 73
nationalisation 144, 145
nationalism 17
National Key Results Area (NKRA) 112
National Language Act 8
National Occupational Skills Standards (NOSS) 94, 95, 96, 98
national schools 33, 34
National Secondary School (NSS) 35, 36
National Skills Development Act 2006 91, 94, 95
National-Type Chinese Secondary Schools (NTCSSs) 36
National-Type Secondary School (NTSS) 36
National Vocational Training Council (NVTC) 95
nation building 1, 2, 6, 10, 12, 13, 16, 142, 143, 144, 150, 151
New Economic Model (NEM) 46, 75, 106
New Economic Policy (NEP) 8, 10, 11, 12, 19, 38–9, 41, 45, 47, 106, 146, 147, 148, 149; ethnic quota system 39; General Election 38; Malay educational mobility 38–9; MARA Institute of Technology 39; MARA Junior Science Colleges 38–9; MARA University of Technology 39; science secondary schools 38–9
Ninth Malaysia Plan (2006–2010) 33
NOC 56
non-Bumiputera 47, 56, 70, 72
non-Malays 37, 38, 39, 40, 41

OECD 45, 55

participation rate 55, 56, 63
Pekan Baru Vision School 32

Peninsular Malaysia 45, 55
performance 87, 90, 91, 96, 97, 98, 100, 101
performance gap 105
PISA (Program for International Student Assessment) 24, 150
pluralist dilemma 29
pluralistic minority 41–2
pluralist ideology 150
pluralists 29
plural society 21
policy 86, 87, 90, 91, 92, 96, 99, 128
policy discourses 2, 3, 143
political and cultural supremacy 10
political bargaining 19, 28
political liberalization 27
political parties 22
polytechnics 48, 59
population age 18–24, 49
preferential policies 29, 31, 37–40
premier school 117
pre-school 112
pre-university science centres (Pusat Asasi Sains) 54
Prime Minister's Department 91
private colleges 48
private education 27
private higher education 109, 118, 119, 123
Private Higher Education Institutions Act 9, 47
Private Higher Education Institutions Act 1996 96, 109
private sector 91, 92, 95, 98
private universities 48
Program of International Students Assessment (PISA) 87
public higher education 118, 119
public sector 87, 92, 96, 98, 100
public universities 46, 48, 57
Pundut Vision School 33
Pupils' Own Language (POL) classes 33

QS world ranking 150
quality 46, 55
quality assurance 114
quality education 105, 106, 108, 109, 110, 113
quasi democratic 38

racial riot 10
Rahman Talib Report 7, 36; Chinese secondary schools 36; Integration Plan for Unity among Students 34

Razak Report 7, 31, 36–7; Chinese secondary schools 35; common language policy 35; Federal Legislative Election 31; Malay as the main medium of instruction 35; multilingual primary school system 31, 35; public examinations 35
regional differences 46, 64
regional languages 71, 72, 73
religious education 26
religious issues 28
reward system 96

scholarships: overseas scholarship programmes 46, 56, 66, 67, 68, 70, 71, 72, 73; Public Services Department 63; Yayasan Mara 65
School Improvement Toolkit 118
science 25
science and technology 105, 109
semi-authoritarian 38
semi-democratic 38
Senior Middle III Examination 35
Sijil Tinggi Pelajaran Malaysia (STPM) 40
smart school 117
social capital 23
social contract 6
social equality 29
social equity 29
social science 25
socioeconomic disparity 37–9
socioeconomic restructuring 145, 146, 149
soft skills 108, 119
stakeholders 91, 96, 98, 130
Strategic National Higher Education Plan 119
students (postgraduates), 49
subsidies 66, 74
supply driven approach 96
sustainability 108

Taman Aman Vision School 32
Tamil 73, 74, 75
Tamil language 33
Tamil primary schools 34
Tasik Permai Vision School 32
technical and vocational education and training (TVET) 86, 87; continuing vocational education and training (CVET) 92; initial vocational education and training (IVET) 90; performance 90, 92; policy and strategic direction 90; policy-making 87; program delivery 87, 96–8, 99;

system 86, 87, 88, 95, 96, 98; system oversight 87, 92–6, 99; top-down approach 96; Trends in Mathematics and Science Study (TIMSS) 87; vocational education 87, 90; vocational stream 88, 92
Technical Vocational Education (TVET) 11
technological advancement 28
Teluk Sengat Integrated School 32
Teluk Sengat National School 32
10th Malaysia Plan 59, 105, 106, 107, 111, 112, 115, 119
Trust school 118
Tun Tan Cheng Lock Chinese Primary School 33

underprivileged majority 42
United Chinese School Committees' Association (UCSCA or Dong Zong) 30
United Chinese School Teachers' Association (UCSTA or Jiao Zong) 30

United Malays National Organisation (UMNO) 31, 38
Universiti Kebangsaan Malaysia (UKM) 48, 57
Universiti Malaya 48, 55, 56, 57, 58, 75
Universiti Putra Malaysia (UPM) 56, 57, 62
Universiti Sains Malaysia (USM) 56, 58
Universiti Teknologi Mara (UiTM) 59
University of Malaya (UM) 39
USJ 15 Vision School 33

vernacular primary schools 30, 31, 34
vernacular schools 17, 22, 149
Vision 2020 16
vision school 117

workforce 127, 128, 134, 138
World Bank 46, 74, 75

Yang di-Pertuan Agong (King) 46, 47